Telling Tales

COMPANION VOLUME

The companion volume in this series is:
Taking Issue: Debates in Guidance and Counselling in Learning
Edited by Megan Crawford, Richard Edwards and Lesley Kydd.

Both of these Readers are part of a course, Guidance and Counselling in Learning, that is itself part of The Open University MA Programme.

THE OPEN UNIVERSITY MA IN EDUCATION

The Open University MA in Education is now firmly established as the most popular post-graduate degree for education professionals in Europe, with over 3,500 students registering each year. The MA in Education is designed particularly for those with experience of teaching, the advisory service, educational administration or allied fields.

Structure of the MA

The MA is a modular degree, and students are therefore free to select from a range of options the programme that best fits in with their interests and professional goals. Specialist lines in management, primary education and lifelong learning are also available. Study in The Open University's Advanced Diploma and Certificate Programmes can also be counted towards the MA, and successful study in the MA programme entitles students to apply for entry into The Open University Doctorate in Education programme.

COURSES CURRENTLY AVAILABLE:

- Management
- Child Development
- Primary Education
- Learning, Curriculum and Assessment
- Special Needs
- Language and Literacy
- Mentoring

- Education, Training and Employment
- Gender
- Educational Research
- Science Education
- Adult Learners
- Maths Education
- Guidance and Counselling in Learning

OU supported open learning

The MA in Education programme provides great flexibility. Students study at their own pace, in their own time, anywhere in the European Union. They receive specially prepared study materials, supported by tutorials, thus offering the chance to work with other students.

The Doctorate in Education

The Doctorate in Education is a new part-time doctoral degree, combining taught courses, research methods and a dissertation designed to meet the needs of professionals in education and related areas who are seeking to extend and deepen their knowledge and understanding of contemporary educational issues. It should help them to:

- develop appropriate skills in educational research and enquiry
- carry out research in order to contribute to professional knowledge and practice.

The Doctorate in Education builds upon successful study within The Open University MA in Education programme.

How to apply

If you would like to register for this programme, or simply to find out more information, please write for the *Professional Development in Education* prospectus to the Course Reservations Centre, PO Box 724, The Open University, Walton Hall, Milton Keynes, MK7 6ZS, UK (Telephone 0 [0 44] 1908 653231).

Telling Tales

Perspectives on guidance and
counselling in learning

Edited by
Richard Edwards,
Roger Harrison
and Alan Tait
at The Open University

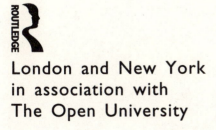

London and New York
in association with
The Open University

First published 1998
by Routledge
11 New Fetter Lane, London EC4P 4EE

Simultaneously published in the USA and Canada
by Routledge
29 West 35th Street, New York, NY 10001

© 1998 Compilation, original and editorial matter, The Open University

Typeset in Garamond by The Florence Group, Stoodleigh, Devon
Printed and bound in Great Britain by Page Brothers (Norwich) Ltd

British Library Cataloguing in Publication Data
A catalogue record for this book is available from the British Library

Library of Congress Cataloging in Publication Data
Telling tales : perspectives on guidance and counselling in learning /
    edited by Richard Edwards, Roger Harrison, and Alan Tait.
        p. cm.
    Includes bibliographical references and index.
    1. Educational counselling.   2. Counselling in adult education.
    3. Student counsellors.   4. Educational counselling–Vocational
    guidance.   5. Storytelling.   6. Discourse analysis. I. Edwards,
    Richard, II. Harrison, Roger. III. Tait, Alan.
    LB1027.5.T37   1998   98-17803 CIP
    371.4–dc21

ISBN 0–415–19443–1

Contents

Figures

Acknowledgements

While the publishers have made every effort to contact the copyright holders of previously published material in this volume, they would be grateful to hear from any they were unable to contact.

Chapter 2 Hodkinson, P. and Sparkes, A.C. (1995) 'Taking credits: a case study of the guidance process into a Training Credits scheme', *Research Papers in Education*, vol. 10, no. 1:75–99. Reprinted by permission.

Chapter 5 Williams, J. (1993) 'What is a profession? Experience versus expertise', in Walmsley *et al.* (eds) *Health and Welfare Practices*, London: Sage.

Chapter 6 Collin, A. (1996) 'Re-thinking the relationship between theory and practice: practitioners as map-readers, map-makers – or jazz players?', *British Journal of Guidance and Counselling*, vol. 24, no. 1: 67–81. Reprinted by permission.

Chapter 7 Unit for the Development of Adult continuing Education (1986) *The Challenge of Change: Developing Educational Guidance for Adults*, Leicester: NIACE.

Chapter 8 Miller, J., Manthei, R. and Gilmore, A. (1993) 'School counsellors and guidance networks: roles revisited', *New Zealand Journal of Educational Studies*, vol. 28, no. 2: 105–24. Reprinted by permission.

Chapter 9 McLaughlin, C. (1993) 'Counselling in a secondary setting – developing policy and practice', in K. Bovair and C. McLaughlin (eds) *Counselling in Schools: A Reader*, London: David Fulton. Reprinted by permission David Fulton Publishers Ltd.

Chapter 11 Watts, A.G. and Young, M. (1997) 'Models of student guidance in a changing 14–19 education and training system', Hodgson and Spours (eds) *Dearing and Beyond: 14–19 Qualifications, Frameworks and Systems*, London: Kogan Page. Reprinted by permission.

Chapter 13 Bates, I. (1990) 'The politics of careers education and guidance: a case for scrutiny', *British Journal of Guidance and Counselling*, vol. 18, no. 1: 66–83. Reprinted by permission.

Chapter 14 Wijers, G.A. and Meijers, F. (1996) 'Careers guidance in the knowledge society', *British Journal of Guidance and Counselling*, vol. 24, no. 2: 185–98. Reprinted by permission.

Chapter 15 Usher, R. and Edwards, R. (1995) 'Confessing all?: A "postmodern guide" to the guidance and counselling of adult learners', *Studies in the Education of Adults*, vol. 27, no. 1: 9–23. Reprinted by permission.

Chapter 16 Mercer, N. and Longman, J. (1992) 'Accounts and the development of shared understanding in employment training interviews', *Text*, vol. 12, no. 1: 103–25. Reprinted by permission.

Introduction

Telling tales in guidance and counselling in learning

Richard Edwards, Roger Harrison and Alan Tait

'Telling tales' may be a surprising title for a book on guidance and counselling in learning. It may even offend in seeming to trivialise the importance of guidance and counselling in assisting people with their problems, transitions and goals. While the element of surprise is intentional on the part of the editors, we view the notion of tale-telling as very serious, opening up different possibilities for the understanding of guidance and counselling practices; possibilities which we hope are exemplified in the structure and content of this text. For us, the telling of tales, the narrating of one's past, present and possible futures is at the heart of guidance and counselling in the interactions – individual, group, face-to-face, at a distance, etc. – between practitioners and users. There is a huge variety of tales told, supported, listened to, challenged, the result of which can itself be thought of as the capacity to tell different tales or make a different sense about oneself. In this sense, guidance and counselling act as forms of learning as well as being part of learning. Similarly, a large number of different tales are told about guidance and counselling in learning by, for instance, practitioners, managers, policy-makers and academics.

Telling tales carries with it a number of possible meanings and implications. It can mean simply the telling of a story, as we do inevitably in our everyday encounters with other people, or even in the stories we tell ourselves. Some of this story telling may be more formal and formalised than others – reading a book to someone, chatting in the pub, giving evidence in court, or attending a guidance or counselling session. Here telling tales may or may not involve telling fictions, but will none the less involve narrating stories to others. A second notion of telling tales is in its more derogatory sense of talking about other people in a negative or unfounded sense. Children are told 'not to tell tales', even when the adults asserting this are often not averse to a 'good' gossip. There is a third sense to the notion which is also important. This emphasises the tellingness of tales, that is that some are more telling, more powerful, than others. Indeed, in the telling of certain tales there are implicit and explicit strategies to make them more or less telling, more or less powerful. It is in these multiple senses that we have adopted telling tales as the title of this book.

Guidance and counselling in learning is a large, diverse and growing arena of practice with a range of professional bodies, codes of practice, structures of practice and disciplinary knowledge informing and being part of it. It is a terrain traversed by and about which there is an increasing amount written, signed and spoken and over which there is much contestation. For us, this means that there are a lot of tales told in and about these practices. Which tales are told, whose tales are more telling/powerful and, of course, who is heard all become important questions if we seek, as we do here, to tell some tales about guidance and counselling in learning as a whole terrain rather than tales about a particular area of practice, setting of practice, approach to practice, client group, etc., etc. In other words, we want to engage in and enable some informed interchange by allowing a variety of tales to be told, to begin to provide a framework for making sense of the tales that are told (itself another story of course!). In this way, what may appear as jokey word plays have a very serious intent. How do we make sense of the variety of tales told in and about guidance and counselling in learning?

To assist in that process we have turned to the notion of discourse. The latter has proved an influential way of framing practices in recent years in a range of human and social sciences. The literature on the reasons for this is extensive, as are the different possibilities that exist for examining discourses (Macdonell, 1991). A certain amount of work of this type is to be found in the arena of guidance and counselling, some of which is represented in this book (see the chapters by Collin, Usher and Edwards, Mercer and Longman,).

Discourses produce specific ways of speaking, signing, writing, of telling tales. These tend to be constituted as universal ways of doing things when they have a specific cultural location which can be mapped. Different locations bring forth only certain possibilities for certain forms of discourse. For instance, universities provide the possibilities for certain forms of academic discourse which are then assessed and accredited. Guidance interviews governed by bureaucratic procedures and specified action plans provide only certain possibilities for what the client can say, how and when. These examples bring out the locatedness of discourse and questions of power. Who is speaking? Where are they speaking from? What effects are they trying to produce?

> Discourses are . . . about what can be said, and thought, but also about who can speak, when, where and with what authority. Discourses embody meaning and social relationships, they constitute both subjectivity and power relations . . . Thus, discourses construct certain possibilities for thought. They order and combine words in particular ways and exclude or displace other combinations.
>
> (Ball, 1990: 17)

Securing meaning is therefore powerful, if always incomplete, as it validates certain discourses as more telling than others.

A discursive approach is therefore one which involves an examination of the exercises of power at work in the micro-practices of daily life (Foucault, 1980). For instance, practitioners may find that their own discourse is legitimate in the workplace, but that it does not translate immediately into management discourse of quality, efficiency and effectiveness or the academic discourses of knowledge legitimate to universities. Similarly, clients may have to translate their own discourses into the practitioner discourses of, for instance, 'learning needs', 'career interests', 'behavioural problems' and 'character traits' to find themselves legitimised within the practices of guidance and counselling. In other words, there is always a powerful struggle to establish certain tales as legitimate within the differing locations of guidance and counselling and, with that, processes of identification, counter-identification and dis-identification (Pecheux, 1982) on the part of both practitioners and users. Meaning is contested, even as attempts to secure meaning remain powerful.

A discursive approach therefore results in and from not seeking a universal explanation of practice or a single way of doing and understanding things. It entails recognising practices as ongoing processes of meaning-making and tale-telling, in which there are many discourses. Capability involves being able to negotiate one's own position as for instance, a practitioner/manager/academic and that of others, including the user, in relation to the range of different discursive possibilities. Locating, mapping and translating within and between the different discourses of guidance and counselling in learning becomes a goal for practice and lifelong development (Edwards, 1998).

This approach echoes other work already in existence. Collin and Young (1992) for example, draw upon a hermeneutic tradition of meaning making in their study of guidance. This is suggestive of the interpretative nature of practice and the need to approach practice in an interpretative way. Drawing on Heidegger's distinction between the 'present at hand' and 'ready to hand' they illuminate that which is immediate in experience and that which emerges through reflection. Instead of the often taken for granted and powerful divide between theory and practice, these spatial metaphors are suggestive of the importance of mapping and locating in processes of interpretation and understanding. Here it is not so much applying theory to practice, but of a reflective and reflexive interpreting and understanding the different possibilities for practice. McLeod (1996a) outlines the implications for counsellor competence of a social constructionist conception of therapy as a particular form of discourse. Law (1996) argues that career behaviour and, with that, senses of the self are learnt, subject to change and therefore capable of development through educative interventions. It is not a question of finding the 'natural' traits, abilities and interests in the person and matching them to certain possibilities, but rather one of engendering certain possibilities for persons by engaging them in educative processes about themselves and their capabilities, about who they might be. Law introduces the notion of maps as metaphors in career narratives. His position is also suggestive of the ways guidance and counselling produce certain effects – are educative – rather than simply uncover or discover what is already there. Guidance and counselling do not find what is already existent, but construct certain possibilities for subjectivity and identity. Implicit in all practices therefore are specific pedagogies of the self – for the practitioner being developed and for the user being guided or counselled. As we suggested earlier, this means that we can not only talk of guidance and counselling *in* learning, but also of them *as* forms of learning.

Mapping and locating the already existing discursive understandings traversing 'practice' is integral to the process of critically reflecting on, interpreting and translating the different possibilities for practice. Capability requires practitioners to be located and locate themselves within a range of discourses, able to map and translate discourses into one another and constantly renegotiating the meanings and significance of their work across domains, a capability which is itself of use to the users of guidance and counselling. Thus there are many discourses traversing the area of guidance and counselling and mapping and locating practice in relation to these discourses and being able to translate meanings between them becomes a central but unending and incomplete dimension to development for knowledgeable practice. Here practices may be more ambivalent, hybrid and open to multiple interpretation, opening different possibilities and raising different constraints. It is on the basis of such practices that boundaries of capability are negotiated as some tales are more telling than others, dependent upon situation, setting, etc.

While it is not feasible to outline all of the possible discourses here, and different ones will emerge over time, there is none the less a number which can be used to illustrate the different discourses of guidance and counselling and with that, some of the different meanings which are possible. McLeod (1996a: 46) identifies six 'perspectives' on counselling competence: the client; the therapist; the supervisor or trainer; peer group; manager; and external assessor. This reflects the particular focus of his discussion on counselling training. By contrast, we wish to outline a framework of six major discourses or forms of tale-telling: user; practitioner; professional; manager, policy-maker; and academic. Some are discourses in guidance and counselling and some about them, where the boundaries between in and about are themselves not firm. These discourses overlap and inter-penetrate each other and they are themselves diverse and contested. For instance, policies to introduce market mechanisms into the provision of guidance may result in practitioners reconstructing users as 'customers' rather than 'clients'. However, where practitioners adhere to a code of practice which lays emphasis on a professional–client relationship, they may continue to work as if the users were 'clients' and indeed, in their professional groupings refer to users as clients. The chapters within each strand have been identified as illustrating the particular form of tale-telling associated with a discourse, telling a user's tale, policy tale, etc. Each offers a way of meaningful tale-telling in and about guidance and counselling in learning and together demonstrate the ways in which practice can be located within each of the discourses available. This book offers therefore a range of tales and tale-telling through which stories of guidance and counselling are told, some more telling than others, all of which are subject to your own interpretation and judgement as a reader.

This attempt to conceptualise the discourses traversing the fields of guidance and counselling is highly schematic at this stage. Further mapping, locating and translating is necessary. The picture is a complex and shifting one. Locating guidance and counselling practices in discourse has a somewhat kaleidoscopic impact, in which meaning-making, the mapping of meaning and the translations of meaning between and within different discursive locations results in a changing of the subject – of the understandings of guidance and counselling, the person who is being guided or counselled and the identity of the practitioner. In this way, this book does not only represent some of the different tales that are told, but itself begins to develop a different tale of and for guidance and counselling in learning. How telling the tales in this book are and indeed the tellingness of this tale of tales we now leave to the reader to decide.

BIBLIOGRAPHY

Ball, S. (1990) *Politics and Policy Making in Education: Explorations in Policy Sociology*, London: Routledge.

Collin, A. and Young, R. (1992) in R. Young and A. Collin (eds) *Interpreting Career: Hermeneutical Studies of Lives in Context*, Westport, Conn.: Praeger.

Edwards, R. (1998) 'Mapping, locating, translating: a discursive approach to professional development', *Studies in Continuing Education*, vol. 20, (1) pp.23–38.

Foucault, M. (1980) *Power/Knowledge: Selected Interviews and Other Writings 1972–77*, Brighton: Harvester.

Law, B. (1996) 'A career-learning theory', in A.G. Watts, B. Law, J. Killeen, J. Kidd and R. Hawthorn (eds) *Rethinking Careers Education and Guidance: Theory, Policy and Practice*, London: Routledge.

Macdonell, D. (1991) *Theories of Discourse: An Introduction*, Oxford: Basil Blackwell.

McLeod, J. (1996a) 'Counsellor competence', in R. Bayne, I. Horton and J. Bimrose (eds) *New Directions in Counselling*, London: Routledge.

McLeod, J. (1996b) 'Working with narratives', in R. Bayne, I. Horton and J. Bimrose (eds) *New Directions in Counselling*, London: Routledge.

Pecheux, M. (1982) *Language, Semantics and Ideology: Stating the Obvious*, London: Macmillan.

Part I

User and practitioner discourses

Chapter 1

The client's perceptions of guidance

Amy Blair, Joanna McPake and Pamela Munn

INTRODUCTION

This chapter concerns an in-depth, qualitative study of adults' perceptions of guidance in different education settings. The chapter opens with a brief discussion of the key literature concerning life-long learning before moving on to a summary of the research itself. The authors then discuss clients' perceptions of guidance at three stages of participation: when making choices about providers and courses; whilst on course; and when leaving courses. The chapter closes with a consideration of the implications for guidance providers raised by salient findings.

LIFE-LONG LEARNING

There is a wide variety of learning opportunities for adults. Providers range from the informal and community-based Community Education Service in Scotland, to formal institutions such as schools and further and higher education institutions. Furthermore, work-based learning opportunities exist for those in employment, and indeed, individual self-directed learning, whether supported via information technology or by other means, is a vast field in itself. The notion that 'education' is something which happens to young people between the ages of 5–16 and takes place in schools is passé. It has been replaced by the idea that education is life long and can take place in many forms in many different kinds of settings.

One of the major forces behind the move towards life-long learning has been government emphasis on the need for a flexible and adaptable work-force if Britain is to succeed economically. This is a rather instrumentalist view of the purpose of education, which others have termed the human capital rationale for learning. In broad terms, this rationale holds that 'knowledge and skills add to the economic performance of a company or country in the same way as investment in physical plant and equipment' (Schuller, 1997: 55). More specifically, for our purposes, workers along with educational providers are no longer encouraged to think in terms of learning 'one-off' job-specific knowledge and skills. Rather, the emphasis is upon developing the ability to adapt quickly to the ever-changing demands of the market place, and the ever increasing pace of technological change. As we shall see below, this instrumentalist view of learning (learning for employment) is prominent amongst adult learners and has a number of implications for guidance.

A second stimulus for life-long learning has been the personal and social development gains obtained. Apart from offering enhanced career opportunities, it is held that 'being an educated person' leads to greater personal fulfilment and greater involvement in society. Past studies of adult returners have focused not only on the employment gains to be made by returning to education, but also on the ways in which adults' positive experience of education have led to increasing confidence and self-awareness and a greater ability and willingness to contribute to society (see Merriam and Caffarella, 1991, for a discussion). Interestingly, children are also thought to benefit from their parents' return to education: the more educated their parents become, the more likelihood there appears to be of children following suit.

Some commentators, however, have countered this view by arguing that adult education (and indeed, all forms of formal education) seeks to perpetuate social norms rather than transform them. Certain groups of people are considerably less likely to participate in adult education than others (Munn and MacDonald, 1988; McGivney, 1990). Researchers in the field of adult basic education in the United States, for example, have described the situation there as a 'creaming operation' (Hayes and Darkenwald, 1988) attracting only those individuals in tune with middle-class values and norms. In the United Kingdom, Jarvis (1987: 209) has pointed out that adult participation 'is something that is clearly related both to the individual's position in the social system and also to his [sic] position in the life cycle'. The variables of age, gender and educational background can be understood more generally as reflecting social class and structure. Keddie (1980) has commented that the difficulty of attracting adults from lower socio-economic groups to education is a reflection of the divisions in society, rather than a failing on the part of providers.

In recent years, there has developed, in response to this critique, a third perspective, which holds that a radically different educational culture is required in order to create what is termed a 'learning society' (Ranson, 1992), from which all would benefit. This view advocates an 'empowerment curriculum', which values the potential of the individual and seeks to develop positive attitudes and self-esteem among students. This perspective emphasizes active learning styles and constructive assessment methods; encourages awareness among students of their responsibility to the community; and invites the community to take a more active role in helping educational institutions to develop a shared understanding of the curriculum. Though controversial, this notion of a learning society (there are others) has been influential in focusing attention on the potential of adult education as a force for beneficial social change.

THE RESEARCH

In the light of the increasing numbers of opportunities for adult learning and of the numbers of adults participating in these opportunities, it is important to understand the processes at work in encouraging and enabling adults to participate. A key process is that of guidance. The research reported below is a small part of four linked investigations into adults' participation, guidance and progression in formal educational opportunities provided by a range of educational organizations in Scotland. The study reported here is a qualitative one which gathered accounts from fifty adults in different education settings (schools, community education, and further and higher education), studying different kinds of courses. The research questions asked were concerned with:

• their reasons for returning to education and for choosing particular forms of provision;
• the kind of help received in making choices;
• the progression (actual or intended) from one learning opportunity to another.

The research design and methods mean that our findings are illustrative rather than generalizable in a statistical sense. Our findings convey some of the issues and challenges facing adult returners to education. Paramount among these is the quality of information and advice received to enable adults to:

• choose an appropriate 'course' and provider;
• enable them to complete their course successfully;
• progress to further appropriate learning opportunities.

Further details of the research design and methods are contained in Blair et al., (1993).

MAKING CHOICES

Our research, in common with a considerable body of earlier work, showed that adults return to education either for work-related reasons and/or to satisfy personal goals: the latter can range from interest in a particular field to finding a reason for getting out of the house. Adults' life circumstances (most commonly age, gender, family situation, employment and educational experience) interact with these goals in ways which either support or hinder the initial impulse to return (see Blair *et al.*, 1995). The intention to participate, however, is only the first step in the process of re-entry to learning. What do adults do next? How do they go about determining the most appropriate setting for their return? How do they identify the subjects and the types of courses they need to take to achieve their goals? What guidance do they look for and how influential is formal guidance in particular in shaping their choices?

Taking the plunge

Although the most obvious 'logical' approach to planning a return to education would seem to be to decide what to do and then to look for appropriate providers, in our research, most of the fifty adults interviewed started by identifying a provider (usually they were aware of only one) and then considered which courses would best fit their circumstances and educational goals. The very limited role which 'choice' played in their decision to return to education was striking. It is, in fact, well-documented that a major difficulty facing adult returners is knowing where and how to get information (Alexander and Steward, 1988; Hillier, 1990; Howieson, 1992). This is particularly the case for those with little or no educational experiences since leaving school (Eagleson, 1991).

Our research supported these earlier findings. Furthermore, few of the respondents had become aware via formal guidance routes of the particular provider they decided to approach. Over half reported that they had consulted family and friends rather than more official guidance sources. It seemed that they did not know where to go to begin looking for information:

> There wasn't any one person you could go to and they could say, 'This would enhance your career' or 'This would enhance your chances of getting on that course.' My husband and I just discussed it ourselves, and read through the papers and talked to people who'd been on the courses before and what they'd found. . . . If you don't know people, it can be difficult to know what to do for the best.

However, a number of respondents also argued that, as adults, they did not want to abrogate their responsibilities to make their own decisions without the involvement of outsiders:

> You can only get so much help without acting like a bit of a wimp and being a bit stupid. You have got to have the balls to go for it yourself.

This notion that adults ought to be able to cope on their own may be one factor deterring some returners from seeking formal guidance before enrolment.

Those who did not have personal contacts able to provide the basic information about the whereabouts of providers were therefore at a considerable disadvantage. Their experiences of seeking information and advice at the outset of their route to return are not encouraging. Often they went round in circles before fortuitously stumbling upon a formal source of help. Several respondents lamented the amount of money they had spent on telephone calls before eventually finding someone able to give them the information they sought:

> There's [sic] no sources [of information] for people like me who all the years have desperately wanted to face my big fear and get educated. . . . I started off in the Yellow Pages and everything that said education department I rang and tried to explain . . . I just got mucked around from one person to the next. Nobody knew anything. Spent my money on the telephone bill.

Moreover, their expectations of what could be provided were low: many were satisfied with the name of one provider – and were fortunate if this turned out to be suitable. None of our respondents reported the kind of in-depth exploration of the possibilities with formal guidance providers (such as Job Centre staff or initial guidance staff at the provider they first approached) which allowed them to choose from a range of providers and course options.

Choosing the course

It was usually only when adults had chosen a provider that they then sought help in deciding on appropriate courses. However, even at this stage, many adults did not have any personal contact with guidance staff before enrolling on courses. The majority relied on prospectuses and other forms of written information in making their decisions. Those who did seek personal contact tended to be looking for *advice* (as to which courses they should take and to what level they should study) and *support* (to encourage and strengthen their resolve) as well as basic information. These adults often thought that they did not have the skills or background knowledge necessary to interpret the information available and, in some cases, needed to be convinced that they could do what was suggested and encouraged to return to education.

Community education services and schools catering for adult students appeared to be more successful than further and higher education providers in supplying the kind of supportive guidance for which such students were looking. These differences in the availability of supportive guidance in different settings may be attributable to differences in the style of provision in further and higher education, which, respondents suggested, tended to be fairly formal compared with schools and community education services which were more informal and personal. Such views are not surprising, given that the remit of community education (and, to some degree, schools catering for adults) is quite specifically to support and encourage mature students returning to learning. Further and higher education providers may, mistakenly, believe that adults fit in more naturally with their 'mainstream' client groups and that their guidance needs are very similar.

Clients' views on guidance

Whether they were simply seeking information or were also looking for advice and support, most of the respondents reported that they were satisfied with what they had received. What mattered was that when they made contact with the provider – whether by telephone or in person – the contact was friendly and encouraging. Someone who could answer queries quickly or who knew the best person to contact was highly appreciated. Adults like being treated as individuals, by someone who cared about them as people as well as potential students. Schools seemed to be particularly good at providing this kind of support. Students in further and higher education who reported that they had received guidance also reported satisfaction, but it was clear that this was minimal in many instances. In any case, client' expectations were not high.

A small number of respondents reported that their experiences of guidance had been negative. In most cases, this was because the information they had received had not been helpful. For example, for those who have been away from education for some time, current terminology, such as 'modular courses' or 'learning outcomes', is not always easy to interpret. Some of those who were dissatisfied with the guidance they had received reported that, even when they had sought help in interpreting written information of this kind, it was not always forthcoming. In addition, the researchers were disturbed by two examples of adult returners who, from the information available, did not appear to have received impartial advice from guidance staff at the providers they had approached. In one case, a man had returned to education in order to qualify as a car mechanic. After discussion with the engineering department of a local college, he found himself enrolled on an introductory course in engineering and construction:

> It's a mistake I'm here. I was under the impression that it was mechanical engineering, as in [car mechanics], but it turns out to be nothing like that. . . . It seemed to me they were desperate to get people to go on the course. When my course started off, there were 13 of us. Now there are only four. I don't know how they selected some of these people. I wouldn't have let them in the garden, let alone the house.

Another woman, aged 55, had contacted her local further education college with the idea of doing a leisure class such as tapestry or sewing. Such courses were unavailable at the college and she was persuaded to take both a modular maths course and a Higher exam course in Anatomy and Physical Health. The student professed to be satisfied with the situation, even though she found the prospect of an exam extremely stressful and had no clear ideas about what she would do with her qualifications afterwards. She also thought that when she had finished these courses, she might still like to pursue tapestry at the college.

STAYING ON COURSE

Current adult education policy emphasizes client-led provision. Since learner choice is a key element in this principle, the question must be asked, 'How can client satisfaction be ensured?'. It appears that the socialization of adults into study affects their motivation and perseverance (Norris, 1985). Whilst expected benefits from a class might lead a student to enrol, the satisfaction gained from a course may be derived from different sources. In other words, although a student may choose a particular course for reasons of convenience and cost, it could well be that other factors – key among these, its facilities and guidance services – become more important as time progresses. By asking students about the formal support they had received during their participation we hoped to uncover the factors and, importantly, the quality of the factors, that were most important in helping them sustain their studies.

Clients' expectations

We hypothesized that adults would find real benefits in their providers' guidance services. How did they conceptualize these services and what did they expect from them? We found that adults distinguished between the guidance they received from their course tutors or lecturers and that which was available from designated, specialist guidance staff. Although almost all of the respondents in our research valued highly the relationship they formed with their teachers, only half our sample made use of their providers' formal guidance networks. Of those who had made use of such services, the vast majority had found the experience to be a positive one. So why didn't half the returners take up the opportunities for guidance that were offered?

Three reasons emerged in interview. The first of these was a belief in *self-reliance*, which was also a factor in adults' rejecting formal guidance at the onset of their courses. Non-users of guidance often expressed the notion that it was their responsibility, as adults, to resolve difficulties themselves. If they did not do so, then they perceived that they had somehow failed, whether the difficulties were personal (such as finance or family issues) or academic. Related to this was the association of guidance with counselling. One individual with whom we spoke talked of the 'stigma' of guidance and explained that he would be worried by what other adults might think if they knew he had sought guidance from his provider. Even adults who were willing to seek help from their teachers were sometimes unwilling to seek support from other, specialized guidance staff. The second reason was the perceived *inappropriateness* of the guidance on offer. Adults often believed that guidance was geared to younger students. This was especially evident in providers where adults were being 'fitted in' to another mainstream culture of younger learners, in particular in higher education. The third and final reason was *fear*. Adults feared to approach strangers with problems but, more importantly, they feared to admit failure, which was how 'going for guidance' was perceived.

> It got to the point where two weeks on the trot I didn't go to my class, with the embarrassment . . . I was frightened to say to the teacher, 'I can't do it'. I feel the help wasn't there for me . . . I thought there was nobody to help me.

What are the consequences for such individuals in admitting they can't cope or are having problems?

Of course, not all students who failed to take up guidance opportunities did so out of choice. Two of the individuals in our sample had no knowledge of any guidance services available from their provider and were relying on friends and family for support. Both were worried about their academic situation and were frustrated at the thought that they had nowhere to go. Two adults in a sample of fifty is not a significant number, but should *any* student be ignorant of the support available, even if they are not having any difficulties?

Clients' experiences of guidance

How did clients construct value in the guidance they received whilst on their courses? Value was, unsurprisingly, inextricably linked to outcome, that is, if guidance was perceived to meet particular needs of the time, then it was reported as a positive experience. However, the difficulties of accessing guidance for many adults meant that outcomes were often elusive. Most respondents, for example, had been reticent about *seeking* guidance. Where guidance was *offered* as a matter of course – at initial interviews, for example – it was much appreciated. Later on in their courses, adults clearly did not see guidance as any sort of 'right' or service 'owed' them by their provider. This was not the case in schools and community education providers, however, where the atmosphere was often relaxed enough to put clients at their ease. Many adults in these settings told us that they had no guidance, just 'chats' with staff in common areas and coffee lounges. Yet it was clear from our interviews that such conversations were extremely important in helping to sort out problems and take decisions. This points out the important distinction between proactive guidance services, built into courses as a matter of routine, and reactive guidance services which students had to access in response to difficulty.

Accessibility of guidance was another area where adults felt there was a good deal of room for improvement. Guidance services were perceived by many of those who used them, particularly for financial purposes, as faceless and bureaucratic. Adults complained that too often, providers' guidance services could not help with external matters, such as loan arrangements or benefits, and where information was required from outwith the provider, it was impossible to find. None of the respondents talked about referral to outside agencies as a matter of course. It was apparent to us that good publicity about the guidance available and skilled staff who can both guide and refer, are vital for effectiveness and client satisfaction.

MOVING ON

Adults typically report a wide range of gains from participation in learning, whether or not they successfully complete their courses (for example Woodley *et al.*, 1987). Increased confidence, new skills, enhanced knowledge, qualifications, social benefits, and greater self-awareness were just a few of the benefits claimed by our respondents. One important outcome of participation was changing goals. As knowledge increased and qualifications were accumulated, adults often set their sights higher than they had originally hoped, as educational success generated the motivation to progress to the next stage of education. Although the single largest group of respondents had originally returned to education in order to find a better job, when we interviewed them this view had changed. Progression to more challenging learning opportunities had become the goal of a significant number of respondents. These changes in plan had serious consequences for clients' guidance needs:

> I don't know where to start looking for a job . . . I am all over the place. It is just like a different language when you start looking at a career. I am just going to keep [doing the modules] until I can't do it anymore.

Clients' expectations

Particular problems emerged for adults leaving their courses and for which they required specialist guidance. The first of these problems arose from adults' uncertainty about their goals, particularly where these had changed during the course of participation. The second problem arose for individuals who were uncertain about the value of their new qualifications. Such clients needed to know whether their new qualifications would be sufficient for meeting these new goals, or what further learning might be required for their realization. Finally, some individuals needed to weigh the benefits and disadvantages of progression against those of entering immediate employment. Would further qualifications enhance employment opportunities or would a longer period of absence from the market be detrimental to job prospects? These were questions that clients were often at a loss to answer for themselves.

To whom, then, did adults go when seeking this advice about what to do after their courses? The single largest group of adults – eighteen of the fifty in our sample – did not know of any formal guidance for progression in their institutions. Many preferred the more informal advice provided by course lecturers and tutors. For the only formal guidance service provided in most institutions – the careers service – only five individuals reported that they had visited it or were intending to visit it. Most of these were in higher education. While self-reliance was often the stated reason for this, many adults were suspicious of the careers service, or felt it was inappropriate to their needs. Considering that careers services often provide the only formal, specialist guidance for students leaving courses, it was quite a remarkable finding that so few adult clients availed themselves of this opportunity.

Of course, for many of our sample it was early days. Those in the first months of a two- or three-year course had not yet investigated their options for progression or employment upon completion. However, as most of our sample had long-term plans, it seemed that such guidance was necessary even at the earliest stages of study. One young man, planning on progressing to higher education after the completion of his present OND course was still uncertain as to the usefulness of his qualifications in the labour market and stated that he wished he had received such advice before starting his course. He lamented, 'They don't tell you what areas or what jobs you can go for [when you first apply].'

POLICY IMPLICATIONS FOR GUIDANCE SERVICES

Adult clients' perspectives on guidance may be considered in terms of their expectations and experiences. To a large extent, the value placed on guidance is determined by the degree of success with which guidance is sought and found. A mismatch between expectations and outcomes was a notable theme running through the study. This final section considers the implications of clients' perceptions for the development of guidance services. The key themes of the study are listed below together with associated policy implications for guidance services, which are presented in bold.

Expectations

All the respondents in the study had questions that needed answering, but few expectations as to what services they might expect from institutions' formal guidance provision. Respondents also had low expectations about the information and advice these services would provide. Almost any guidance was welcomed, regardless of its quality. The key point was an opportunity to talk things over. Adults did not view formal guidance services as a right and were often happier speaking to course tutors or family about both personal and academic difficulties. **Institutions need continually to publicize their guidance services and build in guidance opportunities as part of routine course provision.**

Value

Guidance services which were accessible and proactive and perceived as catering to adults' particular needs and interests were important. As was ethos. Guidance must not be perceived as being 'for other people' and the stigma of 'going for guidance' must be combated by guidance professionals. Most respondents who had personal encounters with guidance professionals reported a pleasant and positive experience, but outcomes were often negligible and people were often satisfied with very little. **Institutions need to be aware of the 'messages' about guidance they are transmitting to students. A message that guidance is for the neurotic or the young is unlikely to attract adult learners.**

Outcomes

The take-up of formal guidance opportunities was low, but respondents expressed a general frustration about the uncertainty with which they were facing the future. Sympathetic course tutors, lecturers and (in schools and community education settings) community workers were seen as providers' greatest assets. Indeed, teachers' overall attitude towards adult students was deemed more important than their skills in the classroom. Interestingly, adults did not generally associate guidance staff with positive or negative aspects of their provider, but focused instead upon the helpfulness and support provided by their course tutors. Successful completion of the course, the most commonly desired outcome of participation, was due largely, in respondents' eyes, to the efforts of their teachers. **Institutions need to recognize the informal guidance role of academic staff and take it into account in, for example, course design and staff development.**

Influence

For our sample, the role of formal guidance in determining educational choices was limited. Adults often had little real choice when choosing courses for a variety of structural and personal reasons: lack of guidance was only one factor. During courses adults were much more likely to consult with course teachers concerning a wide variety of difficulties and a few claimed they did not know what formal guidance services were available from their providers. The same held true for adults seeking guidance about progression and employment opportunities. **This re-emphasizes the need for institutions to publicize their services and target such publicity appropriately.**

We cannot tell from our data how guidance services in respondents' providers projected themselves to students, nor can we discern the ethos they conveyed. It is possible that our respondents were attending classes in providers with particularly inaccessible guidance services. However, given the wide variety of settings in which respondents were participating, it seems that there may be a tension in adults' expectations of guidance, the needs revealed by the data, and providers' perceptions of both. The following list highlights some key findings from the research together with questions with which providers might interrogate their own guidance practice.

- The idea that guidance services are 'geared to other people' combined with guidance's negative image resulted in a low take-up of support services. As our sample included participants only, it was constituted of people who, for the most part, could succeed without such support. What about people who cannot? We know that institutional factors other than guidance services are important for many adults. Is this simply because guidance services are outside many participants' experience? Might clients who profess to believe in self-reliance be more inclined to take up formal guidance opportunities if these opportunities were packaged and marketed in a more informal, pro-active way?
- Some of the adults in our sample preferred to ignore problems rather than approach professional educational staff (teachers *or* guidance staff). To what extent are such problems stigmatized in institutions? How can guidance staff work to overcome the negative image of counsellors for people with 'problems'?
- Many adults sought advice or support from friends and family rather than their providers' guidance services. Whilst all respondents spoke warmly of and were grateful for this informal guidance, we wonder how far it may be viewed as an appropriate substitute for input from trained, specialist guidance staff. Often, well-intentioned advice from

friends could be inaccurate or misleading. Adults would have benefited greatly from professional guidance in these instances, particularly when choosing providers and courses. Although the input and support of informal contacts is often important for students' success, they should not be a sole source of help simply because students do not know where else to go. Do providers know where their adult students are seeking guidance? Do they seek out different sources of support at different stages of their studies? Could a guidance 'audit' help services plug gaps and pinpoint input more effectively?

- Clients felt guidance should be more proactive and would have appreciated regularly scheduled interviews or formalized information networks. Some adults felt it was quite difficult to 'stop by for a chat' and would have preferred appointments to see guidance staff, so they could prepare what they wanted to say and the questions to which they needed answers. How far is such planning desirable for guidance staff?
- When we asked respondents where they would seek help in making decisions about the future, the single largest group did not know. There was frustration over the isolation many adults felt when making decisions about the use they were going to make of their new skills and qualifications. To what degree can careers staff, particularly, be more pro-active in helping such students? At what point in courses is such guidance offered? Are students encouraged to seek careers guidance early enough?
- Some respondents appeared to receive advice at the outset of their courses that may have benefited their provider more than the clients themselves. How can guidance providers ensure that access guidance is impartial?
- Guidance in different settings appeared to operate with different degrees of success. How can schools, community education providers, higher education institutions and further education institutions learn from one another about best guidance practice?
- Adults appreciated responsible guidance provision which treated them like individuals and respected their belief in self-reliance. Clearly, in this as in so many respects, questions about best guidance practice for adults raise questions about best practice for all. In what ways can the interests of adult clients be transferred to improve guidance for all students?

We have seen the importance of coordinated, independent guidance services which adult students can access from a number of sources at any time before, during or when leaving their courses. Such services play a vital role in helping to encourage wider access and sustaining the participation of adults in current and future study.

REFERENCES

Alexander, D. and Steward, T.G. (1988) 'Issues in the development of guidance on adult learning opportunities in Scotland'. *Studies in the Education of Adults*, 20(1), pp. 29–48.

Blair, A., McPake, J. and Munn, P. (1993) *Facing Goliath: Adults' Experiences of Participation, Guidance and Progression*, Edinburgh, SCRE.

Blair, A., McPake, J. and Munn, P. (1995) 'A new conceptualisation of adult participation in education'. *British Educational Research Journal*, 21(5), pp. 629–644.

Eagleson, D. (1991) 'Engaging with guidance: 20 years of educational guidance for adults'. *Adults Learning*, 2(10), pp. 275–276.

Hayes, E. and Darkenwald, G.G. (1988) 'Participation in basic education: deterrents for low literate adults'. *Studies in the Education of Adults*, 20(1), pp. 16–28.

Hillier, Y. (1990) 'How do adult students learn about educational opportunities?'. *New Era in Education*, 71(1), pp. 6–10.

Howieson, C. (1992) *The Guidance Project: Final Report*, Edinburgh, University of Edinburgh.

Jarvis, P. (1987) 'Adult learning in the context of teaching'. *Adult Education*, 60(3), pp. 261–266.

Keddie, N. (1980) 'Adult education: an ideology of individualism'. In Thompson, J.L. (ed.) *Adult Education for a Change*, London, Hutchinson.

McGivney, V. (1990) *Education's for Other People: Access to Education for Non-Participant Adults*, Leicester, National Institute of Adult and Continuing Education.

Merriam, S. and Caffarella, R. (1991) *Learning in Adulthood*, Oxford, Jossey-Bass.

Munn, P. and MacDonald, C. (1988) *Adult Participation in Education and Training*, Edinburgh, SCRE.

Norris, C. (1985) 'Towards a theory of participation in adult education'. *Adult Education*, 58(2), pp. 122–126.

Ranson, S. (1992) 'Towards a learning society'. *Educational Management and Administration*, 20(2), pp. 68–79.

Schuller, T. (1997) 'Building social capital: steps towards a learning society'. *Scottish Affairs*, 19, pp. 77–91.

Woodley, A., Wagner, L., Slowey, M., Hamilton, M. and Fulton, O. (1987) *Choosing to Learn: Adults in Education*, Milton Keynes, The Society for Research into Higher Education and the Open University Press.

Chapter 2

Taking credits

A case study of the guidance process into a Training Credits scheme[†]

Phil Hodkinson and Andrew C. Sparkes

The transition from school to work is a crucial time in the lives of young people. How and when this transition is made can have a major impact upon the sense of identity young people develop, the importance they feel they have in the eyes of others, the kind of person they want to be and their view of the world in general. Young people do not make the transition in a social vacuum and their destinies are interconnected with the lives of other young people, parents, teachers, friends and careers officers, to name but a few. Within such an embedded network of relationships, multiple meanings are constructed, reconstructed, deconstructed or maintained concerning the nature of schooling, work, appropriate career pathways and favoured ways of living. In turn, these personal meanings are themselves socio-historically, economically and politically shaped in a variety of ways.

In this chapter we focus upon career decision-making and guidance as one aspect of this transition. We highlight the views and experiences of the young people themselves and examine the experiences of careers officers and careers teachers who play a part in the guidance process. These groups were involved in new careers guidance procedures, associated with one of the original Training Credits (TCs) pilot schemes started in September 1991. We begin this chapter by describing the TCs initiative and the methodology that underpins our research project. Following this, the views of young people, careers teachers and careers officers are presented. Finally, we explore issues of culture, context and technical rationality which arise out of those views.

TCs[1] are a model for the provision of training for those leaving full-time education between the ages of 16 and 18 in Britain. The initiative was strongly influenced by the Confederation of British Industry (CBI, 1989), with its proposal that a 'careership profile' be developed to place individuals in control of decisions about their own education and training. The CBI

[†] This chapter is an edited version of an article in *Research Papers in Education*, 1995, 10(1): 75–99.

saw TCs as a mechanism for raising standards in training. Young people would be given control over their own training by giving them improved careers education and guidance and by issuing them with vouchers (TCs) to spend on the training of their choice. The young person with the credit would be the customer, and trainers or employers would have to improve their 'products' so that they would attract the spending trainees. Trainers' income would come from persuading the trainees to spend the credits with them and from the achievement of specified outcomes, usually a National Vocational Qualification (NVQ) at level 2. There would be further quality control, because only trainers approved by the Training and Enterprise Councils (TECs) in England and Wales would qualify to use TC funding.

The success of TCs was seen partly to depend on the way in which careers education and guidance helped young people to identify future career pathways and, where appropriate, make maximum use of the Credit. This is the focal point in the new market system – when the young person as 'customer' makes the first, and arguably most important, decision about the future. The importance of careers education and guidance was recognized in the CBI (1989) paper that heralded the TC initiative and in the official TC prospectus (DE, 1990). Both required improved, 'neutral' careers education and guidance to better enable the young person to make a sensible and informed career choice. Funding was provided to appoint additional careers officers to enhance guidance provision. The TCs prospectus specifies that 'the outcome of this interview [with the careers officer] must be written down and the record kept by both the young person and the Careers Service' (DE, 1990: 20).

A Careers Guidance Action Plan (CGAP) was developed using four sequential parts. Part 1 explored the young person's existing achievements, with a particular focus on 'the skills I have gained'; Part 2 specified career aims, the skills required for these aims, and 'how I can work towards my aims'; Part 3 described the planned learning programme. The actual TC could only be issued once this Part 3 had been completed. This was because it specified the relevant occupational area to which it applied, which in turn affected its financial value. Different Credits in this scheme have different values, in recognition of the fact that training in some occupational areas is more expensive to provide than in others. Part 4 of the CGAP, which was to be undertaken after training was completed, was a review of the learning programme.

The introduction of TCs as an approach to training has raised a number of issues, some of which are discussed in Unwin (1994) and MacDonald and Coffield (1993). Of particular interest to us was the wide range of different groups involved in the operation of a TC scheme. In addition to the young people who would use the Credits, others involved include their parents, careers officers concerned with providing guidance, careers teachers, the employers for whom the young people work, private trainers and further education lecturers, who provide the off-the-job training, and TEC officials concerned with the operation of the scheme. These can be seen as stakeholders in the initiative. That is, they have a legitimate personal and/or professional interest in its operation and are potentially 'winners' or 'losers' as a result of its introduction (see Brown and McIntyre, 1982; Sparkes, 1989).

This project set out to investigate these different stakeholder experiences of TCs in one of the original pilot schemes. Our investigation was designed to explore their different perceptions over a period of 18 months. This was done by taking 11 trainees and following them through the first part of the training process. Each trainee was the centre of a stakeholder network and, at each stage in the research, we interviewed those other stakeholders with whom each of the sample trainees came into contact. The fieldwork was organized in four sweeps. The findings reported here are from the first sweep only.

METHODOLOGY

This project is rooted in the epistemological and ontological assumptions associated with interpretive educational enquiry (Smith, 1989). Our concern was not to impose external researcher categories upon the situation but to seek the subjective meanings attributed to TCs by the stakeholders involved. To gain access to this subjective dimension, semi-structured interviews were adopted that used a short list of open-ended questions to ensure some common coverage. Interviewers were free to ask these questions in their own way and in any order, so as to sustain a conversational flow with the interviewee. This would include following up areas of importance for the subject that went beyond the basic questions.

In order to investigate the guidance process we decided to conduct our first interview sweep while the young people were still in school. This presented us with a methodological problem because we did not know which young people were eventually going to take up and use TCs and could not immediately identify our sample to follow through. We decided to interview small groups of 16-year-old (year 11) and 17-year-old (first-year sixth form) pupils who might be seriously considering leaving school, together with the careers teacher and careers officer at each school. We chose six schools, from different geographical locations across Devon and Cornwall. All were mixed-gender comprehensives, five took pupils from 11 to 18 and one from 11 to 16 years of age.

Within these schools we interviewed 115 pupils, mainly in small, single-gender groups. Of these pupils, 91 were in year 11 and 26 in the sixth form, 59 were boys and 56 girls. We also interviewed individually ten careers officers and eight careers teachers. Interviews were conducted between

March and May 1992 and tape-recorded. The pupils were selected by the careers teachers in the schools as being likely either to take up TCs or at least to consider them. Perhaps because of this selection by the school, we interviewed only a few pupils who clearly belonged to the type of counter culture identified by Hargreaves (1967) and Willis (1977). Most of our interviewees were what Brown (1987) calls 'ordinary kids'. One pupil, a sixth former, had been statemented for special educational needs.

The responses from pupils, careers teachers and careers officers were examined separately. They were analysed by identifying core categories of meaning which arose from the interviews so that, as far as possible, our findings were grounded in the data. The data were examined to see if there were any significant differences between schools or between gender or age group of pupils. Despite our original expectations, these were found to be slight in comparison with the general range of views expressed, except for some differences between the responses of year 11 pupils and sixth formers, which are explored later.

Given the number of people interviewed and the hours of conversation available we have had to make strategic choices about the manner in which the data are presented. Such dilemmas of representation are inherent in all interpretive forms of inquiry (Hammersley and Atkinson, 1983; Richardson, 1990; Sparkes, 1994a, b) but are crystallized in this study, which draws upon groups holding divergent views, interests, power resources and shifting realities.

Bearing this in mind, we have opted to tell, in a fashion, what Richardson (1990) has called a *collective story*. This kind of story displays fragments of an individual's story by narrativizing the experiences of the *social category* to which that individual belongs. Consequently, the data contain multiple voices from different people who each belong to a particular social category – young person, careers teacher or careers officer. While we are keen to provide an arena for the voices of the different stakeholders, it goes without saying that we have orchestrated the responses in our editing of verbatim quotations. While recognizing our editorial role, we have attempted not to place too much distance between the reader and the voices of the stakeholders, to invite multiple interpretations from the reader of our findings.

PUPILS' PERCEPTIONS OF TRAINING CREDITS

Many pupils with clear ideas about what job they want to do said that they were influenced by close relatives or neighbours who worked in the same fields:

> Body repair on cars [is what I want to do] . . . well I got the information for work experience from my dad, and then asked them if I

could work for the summer holidays, and then at the end of the summer he asked me if I wanted a job. . . . My dad [got me into cars], he's a mechanic. She [mum] wasn't surprised because she knew I was going to end up in a man's job. It's mostly men that do it, but there's another girl where I'm working . . . I doubt if I'd ever sort of go for that job if my dad wasn't a mechanic or anything. [I would have gone for] a window dresser in a clothes shop. (f)[2]

Work experience influenced many pupils and it sometimes helped in getting a job:

I'm getting on to engineering, a firm in [named town]. Well it's a training, a two year training placement, but they're taking me on at the end. . . . It was my second choice, after computer programming. I'm getting a night school course to learn all that stuff. . . . My stepdad works for [named firm] . . . and I started working there. Then when we joined the sixth form we had to do one day a week work experience, so I decided to do it there. (m6)

Some pupils had particular interests which they wanted to incorporate into careers:

Well I've wanted to do that [caring] since I was seven. I wanted to be at work. First I wanted to be a nurse, then I was with my mum in hospital two or three weeks ago and decided I didn't want to be a nurse just in case my family was in there. So I decided to carry on with the disabled . . . I've got a disabled family, disabled cousins and friends. (f)

Some changed their minds, while others were still undecided:

I'm working with my dad painting and decorating . . . because I enjoy doing it. I work like after school and at the weekend, at the moment anyway, and I enjoy doing it. I changed my mind cos I was working with my mum shopwork. But I changed my mind about doing that one cos I thought it might not suit me. So I'm doing this one [painting] now. (m)

Very few pupils described considered decision-making in choosing a job:

I've applied for [National Company] as a plumber, central heating . . . I want to do practical work really. I want to work with my hands. Being out and about, don't want to be stuck in an office. Serving the public really. . . . It's a secure firm, not likely to be made redundant, and they've got their own training and it's quite good money as well. (m)

A few were vehemently anti-school:

> Nah, I don't like it [school]. I don't get on with teachers so much. In the school they seem to boss me about. I can behave sometimes. I behaved better on work experience, better than I do here [in school], cos they just treat you better outside. They just treat you as an adult. (m)

Some could see little advantage in staying in full-time education, especially in the current economic climate:

> I just can't see the point in staying in school and then getting all your different grades. You might get higher grades, but there's no guarantee you're going to get a job at the end of it, so what's the point of waiting another year if you're not going to get a job? (f)

Others saw staying on as a safety net, or the better option in a recession because there were few jobs available: 'I've got a place in the sixth form that's like a safety net. So that if everything falls through I've got something to fall back on'. (m)

We asked the sixth formers why they had returned to school after the fifth year. Only three reasons were given: to improve on grades or results, because they did not know what to do, or because a preferred option was no longer available:

> I got six O-level passes, because I was going to stay on for A levels originally, but I decided against it. But by the time I'd made up my mind I decided I wanted to work, but by that time most of the training places had gone, so I decided I'd make the most of the next year, so I've done a business and admin. course. (f6)

Quite a number of the pupils we interviewed understood the basic purpose of TCs but there were many with misconceptions about the system. 'What they said was that they find an employment for you. But they said that you're supposed to be six months unemployed before you can start on Training Credits'. (f6)

Many found the detail of TC procedures confusing and many others, especially those intending to stay on or already in the sixth form, claimed to know very little. Many pupils talked about careers officers and careers interviews, mainly favourably:

> Well I had my mind set on what I wanted to do when I had my first interview, and she just like helped me. I've had three. . . . The last time I went because I didn't know whether to stay on at school or go hairdressing, and she helped me make up my mind. (f)

Several mentioned the careers officer as the prime source of information about TCs: 'The careers officer mentioned something about it. She tried to explain a little bit. It's quite complicated. You know, I understand the system of payment of your training, that's if you get an apprenticeship.' (m)

A minority did not like their careers interviews, usually if they felt they were being pushed in a direction they did not want to take:

> I had one of them phoning up my house. One of them phoned up my house! 'Can she come up to the careers office to speak about it.' And I went up there and she was there going on about YTS[3] and Training Credits. I didn't want to. I just, I think it's a waste of time to be honest. My mum wouldn't let me go on it anyway. . . . Because she's seen people do YTS and don't get a job at the end of it. You know, now they're unemployed. If you get a job at the end of it, like firm, then you've got everything going for you. But if they say they can't guarantee you a job at the end of it. (f6)

There were fewer comments about careers lessons. When they were mentioned, pupils seemed indifferent and often slightly critical: 'It's [social education] just like to help you with career moves isn't it. But it's like it's either degrees in university or go out and get a job – nothing in between.' (m)

A significant minority were critical of the quality of information they received, from whatever source. They wanted more practical details about how TCs worked:

> I don't understand how I get in to college like you see day release. No one's explained that to me. I know I can go to work . . . but I don't know how you go about going for day release, whether you turn up there and go, or whether you've got to have your name down or something . . . I don't know whether my boss'll do it or I've got to do it or whatever. (f)

Many of the pupils had spoken to parents for advice, and some parents had helped them get information and make decisions: 'I couldn't be bothered really [to talk to people in school]. Don't like teachers – pain in the arse. My dad knows quite a lot about most things, so I discussed it with him. Hopefully I'll get something come up.' (m)

A small number had talked to trainers, often in addition to parents or careers officers. These young people had been proactive in pursuit of fairly clear objectives and were the most knowledgeable about TC:

> When I was at work I talked to the City solicitor and he said about 'would you like to carry on learning' and I said 'yes'. He said, 'well, discuss it with the administrative officer' so I talked to him. He said, 'well, it's not quite as easy as that. There might not be enough money

in the budget'. And I said, 'well, I think I'm still entitled to Training Credits, even though I've spent a year at school'. I said, 'not a lot of people know, but when I went to a college called [named Training Organization] . . . they told me that everybody under 18 was entitled to the training. . . . So I explained that to him, and he phoned a person up and they confirmed what I said. (f6)

Some appeared unconcerned about the recession and seemed to believe that they would be able to get the job and/or training place they wanted. Most of our interviews were carried out during March and April, so that many of the pupils had not yet reached the stage of facing rejections: 'I'm interested in plastering, but I could always become a bricklayer, work for my uncle.' (m)

A few felt there were plenty of jobs: 'There is [jobs], it's just that people can't be bothered to get off their backsides and look for them. If you look in the paper there's loads of jobs in there, and then everybody goes round moaning.' (m) Others expressed concern about job availability: 'There's not many jobs around, everyone says that to me "Oh, you can't get a job in caring there ain't many jobs around".' (f)

A few revealed a lack of self-esteem and blamed themselves for their difficulties in getting employment:

I'd rather be a professional sign-writer [than a painter and decorator] but it's too hard. I can't write. Michael's got about six jobs. He's a painter and decorator, he's an architect, a professional sign-writer – he's covered in gold! He goes 'oh I could get you on with [firm's name]'. I goes 'I ain't good enough'. Cos he's got like seven, eight GCSEs. I won't get one. I'm too thick. Well, when it comes to pricing up rooms, I can't add up. (m)

Careers officers' perceptions of training credits

Of the ten officers interviewed, one was male. Five were new appointments under the TC initiative. Several officers felt that the introduction of TCs had raised the profile of careers education and guidance in schools:

They get a lot more guidance now because it's [the TC pilot] helped us, it's helped our staff, we've got more resources . . . I feel now we're beginning to give the young people the service a lot of us want to give them, that certainly in Cornwall we haven't been able to do before.

We're very stretched. . . . It's very strange, but because we've contracted to give more work, it's spiralling. The schools are actually asking for more . . . it's done a lot for the careers service, this extra funding and everything, extra staff, but it generates more [demand].

When asked for their general opinions about TC, most replied that the idea was good in theory but that either it placed too great a demand on the young person or that it did not work in the recession:

I think in theory it's wonderful, because it does give the young person an opportunity to negotiate their own training. I think in practice not many young people are actually up to doing that. They need a lot of support.

All except one were in favour of action planning, while having reservations about aspects of the procedures and about the appropriateness for some pupils:

I like doing action plans with young people, particularly before they get their job. I find it a bit of a token action plan really if they've actually found a job. OK you can discuss the sort of training, but I think they are more useful if a young person is looking for jobs. You can always suggest that they can use it as a tool in an interview, and I think that's quite useful . . . I always remember the good feedback . . . where young people have said 'I did show my employer my action plan and he was very impressed with it'. So it's worthwhile actually taking a fair amount of time to do this action plan and making sure that that young person owns that action plan, that the words in there are his.

One area of concern for many was Part 3, where specific training needs are identified:

But when you're coming up to actually getting them to write their training plan, and to write a training plan in advance of them actually getting into employment . . . they know the sort of job that they want but they can't seem to grasp . . . the sort of theoretical side of looking at your career aims and how you can achieve them through training, in terms of actually getting those points down: what you need to learn in the workplace, what sort of help you want in the workplace and in terms of what you're going to need away from the workplace.

The rise in staying-on rates post-16 was explained by the officers in terms of the impact of the recession in reducing jobs and training places:

What I see is a lot of youngsters who are so-called more academic, might end up moving away from the Training Credits option because nothing is there for them so they're forced back into education. . . . That could be for less academic students as well say who are forced into things like BTEC[4] 1st Diplomas, who would actually prefer to do Training Credits.

Several officers described pressure from schools to encourage staying on:

> Because they realise what the labour market is like, the unfortunate thing is a lot of youngsters are returning to full-time education (1) when it's not necessarily what they really want, and (2) when they might not be capable of following through the course that they've decided to opt for . . . I tend to feel the schools are encouraging youngsters to go into A levels . . . that aren't necessarily going to get maximum benefits from it.

Several officers identified frustration at being unable to get a placement as a major problem caused by the recession: 'For the kids who can't get a place, they get very frustrated. "Well can't I start training?" is a constant [refrain].'

This was seen as a particular problem for less able youngsters. This TC scheme provided for those identified as having special training needs through transition training. Several officers reported that transition training was being widely used for any youngster who could not get a placement:

> It [transition training] was supposed to be for those youngsters who had absolutely no vocational ideas at all, who would benefit from a period of work experience, job sampling, or for those youngsters who had maybe one or two ideas but wanted to check them out to begin with, or for youngsters who needed additional time on skills that would basically make them work ready . . . but more and more careers officers are slotting youngsters in for transition training when they do know what they want to do, they are quite clear, and vocationally ready, but there's nothing there . . . and at the end of it a lot of youngsters come forward, and they are even more demotivated than they were at the start of it. It's very depressing.

Another theme running through the interviews was the complexity of the scheme: '[there are] stats, reports to fill in. . . . Some of the forms that they need, I think they need revising. . . . There certainly seems to be rather a lot of bureaucracy attached to it'.

CAREERS TEACHERS' PERCEPTIONS OF TRAINING CREDITS

The impact of the recession was a central concern for the careers teachers:

> I don't feel as if I was really able to help some of the really nice kids. I had two lads in this group that I couldn't do anything for. They were

desperate these two boys and they were both nice lads, but they won't set the world alight, but they would work damn hard for somebody. But everywhere they rang, and they wrote, they got turned down. The enthusiasm dies, they get so demoralized.

Some felt that TC was difficult for pupils to understand:

The careers officer, they spend a lot of time, when you think they have nearly an hour with each of them [pupils], the careers officer. And some of them have had 2 or 3 hours with them and they still didn't really know what they were doing. Still didn't really know what it meant.

One of the main problems in gaining an understanding of what was going on was the pace of change within the scheme:

I just feel that the whole thing, it's never been made clear. I suppose it's because they [TEC and Careers Office] haven't known the changes themselves until they've got there. It's always come in so quick. It's all so sudden, 'Right this is out and the next one's in'.

There was general agreement that the literature for pupils and teachers needed to be simplified:

I personally would like something very concise, very direct that told me in a short space of time what I needed to know. What it is, what it does, how it's used, who it's for. As concise as possible.

Many were concerned that the complexity of the TC process acted against the interests of low-ability pupils:

There are a proportion of students who are quite capable with coping with any system that you put into operation. But there are some students at the lower ability level who find making phone calls, writing letters, extremely difficult.

In contrast, one teacher felt that the strength of TCs was the manner in which they placed the responsibility on the pupils:

[The best thing about TCs is] the fact that pupils are free to use a training pathway as suits them best. That they are going out with a positive view, 'This is mine and I can use it'. So they are taking responsibility for themselves, which I think the pupils going out to work, that's what they feel they want to be doing . . . that's the comment

I've had from a few of them this year. They want to be making their own decisions, they are ready to do it.

Some felt that the low training allowance put off some pupils:

For some kids it's absolutely crucial that they go out to work at 16. ... When you think that even as little as five years ago, plenty of companies were offering kids £40 a week to start if they were good kids. We are now told it's £28.50, and they are told it's gold dust and it isn't. ... They'll go and do non-training jobs because they'll get more money, because that type of kid only thinks about the money.

Some expressed concerns over older pupils who were excluded from the scheme:

There has got to be some change or provision for the 18 plus or 19-year-old. There is a lot of the vocational children, too young to leave school, but to get something worthwhile out of staying on at school or college, they need two years and then they've missed their Training Credits. I think that's going to be a major problem.

All except one of our interviewees were teachers of other subjects in addition to being in charge of careers guidance. They often carried out their careers responsibilities in the face of a heavy teaching load that left them little spare time: 'We learn to live with it [lack of time]. What feels sad, you always feel you could do better. ... You always feel that it's never done properly'.

Another concern was the mismatch of conceptions of time between those who work in education and those who work in other areas. This was particularly evident in the timing of the launch of TCs:

Another criticism would be that it was all left so very late. ... The first we knew was when we came back to school in September and it was a *fait accompli*. Then everyone was scrabbling around, 'God, it's here. We've got it. We've got to get organized.' The careers service were running around like headless chickens. Then the actual licences [for training] and so on weren't actually settled until late February ... I was actually in the situation where I said, 'Look I am not going to stand up in front of our kids and in effect tell them, "Look we have got this thing called Training Credits, but what the hell it is I don't know"' (*laughs*) ... Very often people don't understand the time scale of guidance in schools.

The careers teachers thought that CGAP was a valuable process for pupils:

The strengths of it [CGAP] obviously is that the careers officer does sit down with the youngster and there is a pro forma that they have to go through and write up. It ensures that every youngster gets that amount of time and opportunity to plan their careers.

Career officers were thought to be doing a good job under great pressure and the careers service was often mentioned as an 'honest broker' that the teachers would like to see having more control over placements. Some felt that for TC to work properly, careers officers would need to spend even more time in schools:

For a start I think we have got to be able to buy in more time for careers service to come into classes within the schools. We are limited here in that we have got very little time, that they have with children. We have no careers time as such. The only people I think who really can come and do it are the careers service.

It was recognized that TCs had given the careers service a major boost: 'What TCs did was to restore confidence and put money into the system. We've now seen an expansion of the careers service. They are now firmly at the centre of the guidance process'.

CULTURE, CONTEXT AND TECHNICAL RATIONALITY

The views of these stakeholders highlight a range of differences and similarities both within and between the various groups in terms of how they make sense of TCs. This sense-making is framed by their own positioning in relation to the TCs' process, which is specifically culture bound. Culture is a complex and elusive concept. While there is a range of definitions available, Feiman-Nemser and Floden (1986) point out that many studies that have focused upon culture have made the assumption that it provides a common base of knowledge, values and norms for action that people grow into and come to take as the natural way of life. In relation to this, Clarke et al. (1981: 52–3) suggest 'a culture includes the "maps of meanings" which makes things intelligible to its members. . . . Culture is the way the social relations of a group are structured and shaped; but it is also the way those shapes are experienced, understood and interpreted'.

In saying this, it is important to emphasize that while groups such as careers officers, teachers or school pupils may have similarities between them, they are not characterized by cultural uniformity. For example, teachers differ in age, experience, social and cultural background, gender, marital status, subject matter, wisdom and ability. Likewise the schools they work in differ in many ways, as do the groups of students they teach. Each stakeholder operates within the specific culture of their situation and it is from within this culture that TCs as an innovation are given personal, subjective meaning by those involved.

The data presented indicate that TCs were introduced with little awareness of the cultural contexts in which each stakeholder group operated, with their particular maps of meaning. Essentially, the introduction of TCs and the way in which the CGAP procedures in particular were planned and introduced are examples of what, following Habermas and others (Gibson, 1986; Held, 1990), we call technical or instrumental rationality: 'Instrumental rationality represents the preoccupation with *means* in preference to ends. It is concerned with *method* and efficiency rather than with *purposes*. . . . It is the divorce of fact from value, and the preference, in that divorce, for fact' (Gibson, 1986: 7).

A technical, rational approach to TCs judges their introduction and development as an engineering problem, to be externally planned and organized. This ignores the emotions, beliefs and cultural 'situatedness' of the participants and is a top-down, control-dominated approach that risks alienating some of the key players whose support is essential for the long-term success of the initiative. It assumes that there is one 'correct' view of the TC processes and that use of systems and effective communication will eventually ensure that participants share that view and understand it in similar ways.

MAKING CAREER CHOICES

The descriptions by young people of the ways in which they decided on a particular job demonstrated two qualities. Firstly, they described *rational* reasons for making their choices. They were often choosing jobs they knew a lot about and the source of information was often an insider who had no vested interest in 'selling' a vacancy and whose judgment they could trust because they knew them personally. Alternatively, the information came from doing some aspect of the job, for example on work experience.

Secondly, these rational decisions were *pragmatic*, though often in a restricted way. The decisions were based on partial information, which was localized, being based on the familiar and the known. The decisions were opportunistic, being based on fortuitous experiences and local networks (Moore, 1988). Sometimes rapid changes of intention were described, without any apparent link between the early and later choices in some cases, while other young people appeared to have fixated views either about what they wanted, or more likely what they did not want. The timing of the decisions was sporadic, in that decisions were made when the pupil felt able to do so and were reactions to opportunities as they were encountered. Finally, decisions were often only partially rational, being also influenced by feelings and emotions. While we are not claiming that all these characteristics applied to decision-making in every case, the majority of pupils exemplified many of them.

If we consider young people making career choices as having existing schemas that are constructed within a cultural context, it helps explain what happens. Schemas act as a filter, helping the brain ignore 'irrelevant' data which do not fit a person's preconceptions (Rumelhart, 1980). In this way, two pupils can see the same video about TCs and each gain a completely different picture of them, as each pupil makes sense of the programme in terms of their own schematic perceptions. If the schemas are broad or not rigidly formed, then frequent changes can be absorbed and the schematic view a pupil has of their ideal career is modified, provided the new schema does not run completely counter to the old. Even where the schematic view of a career is narrow and rigid, there is no conflict if the desired route is achievable and seen as appropriate by significant others. However, if a pupil wants to get a job now but the careers officer thinks they would be better advised to take a full-time college course, or if a pupil sees TC as beneath him/her but the careers officer sees it as a sensible way forward, then conflicts can occur. In such a situation, neither the young person nor the careers officer may be able to reason with the other, as they approach it with fundamentally different schematic views.

This culturally situated, pragmatically rational decision-making by young people contrasted with the technical rationality of the guidance process and the CGAP (Hodkinson and Sparkes, 1993). The design of this CGAP presupposed that young people should reach decisions in a systematic way, moving logically from considering their own strengths and achievements through to deciding what they wanted to do and then on to exploring how to achieve that aim, including identifying quite specific training needs. Decision-making was seen as an externally planned, controlled sequence aimed at the acquisition of a TC which was normally job specific and which could not be awarded until after the CGAP was complete.

Such technically rational decision-making assumes that all information is available, so that young people have been able to consider everything of relevance. This information is cosmopolitan rather than localized, although local labour-market and training opportunities will form an important focus. The decision is assumed to be context free, in that pupils are expected to consider all opportunities separated from their own life histories and background. Finally, rather than being opportunistic and sporadic, the CGAP procedure assumed that young people reach a decision as they move along the guidance conveyor belt, stage by chronological stage.

The careers officers described problems in the operation of careers guidance which can be explained by the tensions between the pragmatic rationality of pupils and the technical rationality of the guidance process. Some officers question the rigidity of the process. Others described how Part 2 of the CGAP could be modified to help young people face up to a range of personal priorities far wider than the CGAP documents imply. In these ways the mechanistic version of CGAP was being rejected and transformed. The wide-spread problems described in connection with Part 3 were also an acknowledgement of flaws in the technical rationality model. Some felt that specific focusing on one goal was inappropriate and others want the specifics to wait until after a placement has been gained. Both suggestions are prag-matically sensible approaches to career choice.

In other ways, though, the careers officers and teachers locate the prob-lems of CGAP either with the young people or their situation, rather than with flaws in the design. We were told that the procedures may be asking too much of some young people or that others were not committed to it. We were also told that CGAP won't work because the placements are not there, or because it would be employers rather than trainees who decide what training is done and by whom.[5] What they are saying is only a little short of claiming that the technical–rational decision-making of CGAP will only work in an ideal world populated with ideal people.

LEVELS OF AWARENESS AND TRAINING CREDITS

Each stakeholder group expressed a variety of confusions and concerns regarding the TCs process. In particular, the views of the young people about TCs undermine a technical–rational approach to guidance, for they display a wide disparity in levels of awareness running from quite good understanding of the TC scheme to almost complete ignorance, often spiced with erroneous information. This was paralleled by a similar range of attitudes towards TCs, from the generally enthusiastic to the vehemently opposed. These young people would respond in very different ways to the same information and advice about TCs.

Many of the young people interviewed can be classified into four ideal types, lying on a continuum of awareness about TCs.

Knowledgeable and committed

Those who knew most about TCs had clear career objectives involving their use. They had showed some initiative and had directly approached a trainer working within the scheme. Members of this group were most likely to be positive about the value of TCs, though this may sometimes have been based on hopes fuelled by trainers who have an interest in presenting TCs in the best light in order to recruit trainees.

Generally interested

The next group were those pupils, mainly in year 11, intending to leave school but who did not see TCs as relevant to their job aspirations, or who lacked clear objectives as to the chosen career, or who lacked the initiative to make contact with training organizations themselves. This group relied on the careers officer and school to inform them and their comments suggest that the schools were less effective in this role. Many of this group were worried by their lack of understanding of credits. Others saw TCs as something to fall back on if they couldn't get a 'proper job', or they saw the possession of a Credit as something which would make them more attractive to employers.

No knowledge or interest

Those year-11 pupils determined to stay in school formed the third group. They knew very little about TCs and could see little point in finding out. They saw Credits as irrelevant to their own career aspirations and may have felt that they were low status and to be avoided. Many of the careers teachers interviewed saw TCs as something aimed at the least able and some of the pupils who were leaving described feeling like outcasts.

Antipathy and ignorance

The fourth group knew least and were most vehemently opposed to TCs. They associated TCs with YTS and regarded both initiatives as inappropriate and beneath them. Many of this group were sixth-form pupils who had finished a one-year course, but we also identified a small number of year-11 pupils who had much in common with other counterculture groups (Hargreaves, 1967; Willis, 1977). They appeared to be alienated from anything 'official' rather than from TCs specifically.

Recent studies have shown that both careers officers (Lawrence, 1992) and careers teachers (Harris, 1992) are marginal groups within education, and that members of both groups feel insecure and that they lack status. However, in relation to TCs their perceptions of their own positions are different. Careers officers feel that TCs have enhanced their status, evidenced by the predominantly positive comments about the initiative and by the sparsity of the sort of negative comment reported by Lawrence (1992). There is evidence that this enhancement also occurred in the other ten original TC pilot schemes (Sims and Stoney, 1993). The fact that most of the careers officers interviewed saw their status as enhanced by TCs may partly explain why they took a predominantly positive view of the initiative and of the guidance procedures associated with it.

In contrast, many of the careers teachers we spoke to felt marginalized in the TC process. It is hardly surprising that many were sceptical about aspects of the TC initiative and some regretted the change from YTS, which they felt they understood and could deal with. Fullan (1991: 127) notes:

Change is a highly personal experience – each and every one of the teachers who will be affected by change must have the opportunity to work through this experience in a way in which the rewards at least equal the cost. The fact that those who advocate and develop changes get more rewards than costs, and those who are expected to implement them experience more costs than rewards, goes a long way to explaining why the more things change, the more they remain the same.

Careers teachers felt themselves to be under pressure, with little time to get things done in the normal working day. In such a context, any source of change that meant a major investment of time and energy would be defined as costly unless these investments were closely followed by some rewarding circumstance. Several of the careers teachers felt that they were being asked to make a major reinvestment in a system that would not meet the needs of their pupils in a time of recession.

Given the nature of its inception and the speed with which TC was operationalized, it is not surprising that the introduction of TCs into schools was framed within the 'technological perspective' (House, 1979). This perspective incorporates a research, development and diffusion model of change. While the features of this perspective are outlined in more detail elsewhere (Hord, 1987; Nicholls, 1983), it is worth mentioning that it assumes a *passive* consumer who is willing to accept the innovation within a process that involves a division of labour with a clear separation of roles and functions.

Talking of the technological perspective which infused the major centrally funded curriculum projects that were spawned in the 1970s, Rudduck (1986: 9) notes how they were, 'arrogantly simplistic and somewhat neglectful of the school's sense of its own identity. . . . The ownership of meaning remained with its originators. Many teachers felt as though they were puppets dangling from the threads of someone else's invention'. In considering the main achievement in our learning about planned change since the 1970s, Rudduck (1991) points out that we are beginning to see change not simply as a technical problem but a shared cultural problem that requires attention to context, and to the creation of shared meaning within working groups.

Associated with feelings of marginality was the perception of several careers teachers that many of the changes they were being expected to make, due to the introduction of TCs, were conceptualized with little awareness of the school culture. Some commented on the time in the year when TCs were originally introduced, since this seemed completely out of phase with the workings of the school year. Others pointed out that while they were in favour of the CGAP, it placed a heavy demand on their limited resources of time in schools. The gap between the perspective on time of the teachers and that of those responsible for the introduction of the initiative had been a source of stress for some of the careers teachers involved. As Woods (1990: 50) reminds us, 'for ideas to be produced and to take root, inspiration and incubation is needed. The prime element here is time – not just hours or days, but subjective time involving ownership and control'.

CLOSING COMMENT

We have suggested that the TCs initiative, in the pilot scheme studied here, was based on assumptions and principles that are inherently technically rational, both in the innovation process adopted in relation to schools and the guidance procedures of the CGAP. In contrast, we have presented rich, thick descriptions of the perceptions of different stakeholders involved in the TCs process, in the form of collective stories. These stories have been shown to be complex and multifaceted. We have tried to make partial sense of this complexity by seeing the stakeholders concerned as culturally situated, and as interacting with others and with the initiative itself in what Giddens (1990) would call a reflexive way. In doing so, we accept that readers may well draw out different things from the stories and that our data can be interpreted in different ways. Even though it has only been possible to touch on the views of selected stakeholders and despite the focus on a small part of the transition from school to work, we hope our findings have raised some important questions for researchers and policy makers in the education and training arena, which are fundamental to the eventual success of TC, and to other new initiatives in post-16 education and training.

NOTES

1 Training Credits were later called full credits. The research reported here is based on one of the regional pilot schemes. The detailed workings of others were substantially different (Sims and Stoney, 1993).
2 An 'm' of 'f' after a quotation indicates gender, and a '6' indicates sixth former.
3 YTS stands for the Youth Training Scheme. This was the government scheme which was the forerunner of YT, and therefore TC. Some interviewees were largely unaware that YTS no longer existed, and others used it as a reference point to comment on TC.
4 BTEC is the Business and Technical Education Council, one of the main examination boards offering NVQs. The BTEC 1st Diploma is a full-time, one-year vocational course.
5 Findings from later interview sweeps confirmed this view that the notion of a young person acting as a customer for training was largely mythical.

ACKNOWLEDGEMENT

We would like to thank Jane McNeill for her helpful comments on an earlier draft of this chapter.

BIBLIOGRAPHY

Brown, P. (1987). *Schooling and Ordinary Kids: Inequality, Unemployment and the New Vocationalism*, London: Tavistock Publications.

Brown, S. and McIntyre, D. (1982). 'Costs and rewards of innovation: taking account of the teachers' viewpoint.' In: Olson, J. (ed.) *Innovation in the Science Curriculum*. London: Croom Helm.

Clarke, J., All, S., Jefferson, T. and Roberts, B. (1981). 'Subcultures, cultures and class.' In: Bennet, T., Martin, G., Mercer, C. and Wallacott, J. (eds) *Culture, Ideology and Social Process*. London: Batsford.

Coffield, F. (1990). 'From the decade of the enterprise culture to the decade of the TECs', *British Journal of Education and Work*, 4, 1, 59–78.

Confederation of British Industry (1989). *Towards a Skills Revolution*, Report of the Vocational Education and Training Task Force. London: CBI.

Department of Employment (1990). *Training Credits for Young People: A Prospectus*. Sheffield: Employment Department.

Department of Employment (1992). *Progress: Training Credits, a Report on the First Twelve Months*. Sheffield: Employment Department.

Feiman-Nemser, S. and Floden, R. (1986). 'The cultures of teaching.' In: Wittrock, M. (ed.) *Handbook of Research on Teaching*. London: Collier Macmillan.

Fullan, M. (1991). *The New Meaning of Educational Change*. London: Cassell.

Gibson, R. (1986). *Critical Theory and Education*. London: Hodder and Stoughton.

Giddens, A. (1990). *The Consequences of Modernity*. Cambridge: Polity Press.

Hammersley, M. and Atkinson, P. (1983). *Ethnography: Principles in Practice*. London: Tavistock.

Hargreaves, D. (1967). *Social Relations in a Secondary School*. London: Routledge and Kegan Paul.

Harris, S. (1992). 'A career on the margins? The position of careers teachers in schools', *British Journal of Sociology of Education*, 13, 2, 163–76.

Held, D. (1990). *Introduction to Critical Theory: Horkheimer to Habermas*. Cambridge: Polity Press.

Hodkinson, P. and Sparkes, A. (1993). 'Young people's choices and Careers Guidance Action Planning: a case study of Training Credits in action', *British Journal of Guidance and Counselling*, 21, 3, 246–61.

Hodkinson, P., Sparkes, A. and Hodkinson, H. (1992a). Careers Officers and Training Credits. Working Paper No. 1, 'Training Credits in Action' project. Crewe Education Department, Crewe and Alsager Faculty, Manchester Metropolitan University.

Hodkinson, P., Sparkes, A. and Hodkinson, H. (1992b). School Pupils and Training Credits. Working Paper No 2, 'Training Credits in Action' project. Crewe Education Department, Crewe and Alsager Faculty, Manchester Metropolitan University.

Hord, S. (1987). *Evaluating Educational Innovation*. London: Croom Helm.

House, E. (1979). 'Technology versus craft: a ten year perspective on innovation', *Journal of Curriculum Studies*, 1, 1–15.

Lawrence, D. (1992). 'The careers officer: a marginalised member of the education family', *School Organisation*, 12, 1, 99–111.

MacDonald, R. and Coffield, F. (1993). 'Young people and Training Credits: an early exploration', *British Journal of Education and Work*, 6, 1, 5–22.

Moore, R. (1988). 'Education, employment and recruitment'. In: Dale, R., Ferguson, R. and Robinson, A. (eds) *Frameworks for Teaching*. London: Hodder and Stoughton.

Nicholls, A. (1983). *Managing Educational Innovations*. London: George Allen & Unwin.

Richardson, L. (1990). *Writing Strategies: Reaching Diverse Audiences*. London: Sage.

Rudduck, J. (1986). *Understanding Curriculum Change*. Sheffield: USDE Papers in Education.

Rudduck, J. (1991). *Innovation and Change*. Milton Keynes: Open University Press.

Rumelhart, D. (1980). 'Schemata: the building blocks of cognition.' In: Spiro, R. *et al.* (eds) *Theoretical Issues in Reading Comprehension*. Hillsdale, NJ: Lawrence Erlbaum.

Sims, D. and Stoney, S. (1993). *Evaluation of the Second Year of Training Credits*. Slough: NFER.

Smith, J. (1989). *The Nature of Social and Educational Inquiry: Empiricism versus Interpretation*. Norwood, NJ: Ablex.

Sparkes, A. (1989). 'Towards an understanding of the personal costs and rewards involved in teacher-initiated innovations', *Educational Management and Administration*, 17, 3, 100–8.

Sparkes, A. (1994a). 'Life histories and the issue of voice: reflections on an emerging relationship', *International Journal of Qualitative Studies in Education*, 17, 3, 99–118.

Sparkes, A. (1994b). 'Self, silence and invisibility as a beginning teacher: a life history of lesbian experience', *British Journal of Sociology of Education,* 15, 1, 93–118.

Sparkes, A., Hodkinson, P. and Hodkinson, H. (1992). Careers Teachers' Perceptions of Training Credits. Working Paper No. 3, Training Credits in Action Project. Crewe Education Department, Crewe and Alsager Faculty, Manchester Metropolitan University.

Unwin, L. (1994). 'Training Credits: the pilot doomed to succeed.' In: Finegold, D., Richardson, W. and Woolhouse, J. (eds) *The Reform of Education and Training*. London: Longman.

Willis, P. (1977). *Learning to Labour*. Farnborough: Saxon House.

Woods, P. (1990). *Teacher Skills and Strategies*. Lewes: Falmer.

Chapter 3

The counsellor's story

John McLeod

What is it like being a counsellor? What is it like to spend many hours each week listening to the troubles of strangers? What kind of impact does this work have on those who are counsellors? What is the effect of a training that can involve undergoing personal therapy, exploring the influence that the most personal and intimate memories and feelings might have on one's response to clients? It is, of course, impossible to offer any definitive answers to these questions. The experience of being a counsellor is unique to each individual. It is impossible to be prescriptive about the way that members of an occupational group experience their work. Nevertheless, there are certain common themes that emerge when counsellors talk about what it is like to do this job. There exists a set of counsellors' stories that convey the sense of being a counsellor. The aim of this chapter is to describe some of these stories, and reflect on their meaning and implication in relation to the theory and practice of counselling. Throughout the chapter, the terms 'therapist' and 'counsellor' are used interchangeably, to reflect the fundamental similarity of the work done by members of these professions, and also by those who offer counselling alongside other work roles. There is a core experience of listening, attending, and following the other person that is shared by all varieties of counselling activity.

In all areas of life, there can be found an 'official' or 'correct' narrative that dominates discourse on a topic, and also a series of hidden or subjugated knowledges (White and Epston, 1990) that reflect types of experience that are harder to talk about, or to accept, or which threaten the prevailing social order. It is often these whispered stories that provide the most interesting, informative and authentic accounts of what really goes on. Unfortunately, there is a real lack of gutter journalism or fly-on-the-wall versions of the lives of counsellors. This absence is significant, given the importance of therapy as one of the defining cultural forms of late twentieth-century urban-industrial society. The life-world of that other culturally fascinating occupational group, the police, has been dissected in great detail in research studies, autobiographies, novels, films and television series. By contrast, up to now, the therapy professions have been extremely careful about their public image. Only Masson (1988), perhaps, has punctured this image.

Some writers have portrayed counsellors as saint-like self-actualised individuals. An example of this genre of counsellor hagiography can be found in Egan, whose 'portrait of a helper' includes the following descriptors:

> they are 'potent' human beings . . . show respect for their bodies through proper exercise and diet . . . (read actively and hungrily . . . [have] developed an extensive repertoire of social-emotional skills . . . genuinely care for those who have come for help . . . people of imagination . . . people who seize life rather than submit to it.
>
> (Egan, 1986: 28–30)

By contrast, other commentators have characterised counsellors as neurotic and inadequate personalities who have chosen to be counsellors as a way of compensating for an inability to establish satisfactory relationships in everyday life. An example of this perspective is Sussman (1992) who discusses an exhaustive list of unconscious sources of motivation to become a therapist: seeking sexual gratification, aggressive strivings, masochistic tendencies, narcissism and grandiosity, dependency and rescue fantasies.

In reality, the experience of being a counsellor lies somewhere between these two extremes. The over-idealised image of the counsellor presented by Egan carries with it the danger of reinforcing what Gergen (1990) has described as a professional 'language of deficit', in which therapists are regarded as living exemplars of all the virtues, and clients are viewed as bundles of needs and problems. The approach adopted by Sussman, on the other hand, is unremittingly pessimistic and life-denying in its apparent denial of any genuine capacity for caring, creativity and duty to others. Both Egan and Sussman perpetuate an over-individualised, psychologised way of making sense of these issues. For example, the capacity of a counsellor to be empathic with a client may be influenced as much by his or her cultural milieu, or the organisational climate in the counselling agency, as by his or her individual personality or mastery of counselling skills.

The experience of being a counsellor encompasses much more than just being in a room with a person who is seeking help. *Doing* counselling is clearly the core of counselling, but *being* a counsellor is a complex professional role, and a powerful source of personal identity and meaning. Three main areas of counsellor experience are examined here. First, there is a discussion of what it is like to be with a client during a counselling session. Second, there is some exploration of the ways in which being a counsellor can lead to a re-appraisal of one's life before entering the counselling profession, almost a kind of re-writing of life history. Third, the impact of counselling on the counsellor's life as a whole will be considered, for example the effect of the work on relationships at home and at work. In recent years there has been a great deal of interesting material published about the experience of being a counsellor. There are excellent books on this topic by Kottler (1986), Guy (1987) and Goldberg (1988), and useful collections of autobiographical accounts compiled by Dryden and Spurling (1989) and Noonan and Spurling (1992). Alternative discussions of some of the issues raised in this chapter can be found in McLeod (1998).

THE EXPERIENCE OF BEING WITH A CLIENT

All counselling is 'client-centred' in the sense that the counsellor is there in the service of the client and is receptive to whatever the client brings. An important feature of being with a client is, therefore, a process of achieving a sense of readiness or openness to enter that person's world. It is taken for granted that a counsellor should do their best to put to one side their own feelings and preoccupations for the duration of the counselling session, in order to focus exclusively on the needs of the client. Many counsellors employ rituals and routines, ranging from note-writing through to tea drinking or meditation, to clear themselves of 'unfinished business' in advance of a session. Personal therapy, supervision and support networks can also assist the counsellor to achieve this state of readiness. When a counsellor is seeing a series of clients one after the other, it can be difficult to move out of the experiential reality of one client and move into the world of the next person, particularly if the earlier client has recounted emotionally powerful events.

A constant element of the experience of being with a client is that of striving to enter the client's world, to engage with the way that the client makes sense of things. This is empathy. The experience of being as empathic as possible, of seeking to stay with what the client is expressing both verbally and nonverbally is a constant theme in the experience of being a counsellor. 'Being empathic' is in itself a broad category which includes a set of more specific experiences. For example, Buie (1981) argues that there are four distinct ways in which therapists carry out this activity. *Conceptual empathy* occurs when the therapist attempts to construct a cognitive model, drawing upon theoretical insights, which reflects some part of the world of the client. *Self-experiential empathy* is a state of being 'touched' by the client. Buie gives an example of a client exploring an experience of traumatic separation from her mother at an early age. The therapist had himself undergone a similar experience in childhood and was able to draw upon these feelings in the service of understanding the client. The third way is through *imaginative imitation* where the therapist can find no readily available inner referents or self-experiences and resorts to imagining what it must have been like for the client to have been in a particular situation. The fourth strategy identified by Buie, *resonance*, is when patients are about to express or actually express strong feelings or impulses and the therapist experiences 'a similar feeling at a level of intensity exceeding that involved in self-experience reference' (Buie, 1981: 297). His description of this process, drawn from a psychoanalytic case but recognisable as the kind of process that can occur in any counselling encounter, depicts the sense of this type of experience for the therapist:

> when patient A was four and a half, her parents divorced, and she was shuttled between them because neither parent wanted the burden of caring for her. The patient became aware of an intense sadness from that time which she had repressed. Eventually she filled much of several analytic hours with open sobbing. As the analyst listened, he found himself also purely sad; tears often rolled freely down his cheeks. This was not a sadness of his own, and it was not sympathy. Experientially it seemed to be her sadness itself which he felt. He did not, so far as he was aware, convey his resonant empathy. But his experiencing it naturally led him to sit quietly, saying nothing for long periods of time while she cried in the working-through process.
>
> (Buie, 1981: 301)

The experience of being in the role of counsellor can be characterised as ranging along a dimension of *activity–passivity*. Havens (1978) suggests that counselling can sometimes be an active process of 'searching out the other', 'a bold swinging into the life of the other'. Passive engagement with the client, by contrast, is a 'waiting, feeling posture, in which one echoes some of the patient's statements and above all supports and echoes his feelings'. He characterises the passive stance in relation to entering the emotional world of the client in these words: 'we can place ourselves emotionally close to the other person, allowing the reverberations of feeling to occur, and then utter what occurs to us' (Havens, 1978: 344). Alternatively, 'when no feelings occur to us, we can actively search out the other's feelings until we are close' (ibid.).

The modes of engagement in the world of the client described by Buie and Havens require the counsellor to draw upon his or her personal feelings and memories. Self-experiential and imaginative engagement rely on the counsellor being able to access memories of times when he or she had similar feelings to those being expressed by the client, or had encountered a similar situation or dilemma. Resonant engagement with the client involves paying attention to here-and-now feelings triggered by the client's story. These personal memories, images, feelings and intuitions are an essential dimension of the experience of being a counsellor. Effective counselling means listening to oneself at the same time as listening to the client. Part of the skill of counselling is to develop a capacity for maintaining a kind of 'split attention' which keeps these internal and external sources of information in balance. The experience of doing this also includes an ability to monitor and reflect on the relevance of such personal material. The complex movement of the counsellor's awareness back and forward between self and other is captured well by Spinelli (1997).

The experience of working with a client is not only a matter of having a sense of being active or passive in relation to the flow of feelings and meanings being pursued by the other person, it is also a matter of power and control. Most of the time the counsellor may have a sense of being in control, or 'in charge'. Research by Rennie (1994) where clients were interviewed about their experience of counselling showed a strong tendency for clients to *defer* to the counsellor. For example, even if a counsellor said something or made a suggestion that was inappropriate or wrong, most clients would not challenge what had been said but would give the appearance of conforming and agreeing. However, although this may be the norm in counselling, there can be occasions when there is a breakdown or crisis in the relationship or in the therapeutic process. Most commentators have suggested that these events arise from struggles over power and control, or from client 'resistance'. Mearns (1994) has proposed that it might be more useful to understand these issues in terms of the degree of mutuality and depth in the relationship, with impasses being seen as signs that the counsellor could be either *overinvolved* or *underinvolved* with the client.

It can be seen that the experience of being a counsellor working with a client involves achieving the right balance across a number of dimensions: listening to self and listening to the other; actively making thinks happen versus passively waiting; to speak or to be silent; being in control as against being controlled by the client; breaking the rules or doing it 'by the book'; being overinvolved, optimally engaged or underinvolved. It is no surprise, then, that one of the themes running through counsellors' stories is that of difficulty and uncertainty. To be a counsellor is to accept the inevitability of working in a field characterised by unresolvable dilemmas. As Whiteley *et al.* (1967) have shown, to be an effective counsellor it is necessary to possess sufficient cognitive flexibility to live with these dilemmas. Davis *et al.* (1987) and Dryden (1992; 1997) have compiled counsellor and psychotherapist accounts of the kinds of dilemmas that arise in this work.

A dimension of the experience of being a counsellor that has received relatively little attention in the literature is the experience of spirituality. The dominant, 'official' narrative enshrined in mainstream theories of counselling has little to say about spiritual experience and as a result many counsellors find themselves silenced in relation to this facet of their work (Thorne, 1997). Nevertheless, many counsellors know that the discipline of maintaining a selfless focus on the other can lead at times into a region of experience in which something about the sacredness of human being can be revealed (see West, 1997).

No doubt there are many other aspects of the experience of working with clients that have not been touched upon here. Examples of important dimensions of counsellor experience which would repay further study might include: the experience of being an embodied, sexual being; the experience of loss when a client leaves; the experience of getting close to someone from another culture; the experience of deserving payment (or not). What emerges from an examination of the experience of being with a client is just how problematic and challenging this kind of work can be. In their large-scale survey of the in-session experiences of counsellors and psychotherapists, Orlinsky and Howard (1977) found that their respondents reported themselves as feeling *inadequate* and *uncertain* in around one-quarter of all sessions.

BECOMING A COUNSELLOR

The struggle to make sense of the world of the client can often lead a counsellor into a process of remembering what they had thought and how they had felt and acted in situations similar to those being described to them. This experience can either take the form of a conscious searching of past memories, or it is like being 'thrown' back into a re-living of what it was like to be a child with an angry parent, to be in danger, to be in love. The actual process of offering counselling to another person, therefore, tends to stimulate conscious re-examination of one's own life. Counsellor training usually strongly reinforces this tendency. Most training programmes require students to undertake a period of personal therapy so that they can experience at first hand what it is like to be a client. Training courses also demand that students consistently apply the theories and models they are learning to themselves. The meaning of, for instance, Rogerian 'conditions of worth' depends on having an appreciation of the role of this factor in one's own life. People who consult a counsellor expect that person to really believe in the approach that he or she has adopted. Such a genuine belief in a theory can only be achieved by testing it against personal experience. The requirement to engage in ethical practice also leads counsellors in the direction of examining their own motives for entering this area of work.

Training to be a counsellor, of whatever length or intensity, involves socialisation into a culture and social group in which it is expected that one will be able to articulate the story of one's life in terms of the concepts and assumptions of the psychotherapeutic theory that one espouses. From this perspective, an important element of counsellor training (delivered by personal therapy, keeping a journal, participation in personal development groups, etc.) consists of learning how to re-tell or re-author a life narrative. A significant number of people who become counsellors have had some experience of therapy before entering training and have therefore made a start on this process. For those who have not, counsellor training can be challenging and difficult, as the story of 'who I am' that the would-be counsellor had always told to his or her family, partner and friends begins to change. The autobiographies of well-known therapists illustrate the end-point of this process (see Dryden and Spurling, 1989).

The counsellor's story is an account of an individual, unique life, but the way it is told is socially constructed. Being a counsellor usually means participating in a particular type of discourse of self that can be observed in counselling agencies and networks and which, at a more fundamental level, is a reflection of important aspects of contemporary culture, in particular the movement toward self-contained individualism (Cushman, 1990; Taylor, 1989).

LIVING WITH THE WORK

If becoming a counsellor means re-adjusting and re-working the manner in which one defines and understands oneself in ways that have an impact on other roles and relationships, then the experience of working as a counsellor continues that process. The experience of accepting and really listening to the despair, rage or confusion of another person can be hard to shake off. A counsellor who enters the emotional world of a client experiences some of what the client feels. In Buie's (1981) terms, the counsellor *resonates* to the client. It can be hard to switch off these feelings on leaving the office and going home. The impact of some clients can be considerable. One of the areas of counselling where this kind of experience is particularly visible is that of work with victims/survivors of trauma and abuse (Neumann and Gamble, 1995; Pearlman and McIan, 1995). McNeill and Worthen (1989) have used the term *parallel process* to describe the way that the dynamics and feelings exhibited in a counsellor–client relationship can transfer into other relationships.

At the heart of much counselling is the experience of hearing secrets, listening to stories that can be told to no other person. The counsellor is in many ways a *liminal* figure, on the edge of society, between the light and the dark, the holder of secrets and confidences (Mair, 1989). In many ways this is a very practical matter. For example, a counsellor who works in a school may know things about students and staff that cannot be passed on. He or she has to be extremely careful about what is said over the lunch table, or even who is acknowledged with a smile or glance. The counsellor may well seek to be allocated an office in a quiet part of the school, where it is not obvious to others who is attending for counselling and how often.

The personal impact of being a counsellor is reflected in the growing literature on counsellor stress (Dryden, 1995) and burn-out (Farber, 1983; Jupp and Shaul, 1991). For some counsellors, the pressures of the work can lead to an increasing detachment from clients and a continual feeling of emotional exhaustion and insufficiency. In an autobiographical account, Chaplin writes that:

I limit the number of clients that I see in a week and try to see only one or two in the evenings. But it can still be a strain after giving out energy to others all day to have to give more to my daughter at the end of the day . . . relationships with partners and recently with men friends have suffered . . . after being available for clients all day, the least thing I want to do is look after a man friend at night.

(Chaplin, 1989: 186)

Chaplin's comments express some of the subtlety, complexity and difficulty of the interaction between being a counsellor and being a parent, friend or partner. Bayne (1997) has described some of the survival strategies employed by counsellors.

CONCLUSIONS

There are important aspects of the experience of being a counsellor that have not been included in this chapter, for example the experience of being supervised, undergoing training, working in a counselling agency. Nevertheless, it can be seen that being a counsellor is a highly demanding work role which can make a major impact on personal and family life. At one level, listening to other people's problems and pain, and being exposed to the chaos of lives in crisis, can teach counsellors about the value of their relationships with their family, friends and colleagues. It can have the effect of strengthening these relationships. At another level, however, family and friends can be jealous of the amount of time the counsellor devotes to strangers. Emotions triggered by clients can spill over into other relationships. Friends can be exasperated by the intrusion of psychobabble into conversations in the pub. At an even more fundamental level, taking counselling seriously means reconstructing the self within the parameters of the therapeutic theory being used – *really* being a Rogerian, a behaviourist, an analytic psychotherapist.

The experience of being with a client during a counselling session replicates these issues on a daily basis. The discipline of listening to oneself at the same time as listening to the client is a practice that provides constant reminders of personal dilemmas and areas of anxiety in a way that just does not happen in less reflexive occupations. Each utterance or gesture that is made toward a client is a compromise between the response defined as appropriate by the model within which the counsellor is operating and the spontaneous reaction that might be made to a child in distress.

It is necessary to bear in mind that what has been written here cannot be definitive. There is much that remains to be understood about the experience of being a counsellor, many stories that await their telling. For instance, there are undoubtedly significant differences between counselling where the client is met only once or twice (for example in many crisis counselling or telephone helpline settings) and counselling where there is a relationship with the client that stretches over several years. Also, counselling in which the counsellor also fulfils another role in relation to the client (for example as teacher, social worker or nurse) introduces many other possible storylines. There are also important cultural sources of difference. Western culture has tended to construct counselling as an individual, private activity. In other cultures the tradition is to engage in a more communal therapeutic process. Gender is a further key factor in the way that work and relationships are experienced: one might well imagine that there could be ways in which experience of being a counsellor may be different for men and for women.

There are significant practical implications to taking the counsellor's story seriously. In terms of everyday counselling practice, it is important to recognise that the counsellor and client may experience the same session in quite different ways, and construct different stories around what they believe to have happened. For example particularly in early sessions, clients are much more aware than their counsellors of how emotional they feel (Maluccio, 1979). Counsellors are familiar with the situation and are relatively at ease during first sessions. Clients, by contrast, are often highly anxious (even if they strive to conceal this fact). Clients, also, are likely to construct stories around themes of the quality of guidance and advice they have received, while counsellors do not usually view the counselling process in this way (see McLeod, 1990). The type of stories that counsellors tell are also quite different from those told by other professionals with whom they may be in contact, such as psychiatrists, teachers or social workers. Counsellors have a tendency to tell open-textured, reflexive and 'person-oriented' stories about their work, while colleagues may engage in narratives that are more purposeful, objective, task-oriented and funny. This kind of narrative divergence can at times lead to counsellors being perceived by colleagues as somewhat 'precious', as the only members of staff who can spend an hour at a time with a client and who hold secrets. The integration of counselling within diverse organisational settings can be largely a matter of getting the story right. The counsellor's story is increasingly seen as a resource for research and training. Thus Stiles (1995) has argued, the best way to make the link between research findings and practical applications of these findings in training and practice is to express that knowledge in a narrative form, to make it into a story.

BIBLIOGRAPHY

Bayne, R. (1997) 'Survival', in I. Horton and V. Varma (eds) *The Needs of Counsellors and Psychotherapists*, London: Sage.

Buie, D. (1981) 'Empathy: its nature and limitations', *Journal of the American Psychoanalytical Association*, 29, pp. 281–307.

Chaplin, J. (1989) 'Rhythm and blues', in W. Dryden and L. Spurling (eds) *On Becoming a Psychotherapist*, London: Routledge.

Cushman, P. (1990) 'Why the self is empty: toward a historically situated psychology', *American Psychologist*, 45, pp. 599–611.

Davis, J., Eliott, R., Davis, M., Binns, M., Francis, V., Kelman, J. and Schroder, T. (1987) 'Development of a taxonomy of therapist difficulties: initial report', *British Journal of Medical Psychology*, 60, pp. 109–119.

Dryden, W. (ed.) (1992) *Hard-earned Lessons from Counselling in Action*, London: Sage.

Dryden, W. (ed.) (1995) *The Stresses of Counselling in Action*, London: Sage.

Dryden, W. (ed.) (1997) *Therapists' Dilemmas*, London: Sage.

Dryden, W. and Spurling, L. (eds) (1989) *On Becoming a Psychotherapist*, London: Routledge.

Egan, G. (1986) *The Skilled Helper: A Systematic Approach to Effective Helping*, 3rd edn, Belmont, CA: Brooks/Cole.

Farber, B.A. (1983) 'Dysfunctional aspects of the psychotherapeutic role', in B.A. Farber (ed.) *Stress and Burnout in the Human Service Professions*, New York: Pergamon.

Gergen, K. (1990) 'Therapeutic professions and the diffusion of deficit', *The Journal of Mind and Behavior*, 11 pp. 353–368.

Goldberg, C. (1988) *On Being a Psychotherapist: The Journey of the Healer*, New York: Gardner Press.

Guy, J.D. (1987) *The Personal Life of the Psychotherapist*, New York: Wiley.

Havens, L. (1978) 'Explorations in the use of language in psychotherapy: simple empathic statements', *Psychiatry*, 41, pp. 336–345.

Jupp, J.J. and Shaul, V. (1991) 'Burn-out in student counsellors', *Counselling Psychology Quarterly*, 4, pp. 157–167.

Kottler, J.A. (1986) *On Being a Therapist*, San Fransisco: Jossey-Bass.

Mair, M. (1989) *Between Psychology and Psychotherapy: A Poetics of Experience*, London: Routledge.

McLeod, J. (1990) 'The practitioner's experience of counselling: a review of the research literature', in D. Mearns and W. Dryden (eds) *Experiences of Counselling in Action*, London: Sage.

McLeod, J. (1998) *An Introduction to Counselling*, 2nd edn, Buckingham: Open University Press.

McNeill, B. W. and Worthen, V. (1989) 'The parallel process in psychotherapy supervision', *Professional Psychology: Research and Practice*, 20, pp. 329–333.

Mair, M. (1989) *Beyond Psychology and Psychotherapy: A Poetics of Experience*, London: Routledge.

Maluccio, A. (1979) *Learning from Clients: Interpersonal Helping as Viewed by Clients and Social Workers*, New York: The Free Press.

Masson, J. (1988) *Against Therapy: Emotional Tyranny and the Myth of Psychological Healing*, Glasgow: Collins.

Mearns, D. (1994) *Developing Person-Centred Counselling*, London: Sage.

Neumann, D.A. and Gamble, S.J. (1995) 'Issues in the professional development of psychotherapists: countertransference and vicarious traumatization in the new trauma therapist', *Psychotherapy*, 32, pp. 341–347.

Noonan, E. and Spurling, L. (eds) (1992) *The Making of a Counsellor*, London: Routledge.

Orlinsky, D. and Howard, K. (1977) 'The therapist's experience of psychotherapy', in A. Gurman and A. Razin (eds) *Effective Psychotherapy: A Handbook of Research*, Oxford: Pergamon.

Pearlman, L.A. and McIan, P.S. (1995) 'Vicarious traumatisation: an empirical study of the effects of trauma work on trauma therapists', *Professional Psychology: Research and Practice*, 26, pp. 558–565.

Rennie, D.L. (1994) 'Clients' deference in psychotherapy', *Journal of Counseling Psychology*, 41, pp. 427–437.

Spinelli, E. (1997) *Tales of Un-knowing: Therapeutic Encounters from an Existential Perspective*, London: Duckworth.

Stiles, W.B. (1995) 'Stories, tacit knowledge, and psychotherapy research', *Psychotherapy Research*, 5(2), pp. 125–127.

Sussman, M. (1992) *A Curious Calling: Unconscious Motivation for Practicing Psychotherapy*, New York: Jason Aronson.

Taylor, C. (1989) *Sources of the Self*, Cambridge, MA: Harvard University Press.

Thorne, B. (1997) 'Spiritual responsibility in a secular profession', in I. Horton and V. Varma (eds) *The Needs of Counsellors and Psychotherapists*, London: Sage.

West, W. (1997) 'Integrating counselling, psychotherapy and healing: an inquiry into counsellors and psychotherapists whose work includes healing', *British Journal of Guidance and Counselling*, 25(3), pp. 291–312.

White, M. and Epston, D. (1990) *Narrative Means to Therapeutic Ends*, New York: W.W. Norton.

Whiteley, J.M., Sprinthall, N.A., Mosher, R.L. and Donaghy, R.T. (1967) 'Selection and evaluation of counselor effectiveness', *Journal of Counseling Psychology*, 14, pp. 226–234.

Chapter 4

The teacher's experience of guidance

Cathy Howieson and Sheila Semple

This chapter draws heavily on a two-year qualitative evaluation of the effectiveness of guidance in six contrasting secondary schools in four regions of Scotland, from 1993 to 1995. The research studied six illustrative schools in depth. Its findings echoed those in the HMI report based on work in around 200 schools (Scottish Office Education and Industry Department, 1996).

CONTEXT OF GUIDANCE IN SCOTTISH SCHOOLS

The Scottish Education Department (SED) memorandum 'Guidance in Scottish Secondary Schools' (SED, 1968) marked the formal introduction of structured guidance provision in Scottish schools. By 1974 all education authorities had set up guidance systems in their schools, and the system is now well established.

Under the Scottish system of guidance, principal and assistant principal teachers of guidance (PT(G)s and APT(G)s) are responsible for the personal, social, curricular and vocational guidance of a caseload of pupils. Guidance staff are usually also subject teachers.

The recommended staffing for guidance is approximately one promoted post for guidance for every 150 pupils, but in practice this varies. Caseloads might be organised on a 'vertical' basis, i.e. include pupils from each of the year groups S1-S6, or on a 'horizontal' basis covering a separate year group(s).

A Certificate in Guidance and several other relevant qualifications are available but the Certificate is not a mandatory qualification for guidance teachers and the extent to which guidance staff hold the Certificate varies across authorities. The issue of a mandatory qualification continues to be debated.

The reform of the upper school curriculum in Scotland (Higher Still) has led to an increased awareness of the need for guidance, particularly its curricular and vocational aspects, since pupils will face more complex post-16 choices. When the Higher Still curriculum is introduced, pupils will have a 'guidance entitlement' covering pre-entry, induction, on-going and pre-exit guidance. Guidance is, therefore, seen as supporting progress and success in learning and also as encouraging motivation through appropriate choice of subjects and post-16 routes.

The aims and practice of guidance continue to evolve but *More Than Feelings of Concern* (Scottish Central Committee on Guidance, 1986) remains the defining document on guidance in Scotland. The first of its eight objectives for guidance remains the basis of practice: 'to ensure that each pupils knows and is known personally and in some depth by at least one member of staff'.

Most guidance teachers deal with all aspects of guidance provision. There are some 'careers co-ordinators' who typically have the responsibility to liaise with the Careers Service. They may or may not deal with careers education, the careers library or work experience. The vocational guidance role of the careers co-ordinator is limited, reflecting the principle that pupils' own guidance teachers give vocational as well as personal, social and curricular guidance.

Guidance teacher's work

Within their overall remit, the on-going aspects of the work of PT(G)s and APT(G)s in the Scottish guidance system include the monitoring of attendance, review of progress in school subjects, and advising on subject choice. Although guidance staff historically had a direct role in discipline, schools have now generally excluded guidance from the issuing of disciplinary sanctions and instead emphasise their supportive role. Another common feature of the work of guidance staff concerns Personal and Social Education; most guidance teachers having some responsibility for the design and/or delivery of Personal and Social Education provision for pupils.

A major element of the work of guidance teachers is dealing with a range of issues that might concern pupils' relationship with teachers or their peers or behavioural, personal, family or health matters. Some of these cases might require liaison with external agencies such as Psychological Services, Social Work and the Children's Panel.

Guidance has been defined as a whole school responsibility, in which all teachers have a role. Register or form teachers, in particular, are generally encouraged to take on a pastoral role with their register class in addition to administrative duties. Where staff who are not promoted guidance teachers accept a guidance-related role for a particular small group of pupils this is described as 'First Level Guidance' (FLG). Schools are at varying levels of development of FLG and a sophisticated FLG system is still the exception rather than the rule in schools. A key question is: do teachers agree that 'all teachers are guidance teachers?'. Some argue that the existence

of promoted guidance posts encourages other teachers to think that if guidance teachers exist and are being paid to do it, it's their responsibility.
Others suggest that the role of the guidance teacher is as a supporter of all
guidance in the school.

THE RESEARCH

The central aim of the research project was to examine the guidance needs
of pupils and their parents, the organisation of guidance provision and its
effectiveness. Variation between schools was a major focus. While the
research covered all aspects of guidance (personal, curricular and vocational)
there were also specific aims to review the management of careers service
work in schools and links with local employers.

The research involved:

- an extensive programme of interviews with promoted guidance staff, senior
  management, other teachers with a guidance role and careers officers;
- interviews with key informants;
- a postal survey and interview study of parents and guidance (720
  parents);
- group discussions (including questionnaires) with S2, S4 and S5 pupils
  (233 pupils). For readers not familiar with the Scottish system,
  pupils have seven years of primary education from age 5 (P1 to P7)
  and, potentially, six years of secondary education (S1 to S6). S1 and S2
  pupils have a common curriculum, with the end of S2 being the point
  of some limited specialisation in choosing standard grade subjects. S4,
  for many, is the first point at which pupils are legally allowed to leave
  school, having completed Standard grade exams. Many S5 pupils will
  have chosen to stay on at school to sit Scottish Higher grade exams at
  the end of S5.

The six schools were chosen on the basis of: the type of guidance structure;
the socio-economic composition of the school roll; school size; staying-on
rates; attainment; type of location; denominational/non-denominational;
multi-cultural; and local labour market. The aim was to select schools that
were *illustrative* of different types of schools and guidance provision in
Scotland.

The identification and measurement of guidance needs and the evaluation
of guidance provision are difficult tasks. The approach of the study was to
focus on the perceptions and experiences of both the consumers of guidance
(pupils and parents) and the providers of guidance (guidance teachers, other
relevant staff and careers officers), considered against the background of
relevant regional and national policies and guidelines.

OUTCOMES OF THE RESEARCH – TEACHERS' PERSPECTIVES ON GUIDANCE

The identification of guidance needs

When we asked guidance staff to identify the pupils' needs to which they felt guidance should be responding, they frequently began by telling us about needs but quickly moved on to telling us about provision and guidance teachers' tasks at each school stage. A number of reasons may explain this response. At a general level, their response is an example of what seems to be one of the underlying characteristics of guidance in the project schools: that is the implicit nature of much that is assumed and carried out in guidance. Guidance practice seems often to be based on a set of unstated assumptions that are shared by guidance and other school staff. Another reason may be the lack of any sustained attempt to evaluate pupils' needs in the schools concerned. While some staff referred to the range of pupil needs identified in *More Than Feelings of Concern* (Scottish Central Committee on Guidance, 1986) none of the schools in the project had tried to assess pupils' needs in their own school on a regular and systematic basis. Yet when guidance is hard pressed for time and resources, knowing the needs of pupils is a key way to decide priorities.

How are we to find out what pupils' guidance needs are? Asking pupils is one method but can only be a partial one. Pupils are likely to experience more needs than those they are able to articulate. A few staff routinely monitored their pupils' report cards to pick up on any problems; others identified needs during their subject or Personal and Social Education (PSE) teaching and through liaison with other staff. The latter was often on an informal basis. In those schools managing to have at least one guidance interview per year with every pupil, the interviews provided a potential means of identifying needs. However, none of the schools in the project conducted a regular, comprehensive review of pupil needs. Staff comments on pupils' needs were made largely on the basis of personal opinion and experience and there was limited cross-checking and balancing of individual teacher's personal views and experiences. The focus of staff on guidance provision at the various school stages may also reflect how the business of schools is generally conceived, that is schools are concerned with the delivery of stage-related curricula and syllabi. Most guidance staff in the project schools identified a similar range of guidance needs or provision and noted the same sorts of needs and provision at the various school stages. For example, the need to help pupils settle in and to deal with potential bullying in the first year of secondary school; support for subject choice at age 13/14, etc. While stage may be an obvious defining characteristic, guidance staff also commented frequently about the variation in needs within year groups because of different levels of maturity. For example, one guidance teacher spoke about teaching sex education to a group of 14-year old girls: at one extreme one girl was still playing with dolls while at the other another was talking about going to nightclubs.

In considering pupils' guidance needs, there are both pupils' own self-generated needs, and also other needs that arise from the circumstances of how the school curriculum is organised and associated administrative and bureaucratic requirements. The latter type of need is evident from the responses of staff to our questions about pupil needs.

> We have to give priority to helping pupils choose their subjects because the timetabler needs to know.

Teachers frequently translated our question about pupils' needs into pupils' problems. Although most guidance teachers and virtually all pupils thought that guidance was for everyone, many pupils saw guidance as being for pupils who were 'in trouble', and most teachers felt they had too little time and too many pressures to provide the support that ordinary pupils needed.

> It's inevitable, the ones with the most obvious problems get the most attention.

The guidance needs identified by staff

The most fundamental pupil needs commonly identified by staff concerned the need for individual attention, to be listened to, to know that they are valued and taken seriously and to have someone to provide a consistent, non-punitive relationship from year to year.

> They should know they're valued and taken seriously, it's someone to talk to, someone to remember them.

Curricular guidance and review of progress was another commonly mentioned pupil need. Guidance teachers felt that pupils required regular feedback on performance and curricular guidance from someone with an overview of their progress. A number of guidance teachers suggested that, rather than schools seeking to provide pupils with the 'right' answers, pupils needed help to become more aware, to assess and come to their own decisions.

We have noted already that guidance teachers identified stage of schooling as an important factor in determining guidance needs. This raises the question of how far needs are imposed by the school system, rather than being intrinsic to the experience of young people. During the early stages of their time at secondary school, staff felt pupils needed help to settle in and adjust to their new school and to integrate and form new relationships with other young people. Responding to pupils' worries about possible bullying was mentioned by most staff. Falling out with friends, name-calling and bullying were common reasons for pupils to go to their guidance teacher.

The lower school is also a time when pupils begin to explore their identity and test the limits of what they could and could not do within the school situation. This could result in misbehaviour, poor time-keeping and bad attendance – the main reasons for individual intervention by guidance teachers. It was generally felt that boys were more likely than girls to be involved in misdemeanours, especially of a more overt nature. Do boys, therefore, need more or less guidance support?

Although poor behaviour was often a reason to refer a pupil to the guidance teacher, the role of guidance was to provide the support necessary to help pupils change their behaviour in order to allow them (and their classmates) to be more successful in learning. Disciplinary sanctions were therefore not normally applied by guidance teachers but by members of the senior management team.

For older pupils, teachers identified transition needs: focusing on pupils' progression into the upper school and eventually leaving school itself. Pupils needed help to find their way through the educational and career options available to them. Problems relating to pressure of work and exams were also particularly evident at this stage: pupils felt they had to get particular passes to enter the career or course they wanted. Teachers saw a change in individual guidance needs in the upper school away from attendance and disciplinary issues to a variety of personal problems, for example eating disorders, sexual relationships and home or family problems.

> 'They're wanting to be more independent and find their way in the world, but the expectations and pressures can be high.'

Individual pupils might also sometimes require support from their guidance teacher because of health problems, family illness or bereavement.

Teachers in the school with a substantial minority ethnic population made the point that these pupils were themselves diverse, so generalisations about their particular guidance needs should be avoided. Several guidance staff commented that the school could sometimes be unaware of the barriers at home or in their community that some minority ethnic pupils had to deal with, for example, the lack of freedom experienced by some bright, motivated Asian girls. At the same time they felt that pupils needed the school to acknowledge and work with the differences in other communities rather than confront them.

Impact of deprivation

The socio-economic background of pupils was a major source of variation within and across the project schools. At one extreme, one school did not identify deprivation as a key issue. In another school, teachers felt that the level of deprivation that the majority of pupils experienced had a major impact on the ethos of the school, on its guidance provision, and on the level of attention guidance teachers had to provide.

> They're simply needing attention, maybe because of poverty, split families and single parents.

Teachers thought that deprivation had an impact on pupils' guidance needs in a number of ways: lack of confidence, lack of self-esteem and a poor self-image. This lack of confidence might show itself in attention-seeking or misbehaviour and/or in low aspirations even among pupils of high ability. Staff characterised pupils from disadvantaged backgrounds as tending to have limited ideas about jobs, education and training, and as less likely to achieve their potential. These pupils were more likely to experience low parental expectations and to lack parental support in their studies, particularly in the upper school, reflecting parents' own lack of experience of post-compulsory education.

> 'Even intelligent children don't believe in themselves in this area, and have low aspirations: you've got to keep building them up.'

In one school with areas of serious deprivation and unemployment in its catchment, staff were conscious that many pupils experienced a structure-less life outside of school and had few positive adult role models, especially male, in their family and in the wider community. Consequently some children, and boys in particular, might have difficulty relating to male authority figures and staff felt that the school had to act as a substitute.

Teachers in a majority of the schools noted the intrusion of family problems or poor family circumstances into school life, for example pupils coming to school without breakfast, or dirty, or distressed because of family quarrels and unable to concentrate on their school work. Although family break-up is not confined to any social group, staff tended to identify the resulting problems more in relation to pupils from a poorer socio-economic background.

Drug and alcohol abuse and under-age sex were identified as issues by teachers in three of the project schools and they related this to levels of deprivation in the area. While they did not think there was much drug-taking in the school, the effects of drugs were sometimes evident in pupils, for example when they returned to school on Mondays. Pupils' expectations and norms were also perceived as being influenced by the prevailing attitude to drugs, alcohol and under-age sex in the community.

Is there a tendency for teachers to view drugs as more of a problem in schools in deprived areas than in the others? Certainly some of the parents interviewed thought this to be the case.

'My niece goes to . . . Academy (middle-class area) and the drugs thing is just as bad there, but you just get labelled if you come from this area.'

On the whole, staff did not identify particular needs experienced by middle-class pupils although several teachers in one school did mention that middle-class pupils were more likely to have emotional problems associated with the over high expectations of their parents. However, this was the exception. Staff's views may reflect the everyday pressures to respond to pupils with the most immediate and obvious problems. In the absence of a comprehensive evaluation of pupil needs, it is not possible to be sure whether middle-class pupils have unmet needs.

Guidance needs in the senior school

In discussing pupils' needs in the senior school, the more varied composition of pupils emerged as an important change within and across the project schools. A point commonly made by guidance teachers was that the increase in the number of less academic pupils staying on into S5 and S6 presented a new challenge to the school: curricular and vocational guidance was thought to be more complex.

'Guidance needs to help pupils through the minefield of 16+ choices.'

A related concern was that too many pupils stayed on at school because it was a 'safe' environment, avoiding entering the labour market for fear of unemployment, or through reluctance to make a decision about their future. Such pupils, if they did not markedly improve their educational attainment, were thought to be disadvantaged as an *older* school-leaver entering the labour market. How can pupils be helped to make the transition out of school at the most appropriate time? Within each school, guidance teachers thought they were faced with a greater range of pupil needs in the upper school.

Staff in all the project schools believed that not only had pupils' needs changed over time but also that they had increased.

We've got more kids with serious problems in this school, there's less home support . . . it's harder to be a teenager now.

Teachers identified a range of changes in society that added to pupils' guidance needs: greater tensions in family life with higher levels of unemployment or job insecurity, increased family break-up, and the growing number of one-parent families. Pupils themselves were seen to be under more pressure in relation to drugs, alcohol and sex and to be confronted with these pressures at an earlier age so that such problems were now more evident in the lower school.

Staff felt that in a more competitive society, pupils were under growing pressure to achieve at school in order to be able to access worthwhile education, training and employment opportunities. Entry to educational and career opportunities was thought to be more competitive and the possible routes open to young people were more complicated for them to deal with than before. School itself was seen as being more pressurised both because of the need for pupils to achieve the highest possible qualifications and also because of changes to the curriculum.

Perspectives on the tasks of guidance

How do guidance teachers respond to these needs? All the project schools set themselves the target of arranging one-to-one interviews for each pupil every year, but not all managed it. Several which did, identified problems such as the guidance teacher not being clearly focused on the purpose of the interview, or having too short a time (typically around 15 minutes); or the pupil being uncomfortable in the situation.

> Pupils need something to focus on in the interview, not just 'how are you getting on?'

Virtually all pupils thought guidance was important and wanted more contact with their guidance teacher. Sometimes pupils approached their guidance teacher directly. Whether pupils did this (according to both teachers and pupils) depended on how easy it was to find the guidance teacher, whether he/she had time available and, most importantly, whether the pupil found the teacher approachable and easy to talk to. Where guidance was associated with 'getting into trouble' pupils were less likely to approach their guidance teacher.

> I know it can be seen as a problem if your guidance teacher calls you out of class.

It was also common for referrals to come from subject teachers where a child was not performing well, or had spoken about a personal problem, or whose behaviour had changed. Subject teachers were thought to prefer informal rather than formal referrals for guidance, and they were more likely to refer pupils for behaviour or discipline issues than for personal problems. There were some tensions here with guidance teachers suspecting they would be judged by some subject colleagues as 'successful' only if they managed to improve behaviour in the classroom. The guidance teacher would either try to intervene to help with a problem (for example where there had been bullying or where a relationship with a subject teacher was deteriorating) or support the pupil in dealing with it themselves. Another key task for guidance teachers was to be the channel for home/school communication, making direct individual contact when specific problems arose, for example where a pupil's attendance was poor.

A good proportion of teachers' guidance time was absorbed by a small number of pupils with multiple and complex support needs. For these young people, establishing contacts with Social Work, Psychological Services, the Children's Panel and the police would be an important task for guidance teachers.

Most guidance teachers thought it was valuable to teach PSE to pupils on their caseload, although only some were able to do so. It allowed them to see pupils in a different setting and tackled a number of key guidance issues such as careers education, health education, handling bullying, relationships with others and making decisions. PSE commonly covered preparation for work experience and the completion of a record of achievement for the end of schooling. However, most guidance teachers saw individual contact with pupils as their key function. This led us to wonder what was the appropriate balance and relationship between guidance teachers' individual guidance work and their PSE teaching?

EMERGING ISSUES AND CHALLENGES FOR GUIDANCE

When guidance was set up in Scottish schools, some hoped it would make schools more aware of pupils' support needs, and of how the school system contributed to some of the problems pupils faced in being successful learners. Evidence of this was, in fact, very limited. Our view of guidance teachers is of a group of practitioners with a high level of commitment to their caseload of pupils, frustrated by the lack of time available to get to know and support 'ordinary' pupils whose guidance needs were not manifest. They were engaged in a balancing act between the demands of subject teaching and guidance tasks, between school and local and national priorities and thus were in a poor position to challenge the way their school functioned. Many talked about being stressed and tired, feeling they were unduly reactive and problem driven. The problems of guidance staff were compounded by the fact that in not one of the schools did all teachers have even the minimum recommended time for guidance. In this situation, the ability of the guidance team and, even more so, the individual teacher, to influence the school system was very limited.

As we have noted above, guidance teachers felt pulled by the demands of their guidance and of their subject role. However, despite the pressures, they felt that the roles were complementary, could be done by the same person and, in fact, enhanced each other. This was one area where pupil perspectives were markedly different from those of teachers; some found it difficult to respond to teachers in different roles, 'one minute he's giving you a row for not doing your maths homework, and the next you're supposed to tell him all your problems'. Others did not like it when guidance teachers tried to discuss personal guidance issues in subject classrooms. This illustrates another difference between perspectives of guidance teachers and pupils, i.e. pupils expressed a greater need for confidentiality and privacy than guidance teachers expected. Teachers felt that it was important to see the pupil in a class context, that teaching pupils on their caseload helped to 'keep an eye' on them, and, perhaps most importantly, that it was necessary to maintain credibility in the eyes of non-guidance colleagues. But many pupils and some parents felt it would be better to have full-time guidance teachers with professional training and saw the joint role as compromising the impartiality of the guidance teachers.

The system of specialist but part-time guidance teachers who are also subject teachers could thus raise 'boundary' issues for pupils. Other sorts of boundary issues were more evident in relation to other teachers. While guidance is defined as a whole school responsibility with all teachers having a guidance role, some teachers felt that the existence of specialist guidance teachers undercut this philosophy in practice because it encouraged other teachers to see guidance as 'a guidance teacher's job'. This view also affected the development of first-level guidance since some teachers felt this role was properly the function of the promoted guidance teachers.

Another aspect of 'boundaries' concerned the role of guidance staff with class teachers where they had a difficult relationship with a pupil. The guidance teacher had to tread carefully when trying to persuade the class teacher to change his/her approach to the pupil: it was important to avoid conflict about perceived interference in the professional practice of the class teacher. This difficulty could be compounded where the guidance teacher was a more junior member of staff than the teacher concerned. Guidance teachers felt that other teachers often failed to appreciate that they themselves might need to change how they dealt with pupils. The position of guidance staff in schools is an anomalous one since it cuts across both the established hierarchy and also the departmental subject basis of the school.

All the guidance teachers interviewed were committed to the concept of guidance being very important in supporting pupils' learning. They saw themselves as helping pupils to mature, to improve relationships with others, to handle conflict, to achieve better qualifications and to make appropriate choices about their future and present lives. All could point to individuals who had been supported at the right moment. At the same time, they recognised that many of the social and personal problems that some pupils faced were too complex for easy resolution.

IMPLICATIONS FOR POLICY AND PRACTICE

While the Scottish guidance system is peculiar to its own environment, it shares many features and challenges common to other systems and in this final section we consider some issues of general relevance.

We found little structured evaluation of guidance needs. Instead teachers responded to pupils needs as they emerged; their ability to anticipate and offer support before problems became apparent was limited. A key policy issue is to find strategies that will help schools stand back from the provision they offer to allow them to identify needs in a systematic way so that they can set priorities and move away from 'crisis counselling'.

A second important question to consider is society's expectations of schools. Can we realistically expect teachers to make up for the deprivation that their pupils may experience in other parts of their life? If so, how should we organise and resource schools to do this?

Pupils in our research argued that guidance should be for all, that everybody had a right to the support they needed but that 'going for guidance' often had a stigma attached to it precisely because of its focus on problems.

Most teachers who took part in our research felt they were reactive and problem driven in their guidance work. Their energies were absorbed by a minority of young people with complex needs, leaving them with too little time to support the ordinary pupils in their learning. Should guidance primarily be for pupils with problems, especially personal and social problems? Or should it focus on supporting all pupils in their learning and perhaps have clearer aims related to educational guidance?

Many would argue that personal and social problems *do* interrupt the education of individuals, and if expressed in anti-social behaviour, harm the educational progress of non-disruptive pupils. But what should the balance of work be to deliver guidance support for all?

Virtually all our teachers felt that guidance was not sufficiently well resourced to achieve its maximum effectiveness. A small number added, 'but it never could be'. Is guidance support a bottomless pit? Will pupils' guidance needs continue to increase as schools and education authorities try to keep pupils with many different needs within mainstream education?

If there is such a thing as an 'entitlement' to guidance, is there an upper limit to this? Is there a point at which schools must limit guidance support in times of limited resources? In the schools we studied there was a clear link between the level of resourcing and the effectiveness of guidance.

However, resourcing is not the only issue. In the poorest and the best resourced schools alike, pupils identified individual guidance teachers who were effective, and ones who were not: personality, approach, openness were as important as the system. How should guidance teachers be selected and trained, and the effectiveness of their work be reviewed?

Resourcing, identifying need, setting priorities, deciding on roles: these are all important areas on which management must concentrate. We found considerable variation in how guidance teachers were managed and supported, and this, too, had an impact on effectiveness. Good management of those with a guidance responsibility is a key issue across all schools and systems.

In conclusion, guidance teachers saw their role as requiring both high levels of commitment and also particular skills in juggling time and priorities. They felt support for pupils was essential for their success and happiness in school but were well aware of many constraints, including the impact of the demands made by a small number of pupils with complex needs. Guidance was, they thought, based on 'knowing and being known', the personal relationship based on trust between the guidance teacher and the pupil, and the need for structures to support this.

BIBLIOGRAPHY

Higher Still Development Unit (1997) *Managing Guidance Arrangements for Higher Still*, Edinburgh: HSDU.

Howieson, C. and Semple, S. (1996) *Guidance in Secondary Schools*, Edinburgh: Centre for Education Sociology, University of Edinburgh.

Northern College, SOED, St. Andrew's College (1994) *Managing Guidance. A Resource Pack to Promote the Effective Management and Provision of Guidance to Pupils*, Dundee: Northern College, SOED, St Andrew's College.

Scottish Central Committee on Guidance (1986) *More Than Feelings of Concern*, Edinburgh: Consultative Committee on the Curriculum.

Scottish Education Department (1968) 'Guidance in Scottish Secondary Schools', memorandum, Edinburgh: SED.

Scottish Office (1994) *Higher Still: Opportunity for All*, Edinburgh: Scottish Office.

Scottish Office Education and Industry Department (1996) 'Effective learning and teaching in Scottish Secondary Schools – guidance', a report by HM Inspector of Schools, Edinburgh: Scottish Office.

Part II

Professional discourses

Chapter 5

What is a profession?

Experience versus expertise

Jan Williams

WHAT IS A PROFESSION?

The question of what constitutes a profession has long been debated; and attempts have been made to identify a set of distinct traits which characterize all professions. Freidson (1986) centres on the issue of self-direction or autonomy, suggesting that central to a profession is the power to regulate its own affairs – a power which is usually statutorily granted.

Millerson (1964), surveying the work of twenty-one authors on the definition of professions, extracted a total of twenty-three elements used by them to define a profession, though there was little consensus among them. Certain key characteristics are, however, frequently cited. These include:

- skill based on theoretical knowledge
- the provision of training and occupation
- tests of the competence of members
- organization
- adherence to a professional code of conduct
- altruistic service.

With many different perspectives on the traits which characterize professions, there can be no one 'ideal type' profession. Different occupational groups conform more or less closely to the above criteria – and they change over time.

An important element of the professional–client relationship, it is proposed, is that of 'mystification': professionals promote their services as esoteric. They create dependence on their skills and reduce the areas of knowledge and experience they have in common with their clients. In this way they increase the 'social distance' between themselves and their clients, and so gain increasing autonomy (Johnson, 1989).

While a small number of occupations have long held the status of professions, in the past forty years, with growing knowledge and technology, many more have started to 'professionalize'. Occupations such as social work, nursing, health visiting, midwifery and teaching – often referred to as the semi-professions – have sought to enhance their status and earn recognition as full professions.

EXPERT KNOWLEDGE AS THE BASIS OF PROFESSIONS

As suggested above, a key characteristic of traditional professions is the body of theoretical knowledge which forms the basis for applied specialist skills. Hoyle (1982: 48) described the academic community's criteria for valid knowledge as: 'codified, systematized, universalistic knowledge generated by experimentation and independent sceptical scholarship and, where applied to practical and personal problems, applied in a rational and detached manner'.

The possession of such a systematized, theoretical body of knowledge is seen as an essential foundation for any occupational group aspiring to professional status. A professional group's body of specialist knowledge forms the foundation for developing whole philosophies and systems; for example, lawyers define the nature and function of law and the way to administer justice; and doctors define sickness and health and the distribution of medical services. The claim to specialist knowledge is central, for on it rests the professionals' claim to be qualified to advise, the claim to 'know better' than their clients – and hence the claim for autonomy, for being trusted by the public, for reward and prestige.

The traditional professions of medicine, law, architecture, etc. have a well-established base of expert knowledge. In recent years aspiring professions such as social work, nursing and teaching have similarly attempted to define and emphasize the body of theoretical knowledge underpinning their work; they have sought to extend the length of initial training, and grounded it more firmly in academic disciplines; they have argued for all-graduate entry; attempted to remove unqualified personnel; and developed a growing body of research and scholarship to underpin their occupations. In these ways they have sought 'professionalization', attempting to gain full status and recognition as professionals (Hoyle, 1982).

An expert knowledge base, then, is the foundation on which professional status is built; and the purveying of that knowledge is the means by which power and control is maintained. All professions offer a service; and that service includes 'giving advice'. The claim to be qualified to give that advice, like everything else claimed by the professional, rests on the claim to specialized knowledge. According to Hughes (1975: 249) 'Professions *profess*. They profess to know better than others the nature of certain matters, and to know better than their clients what ails them or their affairs.'

Traditionally, therefore, the professionals' approach to client advice, or education, has been a prescriptive one – that is, the professional, as expert, prescribes what the client needs to know, passes on that information/advice and expects compliance. The emphasis is on a one-way transmission of knowledge from expert to lay person: 'knowledge is a gift bestowed by those who consider themselves knowledgeable upon those whom they consider to know nothing' (Freire, 1972: 46). This prescriptive approach to client education conforms to the traditional educational model of pedagogy. Its theoretical basis is rationalism: a belief in scientific objectivity, a belief that knowledge is certain and absolute, and has a status and origin independent of individual human beings.

Yet knowledge is not absolute, but socially constructed. Values are implicit, if not explicit, in these professionally defined bodies of knowledge, and in the selection of knowledge for transmission. With a prescriptive approach to education, these values too are afforded the status of knowledge, and held to be absolute. In this way professionals impose their perspectives and values on the rest of society – and education becomes a means of social control. This is what Jarvis (1985) has termed 'education from above'.

THE RELEVANCE OF EXPERT KNOWLEDGE TO PROFESSIONAL PRACTICE

Increasingly today, professional knowledge is being challenged. Professional prescriptions of what constitutes valid knowledge are being called into question; and the concept of knowledge as absolute and value-free no longer holds sway. There is criticism that professions are out of touch with the perspectives and needs of their clients; and the value of the theoretical knowledge underpinning professions, and the relevance of theory to practice, are being questioned.

The field of health promotion offers some useful illustrations of this. Kemm (1991), for example, discussing the health education advice professionals give to their clients, questions the validity of the knowledge base for this advice. He suggests that knowledge is one class of belief – the others being opinion, dogma, myth and fallacy – and that knowledge differs from the others in that accepting it as true can be justified. But, he suggests, in practice it is a difficult distinction to make:

> Describing the beliefs of health promoters as knowledge rather than opinion is frequently justified by appeal to science. This implies that these beliefs are firmly founded on the failure of attempts to refute them, and that they are the only interpretation admitted by the observational evidence. Alas the reality is more complex and in health promotion it is hard to draw the dividing line between knowledge and opinion.
>
> (Kemm, 1991: 292)

Considering the question of lifestyle and health, he goes on to suggest that what is accepted as knowledge in this field has changed over time, and that much of the 'knowledge base' for health promotion falls far short of evidence tested and proved 'beyond reasonable doubt', and is usually closer to the 'balance of probability'. So, he proposes, rather than talking of the 'knowledge base' which underpins health education advice, health professionals should describe it as 'best available opinion'; opinion which, while providing a reasonable basis for action, should not be assumed to be infallible nor equated with knowledge (Kemm, 1991).

A growing interest in 'lay epidemiology' again illustrates the limitations of 'expert' knowledge alone. Lay epidemiology looks at the ways in which lay people perceive issues of health and illness and how they incorporate professionals' health messages into their own health culture. Frankel *et al.* (1991: 430), reviewing health education messages regarding coronary heart disease, suggest that health professionals simplify the messages to the point of distortion, and that this brings them into disrepute – so that 'there is public delight when the experts are seen to have "got it wrong"'. The importance for professionals of recognizing and understanding lay epidemiology is stressed, since one-way communication, based on health professionals' prescriptions alone, results in health education messages being widely ignored.

As the professional knowledge base for health education is being challenged, so too is the *way* in which expert knowledge is being used by professionals. Harding *et al.* (1990), discussing the educational role of the pharmacist, warn against the traditional didactic approach as being too narrow, and failing to take account of the sociocultural context in which people operate. Drawing on a critique by Rodmell and Watt (1986) of traditional health education practice, they suggest that: 'an implicit assumption of the traditional health education philosophy is an absence or inappropriateness of the lay person's own health knowledge. Thus health educators may assume that their interpretation of health and illness is better or more appropriate than the interpretation of lay people' (Harding *et al.*, 1990: 89). They criticize health education which is not tailored to the clients' needs, and in which clients are told not what *they* want, or need to know, but rather, what the professionals want to tell them. Failure to accept and act upon inappropriate health education messages is then deemed irresponsible or intransigent.

AN ALTERNATIVE APPROACH TO THE USE OF EXPERT KNOWLEDGE

An alternative approach is one based on partnership, in which professional and client together identify what the client wants and needs to know.

Instead of a one-way transmission of knowledge from professional to client, there is a two-way transaction, building on the existing knowledge and experience of the client, according to the client's perceived needs, and the professional's response to these.

This approach recognizes that knowledge is socially constructed, and acknowledges the value-laden nature of the definition and transmission of knowledge. No longer is the professional seeking to impose her view of what constitutes knowledge on her clients, with the goal of attaining compliance. Her role has changed from one of controlling to one of supporting and enabling, helping the client to draw on and think through his own experiences, and sharing her expert knowledge to help him develop his understanding. The goal of the professional becomes the personal growth and development of the client. Thus the professional–client relationship changes from one of superior–subordinate to one of partnership; it becomes, in Jarvis' terms (1985) the 'education of equals'.

It can be seen that an approach to education based on the philosophy of the 'education of equals' poses a challenge to the way in which the professional's expert knowledge is viewed and utilized. Thus it strikes at the heart of professionalism. Approaches to education based on the 'education of equals' recognize clients' experiential knowledge as the foundation for learning, with the professional's expert knowledge at the *service* of the client. For professionals who have trained for many years to acquire a body of expert knowledge, who have passed examinations to gain qualifications and entry to the profession, to challenge the pre-eminence of their professional knowledge base constitutes a grave threat. It removes power from them and hands it over to the client; and locates their base of power with their clients rather than with their professional body.

A NEW FOUNDATION FOR PROFESSIONAL PRACTICE

If traditional professional practice is being called into question, and the place of expert knowledge is being challenged, what is the foundation for the professional–client relationship? Halmos (1965) has suggested that personal service professions in fact belong to a single profession – that of 'counselling' – a profession which includes all those people whose principal means of helping their clients is through the medium of the personal relationship. In personal service professions, it is suggested, professional effectiveness depends more on the quality of the relationship between professional and client than on a body of expert knowledge.

In social work, for example, it is being suggested that expert knowledge has been given false precedence; that in reality, 'to do social work is to do purposefully and deliberately that which is primarily intuitive' (England,

1986: 39). England describes the central process in social work as the 'intu-itive use of self'. He suggests that the social worker's central function is to develop an understanding of her client, his needs and his worldview. He goes on to suggest that the basis for that understanding is the social worker's own personal experiences; that the worker uses her intuition to understand and communicate with her clients – and that to achieve her intuitive self, she needs self-understanding, understanding which comes from *within*, not from external, generalized, expert knowledge.

In nursing, too, it may be suggested that the central function is the creation of a relationship – that 'nursing is a special case of loving' (Jourard, 1971). Jourard suggests that technical care – the hygienic surroundings, medicine and rest – is insufficient, and that patients need 'human warmth, love and responsive care'. The healing relationship is the relationship between nurse and patient which makes the patient feel valued as an individual, offers him understanding and empathy, and serves to 'increase his sense of identity and integrity'. The same healing relationship, Jourard suggests, is central to the role of physicians, teachers, clergymen, dentists, lawyers, coun-sellors, psychotherapists and every other helping profession.

From this perspective, the most important foundation of the helping professions – and one which they all have in common – is the 'self' of the professional, the way in which she relates to her client, and the interper-sonal skills she brings to the transaction.

Professional practice from this perspective has less to do with the applica-tion of esoteric knowledge, more to do with intuition, common sense, tech-niques for helping and interpersonal skills – a core of skills which should be common to all helping professions. The primary focus of professional train-ing thus becomes, not the inculcation of a body of expert knowledge, but the identification and development of personal and interpersonal skills; and pro-fessional knowledge has a lower priority than the quality of the professional's relationship with the client. Thus a shift is apparent from seeing the foun-dation of the helping professions as scientific rationalism to recognizing it as art. In emphasizing the personal qualities needed for effective professional practice, this is not to suggest that expert knowledge has no relevance, but to see its role as being to *support* the helping relationship. Very few, Hoyle (1982) suggests, have as much genuine hard, scientific knowledge as they profess as the foundation for their practice. Rather, it is suggested, profes-sionals have 'dressed up' common sense as theoretical knowledge to enhance their own status. The traditional professional emphasis on a body of acade-mic knowledge has been designed, not to enhance the effectiveness of pro-fessional practice and hence to benefit clients, but to advance the cause of professionalization. Expert knowledge gives an image of omniscience: it is this which gives professionals power and control over their clients. As Cohen (1985: 175) expresses it: 'Most of the terms used by the helping professions combine a high degree of unreliability (in their diagnoses, prognosis and prescription of the right treatment), with an unambiguous set of constraints upon clients.'

PROFESSIONALIZATION OR PROFESSIONAL DEVELOPMENT?

The quest for professionalization has led to an emphasis on scientific absolutes and material precision. The new approach to professional practice calls for a broadening of perspectives on what constitutes knowledge, and the recognition of the validity of experiential knowledge and intuition. Where, then, is the place for theoretical knowledge? England suggests that theoretical knowledge is valuable only in so far as it serves the professional's intuition and understanding of her clients. It is valuable in so far as it is *indistinguishable* from personal knowledge. Theoretical knowledge, as he sees it:

> is useful only in as much as it is incorporated into the worker's general . . . knowledge and available to inform his intuitive knowledge and intuitive behaviour. The real test of the worker's learning is never in his ability to show mastery of abstract knowledge, but in the way such knowledge is plundered and fragmented to inform his practice; his formal learning becomes useful in as much as it is inseparable and indistinguishable from his colloquial learning.
>
> (England, 1986: 35)

Theoretical knowledge, as the philosophy of the 'education of equals' proposes, thus loses its centrality in the professional–client interaction. It moves from a position of dominance to one of support. This has implications for the whole of the nature of the professional–client relationship. When expert knowledge ceases to be central, the professional's worldview no longer takes precedence over the client's. Nor does the professional have the right to set the terms of the relationship, to prescribe behaviour and to expect compliance. The relationship is now a negotiated one; and the role of the professional is to develop an understanding of her client's perceived needs, and to share her expert knowledge and skills, in so far as they serve these needs.

However, this development poses a dilemma for professionals. In order to further the cause of professionalization, professional training needs to focus on a body of expert knowledge as the foundation for professional practice. But for professional development – to develop practitioners who are more effective at helping their clients – the need is for training which focuses on personal and interpersonal skills, on building on experience, developing intuition and common sense. Thus, there are forces pulling in two different directions. The question is, will professionals and aspiring professionals see this new development as threatening their professional identity? Or can it offer a new model for professional practice?

REFERENCES

Cohen, Stanley (1985) *Visions of Social Control: Crime, Punishment and Classification.* Cambridge: Polity Press.

England, Hugh (1986) *Social Work as Art: Making Sense for Good Practice.* London: Allen & Unwin.

Frankel, Stephen, Davison, Charles and Smith, George Davey (1991) 'Lay epidemiology and the rationality of responses to health education', *British Journal of General Practice,* 41: 428–30.

Freidson, Eliot (1986) 'Professional dominance and the ordering of health services: some consequences', in P. Conrad and R. Kern (eds), *Sociology of Health and Illness,* 2nd edn. New York: St. Martin's Press.

Freire, Paulo (1972) *Pedagogy of the Oppressed.* Harmondsworth: Penguin.

Halmos, P. (1965) *The Faith of the Counsellors.* London: Constable.

Harding, Geoffrey, Nettleton, Sarah and Taylor, Kevin (1990) *Sociology for Pharmacists: An Introduction,* Basingstoke: Macmillan.

Hoyle, Eric (1982) 'The professionalisation of teachers: a paradox', in P. Gordon, H. Perkin, H. Sockett, E. Hoyle (eds), *Is Teaching a Profession?* Bedford Way Paper 15, University of London, Institute of Education.

Hughes, E. (1975) 'Professions', in G. Esland, G. Salaman and M.A. Speakman (eds), *People and Work,* Edinburgh/Milton Keynes: Holmes McDougall/Open University.

Jarvis, Peter (1985) *The Sociology of Adult and Continuing Education.* Kent: Croom Helm.

Johnson, T. (1989) *Professions and Power.* London: Macmillan.

Jourard, Sidney M. (1971) *The Transparent Self,* 2nd edn. New York: D. Van Nostrand.

Kemm, John (1991) 'Health education and the problem of knowledge', *Health Promotion International,* 6 (4): 291–6.

Millerson, Geoffrey (1964) *The Qualifying Associations.* London: Routledge & Kegan Paul.

Rodmell, S. and Watt, A. (1986) *The Politics of Health Education.* London: Routledge.

Chapter 6

Re-thinking the relationship between theory and practice

Practitioners as map-readers, map-makers – or jazz players?[†]

Audrey Collin

INTRODUCTION

Although there may be 'nothing so practical as a good theory' (Lewin, 1951: 169), it is not evident that all practitioners see it that way. They often express considerable unease with and ambivalence towards research and theory, dismissing the value of theory, and being seemingly 'hostile' to it (Kidd *et al.*, 1994: 391). At times, Killeen and Watts (1983: 15) suggest, they assume that research will reveal 'unassailable truths' and solve their problems, while at others they regard it 'with a mixture of impatience and derision', denying its relevance to their practice.

Nevertheless, pure and applied theory, which provides the basis for the practitioner's diagnosis and problem-solving, and the skills and attitudes to apply them to a particular client's needs, constitute 'professional knowledge' or expertise (Schon, 1983: 24). Widespread scepticism among practitioners about the value of theory must, therefore, be a matter of concern, raising issues about its nature and relevance, and how it is introduced to and used by practitioners. With the restructuring of training and the delivery of guidance, and changes in the clients' world, these issues become even more critical, as a number of recent publications discussed below demonstrate. This chapter extends the discussion by examining the relationship between theory and practice, noting its significance within two ongoing debates: between the work-based competency and the academy-based approaches to training, and between the 'modern' and 'post-modern' understandings of theory and practice.

This chapter is concerned with theory and practice in the field of career in particular, but because many of the issues addressed are also encountered in other fields, such as management or counselling generally, its conclusions may have a wider applicability. It argues that practitioners need to become

---

[†] This chapter is an edited version of an article which appeared in the *British Journal of Guidance and Counselling*, 1996, 24 (1): 67–81.

not only 'reflective' (Schon, 1983), but also researchers and theorists themselves, using approaches appropriate to their practice. Thus they will develop the frameworks needed to improvise effective responses to their clients' changing situations. Not only would this have implications for initial and in-service training, supervision and policy, but it would also challenge hitherto accepted relationships between researchers, theorists, practitioners and their clients.

THE ROLE OF THEORY IN PRACTICE: A SENSITIVE TOPIC

This proposal may appear to be at odds with current developments in education and training, which disregard the knowledge inputs into training but emphasise effective performance assessed through standards of competence. Embodied in the national framework of qualifications by the National Council for Vocational Qualifications (McNair, 1992), this approach is being felt in the counselling field through the work of the Advice, Guidance, Counselling and Psychotherapy Lead Body (McNair, 1992; Watson, 1994) and the new competency-based forms of training (e.g. Ford and Graham, 1994; Kidd *et al.*, 1994: 138). The model of management increasingly adopted in counselling and guidance organisations also emphasises performance. With the introduction of competitive tendering and a 'contract culture' (Watson, 1994: 357), and the need for accountability (McChesney, 1995), managers are having to define the nature of the guidance they have contracted to deliver and ensure that it achieves the required standards (Watson, 1994: 357). However, one of the effects of these changes, McNair (1992: 135) suggests, will be to focus on guidance workers' understanding of what they do. To ensure that their professional expertise is fully used, and their training needs identified, practitioners will have to contribute to their managers' definition of the guidance offered (Watson, 1994). Despite today's emphasis upon performance, therefore, the changes taking place may well also encourage counsellors to examine their own practice – a key element of this chapter's argument – and to generate a readiness to develop it.

Nevertheless, it is a 'critical and sensitive time' (Bimrose and Bayne, 1995) to be examining what are key issues in the argument between the proponents of the continuation of academy-based initial training for practitioners and those who argue for a change to a work-based competency approach. This is evident in the recent interchange between Bimrose and Bayne (1995) and Killeen and Kidd (1995) over the paper by Kidd *et al.* (1994: 388) on 'the link between theory and practice in interviewing'. Entitled 'Is guidance an applied science?', the conclusions of the latter paper 'cast doubt on the view' that (p. 385): 'training enables careers officers to be *effective practitioners*, not *reflective professionals*' (p. 392). This is a matter of some significance in the competency debate. Bimrose and Bayne (1995) appear to be guarding against the possibility of these conclusions being marshalled by the pro-competency camp, but Killeen and Kidd point out that their study has indeed shown that theory has some influence upon practice.

The role of theory in practice is, therefore, in terms of the competency debate, of topical, even political, interest. Having noted something of how practitioners learn about and use theory, and examined the relationship between theory and practice, this chapter will then show how this relationship is also significant for another contemporary debate, that concerning modernism and post-modernism.

LEARNING TO PRACTISE CAREERS GUIDANCE AND COUNSELLING

Despite the belief that practitioners find little relevance in theory, the very existence of studies such as that of Kidd *et al.* (1994), referred to above, and of careers officers' 'mental processes' when interviewing (Clarke, 1994), and their 'theoretical framework and model of professional practice' (Watson, 1994: 360), suggests that much remains to be known about the relationship of theory to practice. Watson (1994: 358) notes the lack of published research on how careers officers developed their 'personal models of guidance', and Irving and Williams (1995: 107) infer that 'counsellors rely primarily on ... [an] intuitive approach'. This section will note some of the issues that emerge from these studies.

Students have to learn about the nature of career ('career theory') and of the counselling process itself ('guidance theory') (Kidd *et al.*, 1994; Watson, 1994), and need both to 'know what' and 'know how' (Savickas, 1994a: 240). They have to acquire 'know what' about both careers and counselling, but also the 'know how' of counselling, and how to translate the 'know what' about careers into the 'know how' of practice. Kidd *et al.* (1994: 386) note that it is difficult to achieve a balance between theory and practice in training, but Irving and Williams (1995), Kidd *et al.* (1994) and Watson (1994) all indicate that in initial training greater attention has been paid to the guidance than to the career theories, and to skills training rather than an appreciation of theoretical approaches. For example, Irving and Williams (1995:107) note that the 'systematic, cognitive exploration of practitioners' knowledge' is viewed as of 'secondary importance', or ' "unnecessary clutter"', while 'a critical analysis of the ideas and assumptions that guide practice is often frowned on as "intellectualising" and is less valued than other ways of knowing'.

The study by Kidd *et al.* (1994) illustrates the perplexing task for trainers and students of addressing both theory and practice. It found 'little evidence'

(p. 390) that students had first been introduced to guidance theory and then helped to apply it in practice; 'theoretical perspectives' and practical skills were taught in parallel. However, guidance theories were more influential on interviewing practice than were career theories. The latter appear to have been introduced with 'little regard for academic criteria of validity or coherence' (p. 390), and although students need to be able 'to relate theories and concepts and eventually to integrate and reconcile them', most courses introduced theory pragmatically (p. 390). 'Conceptual integration seemed to be an infrequent activity', students being encouraged 'to make their own connections' (p. 390). Moreover, the implications for practice were paid little explicit attention. 'With respect to the best known career theories, then, guidance is not a direct application of theoretical principles' (p. 402); trainees 'do not learn practical skills by applying theory' (p. 390).

Kidd *et al.* note potential contradictions between some of the career and guidance theories in initial training. Watson (1994, p. 367) refers to conflict between the theoretical approaches taught: between the trait-and-factor approach, in which the careers officer has the role of expert, and the client-centred approach. There is, furthermore, conflict between the use of a 'rigid structure' and 'flexibility of approach' in interview training (p. 363). The tensions experienced in training persist into practice, Watson indicating that novices have difficulty in applying the theory learned and 'struggle to avoid the set structure they felt they had been taught' about interviewing (p. 366). The 'confusion' of and conflict between the two theoretical approaches referred to above creates further difficulty for them (p. 367), and casts doubt upon the purpose of the interview.

It takes several years of experience (Watson, 1994: 366) for 'the interplay of theory with practice' to create a 'personal philosophy and model of careers guidance' (p. 369). This involves 'the fusion of skills and theory', and is 'a complex and individual process, involving self-awareness and a thorough working knowledge of theories and models' (p. 367). Nevertheless, careers officers in the study by Kidd *et al.* (1994: 401) did not view theory 'as more relevant' as they gained in experience. The group discussion participants had a poor memory of and made a 'virtually unanimous' 'dismissal of the value' of theory, apparently considering it 'remote, abstract, irksome and not actually applied in practice'; some were seemingly 'hostile' to it (p. 391). However, the questionnaire respondents' prompted recall showed a more positive evaluation of the relevance to their practice of some theories, such as the client-centred approach and developmentalism (pp. 391–2). This should be interpreted in the light of the view expressed by Irving and Williams (1995: 108) that counsellors 'are not aware of the theories they use to inform their actions' and that they 'say what they *believe* they are doing rather than what they are *actually* doing'. Nevertheless, the explanation Kidd *et al.* propose for this discrepancy offers potential insight into the process of 'fusion' (Watson, 1994). It is that 'theory has "done its job" when its key messages have been communicated, internalised and assimilated as working assumptions' (p. 392). Guidance theory, in particular, appears to provide 'axiomatic assumptions which subsequently act as premises in interview practice' (p. 402). Practitioners do not apply theory directly, but apply 'broad *principles*, rather than specific *formulas*' (p. 392).

These reports demonstrate how the nature of theory and practice generates tensions in training, and presents practitioners with paradoxes which have to be resolved through their own personal 'fusion' (Watson, 1994). The relationship between theory and practice will now be examined more closely.

THE RELATIONSHIP BETWEEN THEORY AND PRACTICE

Theory and practice appear very different in kind, as may be glimpsed in the contrast Parker and Shotter (1990: 2–3) draw between academic text and 'everyday face-to-face talk'. Academic text, through which practitioners will largely have encountered theory, needs to be comprehensible to a wide audience. It is, therefore, decontextualised, standardised, and expressed through predetermined meanings, even when it concerns contextualised practice (e.g. counselling) or argues for the need for contextualisation (Collin and Young, 1992). By contrast, 'everyday face-to-face talk', which approximates to the way in which practitioners and their clients engage, is contextualised, and 'marked by its vagueness and openness . . . only those taking part in it can understand its drift; the meanings are not wholly predetermined, they are negotiated by those involved'. Whereas academic text embodies bounded, systematic, rational, propositional, forms of knowledge, practice embodies contextualised, tacit (Polanyi, 1966), emotional, moral, and relational (e.g. Gilligan, 1982) forms, uses interpretation and analogy, and draws on 'social' and 'practical' intelligences (Sternberg, 1985).

'Theory' is a portmanteau term, but its core meaning is a systematic and organised set of propositions and of 'abstract, decontextualized principles and categorical definitions' (Savickas, 1994a: 240) which is used to conjecture about, describe, explain and predict a part of reality. Krumboltz (1994: 9), for example, sees career theory as a way to explain what is observed, make sense of experience, and summarise a large number of observations into 'a few general propositions'. Theory varies in kind and range, from 'sophisticated overarching theories' to 'systems of interrelated concepts' (Kidd *et al.*, 1994: 386) (to be referred to below as 'formal theory' and 'models' respectively). These are clearly not discrete nor well-defined categories, and Kidd *et al.* (1994) themselves apply 'theoretical' to a variety of terms apparently interchangeably: 'approaches' (p. 386), 'models' (p. 388), 'frameworks' (p. 391), and 'principles' (p. 392). 'Theory' may also express less structured constructs. In everyday speech, it may be used to denote abstractions of various kinds, while a focus on the process of theorising rather than its outcomes can embrace the notion of personal constructs (Kelly, 1955). By making and interrelating assumptions and building propositions upon them which, though not always systematic, explicit, rigorously informed and contextualised, nevertheless 'work' in practice, a person has 'personal theories' with which to conjecture, describe, explain and predict.

To understand the relationship between theory and practice, it is not only necessary to take into consideration the differences *between* them, but also those *among* researchers, theorists and practitioners. Some adopt the orthodox, positivist, western approach, which applies the rational principles of the natural sciences to the social world, and accepts the existence of a relatively stable and ordered reality independent of the observer, 'where facts occur in a determinate order, and where, if enough were known, they could be predicted, or at least described' (Pepper, 1942: 143). Others make very different epistemological assumptions, accepting 'real indeterminateness in the world' (Harre, 1981: 3), with 'multitudes of facts rather loosely scattered about and not necessarily determining one another to any considerable degree' (Pepper, 1942: 142-3), and recognising that humans construct their reality from their particular perspective through their interactions and language.

Positivism has been very influential in career research (Walsh and Chartrand, 1994: 193; see also Savickas, 1995), and informs three of the 'four main approaches underlying careers guidance practice in Britain' – the 'differentialist', 'behavioural', and 'structural' (Watson, 1994: 358, largely agreed by Kidd *et al.*, 1994: 392). The total field of career research and theory, however, is much richer than this (e.g. Arthur *et al.*, 1989; Savickas and Lent, 1994), and within it there is a small but growing number of studies and theories which are straining the bounds of positivism, or rejecting it entirely (e.g. Young and Collin, 1992). In acknowledging the lived experience, context and ecology, meaning-making, biography and narrative of career, such approaches are not only framed in ways that are more meaningful to counsellors (Collin and Young, 1992; Young and Valach, 1996), but are carried out in interpretive, collaborative ways which are sympathetic to counsellors' values (Young and Collin, 1988; Collin and Young, 1992; Reason and Rowan, 1981).

Practitioners, too, may espouse positivism which, according to Schon (1983: 21), has given rise to the orthodox 'technical rationality' model of professional knowledge. This approach accords greater value to general principles than to concrete problem-solving: 'the more basic and general the knowledge, the higher the status of its producer' (p. 24). The role of the researcher, 'distinct from, and usually considered superior to' that of the practitioner, is to provide the basic and applied knowledge which leads to diagnostic and problem-solving techniques (p. 26). In order to be accredited and legitimated, novices have to learn this basic and applied science – the formal theories and models – before they can learn the skills of application, which are 'an ambiguous, secondary kind of knowledge' (pp. 27–8). Professionals following this 'traditional epistemology of practice', in which formal theory and models both play a role, impose their 'categories, theories, and techniques on the situation', ignoring, explaining away, or controlling 'those features of the situation, including the human beings within it', which do not fit their prior categories (p. 345). Writing of a number of professions, including psychotherapy, Schon suggests (p. 40) that this process defines both the nature and boundaries of a situation and the means for practitioners to address it. It constructs the reality with which they will then deal: 'we *name* the things to which we will attend and *frame* the context in which we will attend to them'.

Schon's view, however, does not accord with what was reported earlier of the training of careers officers (Kidd *et al.*, 1994) or counsellors (Irving and Williams, 1995). This does not suggest that they are not professionals, in Schon's sense: rather that, because counselling practice 'treats human beings as agents responsible for making informed choices', whereas positivist 'career research essentially puts them in the same category as other natural objects' (Polkinghorne, 1990: 87), they cannot translate much research directly into practice. In attempting to do so, they 'lose much of the sophistication and complexity that theories can offer' (Young and Valach, 1996). Thus they filter the basic theories of their field through their own interpretive frameworks and overlay them with the experiential knowledge gained from trying to apply them in practice. This leads to 'fusion' (Watson, 1994), 'responsiveness and flexibility' (Killeen and Kidd, 1995), the '"common sense", intuitive approach' (Irving and Williams, 1995: 107), and a readiness to adopt an eclectic approach to theory (Bimrose and Bayne, 1995; Savickas, 1995).

This creates considerable tensions and paradoxes in the teaching and learning of practitioners. It is (relatively) easy to teach decontextualised theory, but its very nature makes it difficult to apply in practice, especially when the field is a dynamic one. At the same time, it is difficult to teach practice: it has to be learned from experience in specific contexts. Novices need time to develop their practice, and in its early phases they often find the principles, concepts and classifications that positivist theory offers helpful.

All this points to the existence of an alternative approach to the generation of knowledge, an alternative epistemology of practice. Several are to be found in the literature, but it is not clear how they relate to one another, nor whether they are essentially one. The best known is that which Schon (1983: 295–6) calls 'reflective practice'. With their 'repertoire of examples, images, understandings, and actions' (p. 138), built up from both theory and experience, reflective practitioners are able to see a new situation as both familiar and unique, and to hypothesise about its 'potential for transformation' (p. 166). Approaching it as a 'reflective conversation' (p. 130), the practitioner 'steps into the situation', 'reframes' it, and 'experiments' with it to identify the consequences and implications of this frame. 'The situation talks back, the practitioner listens' (pp. 131–2), and where necessary 'reframes' again. Technical expertise is 'embedded in a context of meanings', creating the possibility of misunderstanding between practitioners and clients, and the need for their relationship, therefore, to take the form of a 'reflective conversation'. Formal theory and models have a role to play, but they are used tentatively and experimentally.

Irving and Williams (1995) identify ways in which counsellors may be helped to become reflective practitioners; Thomas (1993) argues that managers should practise reflectively. This suggests that their practice is not essentially reflective, and that Schon's reflective practice should be recognised as one variant of the alternative to the 'traditional epistemology of practice', characterised by the practitioner's greater awareness of and reflection upon practice. The more common form may be that described by Thomas. He sees managers as 'practical theorists' (p. 211) who have to 'improvise', not simply 'making it up as we go along', but fitting together knowledge from various sources to 'inform practice in fruitful and productive ways' (p. 214). Their 'practical theory' includes personal experiences, assumptions, values, as well as ideas from formal scientific theory, so that it is unique, with little direct overlap with formal theories. This notion accords well with the observation that, in fields like career or management where there are publicly agreed theories, practitioners still draw upon their practical 'theories-in-use' rather than their 'espoused theories' (Argyris and Schon, 1974; Irving and Williams, 1995). Managers' 'practical theory' constitutes a map which helps them locate problems 'in a meaningful context' so that they become manageable. The contribution of social science to this map is less the 'technical, algorithmic knowledge' which allows managers 'to read off solutions to their problems', but rather the 'sensitizing frameworks' of theories, concepts and 'ways of seeing and thinking' that point to 'alternative ways of understanding and hence of managing' (p. 214).

'Practical theory' is thus the 'personal theory' or constructs referred to earlier, but explicitly informed by the theories of the relevant field. It makes a valuable bridge between the concepts of theory and practice, and suggests that, though disparate, they become intertwined. Savickas (1994a) refers to this as an 'intimate relationship', one of 'mutual shaping', and suggests that theory and practice may not be dichotomous but a continuum, with 'theorizing . . . a form of practice, albeit practice at a distance' (p. 239). Hence, 'a theory is constructed through its use', 'the meaning of theory changes as it is used', and 'situated activity, particularly the practice of career intervention, constructs the true meaning of career theories' (p. 240).

It is likely that these interpretations will receive greater attention as the debate about post-modernism grows (see Kvale, 1992; Savickas, 1995), and 'practical theory' is reframed as a post-modern approach. Polkinghorne (1992), for example, distinguishes the 'psychology of practice' from 'academic psychology' because it does not assume that knowledge represents external reality, because it re-interprets formal theories as 'models or metaphors that can serve as heuristic devices' and 'templates for organizing client experiences' (p. 155), because it does not seek overarching explanations but accepts localised, contextualised knowledges, because it recognises that reality is constructed, that constructions can change, and so accommodates previous understandings to each new unique situation, and because it focuses on practical knowledge that achieves intended ends. These, he argues, are characteristics of post-modern thinking, unlike 'academic psychology' which is modern, so that the 'psychology of practice' – or 'practical theory' – is an effective exemplar for a post-modern science (p. 146).

The recognition of this alternative epistemology of practice heightens rather than diffuses the competency debate. It augments rather than diminishes the need for training to attend to theory. This need, which the new challenges in the field of career, outlined in the next section, will increase, will be set out later.

NEW CHALLENGES IN THE FIELD OF CAREER

The relevance to practitioners of much research and theory is already an issue: 'one of the most poignant pleas I have heard in the last few years in counseling psychology is for researchers to do research that is relevant to the practitioner', comments Harmon (1994: 232). Designed to achieve scientific rigour, it has often been too refined for practical application (Young and Valach, 1996), while some was not particularly rigorous in the first place. Nevertheless, like the Seven-Point Plan (see Kidd *et al.*, 1994), many theories have become taken for granted and embedded in the syllabus. However, the world of work is changing, and many theories are 'simply not addressing the problems of most interest to either policy-makers or the public', are 'slow in accounting for recent changes in the world of work' (Harmon, 1994: 231), and so are increasingly irrelevant because of these changes. It is to these that this chapter now turns.

Looking across five countries, Pryor (1991) highlights 'multidimensional changes' in the social, technological, political, economic and labour-market spheres. These changes present new threats and opportunities to clients and, hence, new challenges to career counselling; counsellors themselves are not exempt from some of them. To those already referred to in the introduction can be added the increasing politicisation of careers services (Pryor, 1991; Watts, 1991), exercised through performance measures and financial constraints: 'more than ever before, we are asked to show that we spend both our research and practice efforts wisely' (Harmon, 1994: 233).

Demography, unemployment, the nature of the employment contract, work opportunities for women and men, the information and communications revolution, the decline of some industries and emergence of others, globalisation, privatisation, organisational structures, the nature of jobs and skills: these are only some of the areas in which changes are taking place which impact upon careers. What is relevant to note is that their effects, in concert with those in other fields, are bringing about the recognition that career, as it has hitherto been known by theorists and practitioners, was essentially a 'modern project' (Savickas, 1994b; Savickas, 1995).

What clients are now experiencing and presenting to practitioners is a 'post modern' form of career (Savickas, 1994b; Savickas, 1995). Expressed differently, what was addressed by many theories in the past was largely the 'bureaucratic' form of career, whereas it is the 'professional' and 'entrepreneurial' forms which are becoming widespread today (Kanter, 1989). Or, put differently again, today's organisations are 'self-designing', and call for 'career improvisation' (Weick and Berlinger, 1989). These changes are already calling into question key assumptions about career, such as the nature of the individual, jobs, occupations, organisations and the labour market. Thus the flatter and more flexible organisations required by, for example, business process re-engineering (Hammer and Champy, 1993), the learning organisation (Pedler et al., 1991), or total quality management (Crosby, 1984), blur the nature of roles, organisational moves and view of the future for the individual, demanding instead multiskilling, teamworking, and continuous improvement. The upward movement, and clearly defined roles, rewards and pathways, of traditional careers in large organisations are disappearing, and with them, the traditional prompts and supports for the individual's identity and social status.

The disjunctive nature of such change means that practitioners will increasingly find that existing theories offer them little insight into their clients' situations, and that, as Savickas (1995) notes, practice has advanced further than theory. Where are the theories to 'name' and 'frame' these new experiences (Schon, 1983: 40)? The terrain is changing, and the old maps are no longer appropriate to guide practitioners through it.

The metaphor of the map recurs in this literature (for example, 'cognitive maps of occupations' to match clients with opportunities (Clarke, 1994: 254); the 'redrawing of our maps of employment' by National Vocational Qualifications (McNair, 1992: 148)). It conveys the notion of identifying what was previously unknown or unfamiliar, and of bringing it under control and into a meaningful relationship with what is already familiar. In discussing the concerns that career theorists have about the nature of their theories, the degree of fragmentation in their field, and the implications for counselling practice (see Savickas and Lent, 1994), Krumboltz (1994: 16) suggests that:

We need to draw a different map. . . . We need to see ourselves as career cartographers. Our theories are about as accurate as the maps of the world drawn by cartographers 500 years ago. . . . We need to send out our Columbuses and our Magellans to collect further data to revise our maps.

These references to map-making and map-reading are instructive. They reveal the assumption on the part of theorists that map-making is still feasible, and that it is they who will carry it out; they ignore the existence of 'practical theory'. The role of the practitioner is not in the mapping of the new or changing terrain, but in finding routes through it. This does not, however, represent an adequate response to the nature of the changes being experienced in career, where for many individuals the very ground is in motion, and it is no longer a question of finding a route, but of maintaining one's balance. What may be needed is not maps, but the development of new conceptual and practical map-making skills which will enable practitioner and client to re-orientate themselves even as their ground moves. To change the metaphor, it is the client and the practitioner who are experiencing and dealing with the shocks and after-shocks of career-quakes. Theorists are generally too distant from the action to offer anything but yesterday's solutions. They have not yet constructed early-warning or rapid response systems; they may be more inclined to develop a Richter scale. What practitioners, therefore, need is not new maps, but entirely new ways of thinking about and responding to change. In Harmon's words (1994: 229), 'What we hope to do may require us to adopt new ways of thinking and conceptualizing reality.'

THE WAY FORWARD: REFLECTION, RESEARCH, AND IMPROVISATION IN PRACTICE

The conclusion drawn from this exploration of the 'intimate relationship' between theory and practice (Savickas, 1994a: 239), and the changing field of career, is that practitioners have never been merely map-readers, and that today they cannot be merely map-makers, though they must at least develop map-making skills. They may need to go further and abandon their maps altogether. A more appropriate metaphor might be that of playing jazz. Jazz players improvise, but are not anarchic. They are disciplined, skilled, creative, and intuitive. They make music in relational, collaborative and non-hierarchical ways. For counsellors to 'play jazz' would call for a significant shift in their role and its relationship with those of researchers and theorists.

If – or when – practitioners' 'heuristics and cognitive maps' (Clarke, 1994) become unable to deal with their changing world, and their improvisation falters, they will need to get into a 'reflective conversation' with their clients and the situations they present. They will be able to do this more effectively, and more appropriately for clients and their context, if they pay critical attention to their practice and 'theories-in-use' (Irving and Williams, 1995), and if they consciously adopt reflective practice. It is clear from the studies quoted that many already work in this way (although, as Kidd *et al.* (1994: 392) point out, their training does not prepare them for it), but this chapter concludes that all should be encouraged to do so.

They need new and more appropriate theories to fuse (Watson, 1994) with their own and their clients' new experiences. The re-evaluations currently taking place amongst theorists (Savickas and Lent, 1994; Savickas and Walsh, 1996), as well as the development of alternative research approaches (Young and Collin, 1992), will undoubtedly generate some, and these must be introduced into initial and in-service training. However, academic research and theory will almost always come too late to be practical, so counsellors must also engage in their own research and theorising. The newly developing interpretive and collaborative research methodologies, many of them compatible with counsellors' values, will ease this task for them (Collin and Young, 1988; Young and Collin, 1988). An already established form of research which would be particularly appropriate is action research (e.g. McNiff, 1988), which McChesney (1995) has recently used in relation to careers education. Killeen and Watts (1983: 16), who recognise that it is 'critically important that the roles of researcher and practitioner are not rigidly separated' and that 'at least some practitioners are encouraged to take on a researcher role themselves', suggest that they do this through a postgraduate degree or, working singly or in small groups, through 'more limited enquiries as part of their continuing work' including follow-up studies of their clients, or surveys to collect occupational information. The work by Clarke (1994), McChesney (1995) and Watson (1994), quoted above, was, indeed, of this kind. The means to develop critical thinking – a 'meta-analysis of success or failure' and of patterns of intervention over time – suggested by Irving and Williams (1995: 113) would themselves be reflective research, and could be linked into broader research studies.

These proposals go beyond recommending reflective practice and action research. They are arguing for the recognition of the sophisticated, improvisatory nature of practice and suggesting ways in which this can be facilitated. These include the critical and reflective development of their 'practical theories' and the theoretical models they use; the integration of reflective practice with action research and other appropriate approaches; and collaboration between researchers, theorists and practitioners so that individual small-scale studies can be linked synergistically to produce a wider, yet still current and grounded, picture. These have significant implications for training, supervision, and policy.

In initial training, students would need to be introduced to a wide range of theories, and to learn about the nature of theory, practice, reflective practice, and 'practical theory', and how to develop them (Irving and Williams, 1995).

They would need to develop critical thinking (Irving and Williams, 1995) and crucial 'map-making' skills – that is, the ability to identify and challenge assumptions, recognise the implications of context, imagine and explore alternatives, and engage in reflection (Brookfield, 1987) – and use them in a continuing awareness of their own practice. They would need to be introduced to, and learn to critique, research and theory in both traditional and alternative forms. They would need to develop research skills for use in practice, particularly the non-positivist forms, including action research. Importantly, they would need to become aware of equal opportunities and other ethical and political implications of improvisation.

Such developments take time to put in place and come to fruition, and it would be several years before initial training would achieve these effects. It is, therefore, important that some be introduced immediately through in-service training. Although the significance of such training in updating and questioning existing knowledge is recognised (Kidd *et al.*, 1994; Watson, 1994), and the opportunity for it welcomed by many careers officers, there is a general lack of encouragement, support and funding for them to undertake it (Watson, 1994: 365). The role of the supervisor is, therefore, significant. However, as Watson (p. 362) identifies, many supervisors may not have the appropriate knowledge, and need up-dating themselves. This will be essential if they are to support novices in the development of their critical thinking (Irving and Williams, 1995: 112–13), 'practical theories', reflective practice, action and other research.

Despite the value of these proposals, without professional and political will they may well founder, because they will place additional pressure upon practitioners who are already working under severe constraints on the 'treadmill' (Watson, 1994: 364). They may conflict with the new forms of working practices emerging in the new performance- and accountability-orientated 'contract culture' (McChesney, 1995; Watson, 1994). Clients' expectations must be taken into account (McChesney, 1995), though it is worth noting that the improvising referred to here is what counsellors increasingly aim to facilitate in their clients. Finally, there are wider policy and political implications, given, as noted before, the national commitment to performance measures and competency-based training. These are issues that need wider discussion, and not just within this professional area.

With their changing needs, practitioners would make new demands upon researchers and theorists for more relevant, timely and appropriate research, and for help with their small-scale investigations, which academics could feed into larger, more detached studies and their construction of theories. By developing new and closer relationships with practitioners who may not share the values of orthodox research, researchers and theorists may be encouraged to become reflective practitioners themselves. Engaging in a 'reflective conversation with the situation', and with their practitioner 'clients', they too could find themselves drawn to research approaches more compatible with reflective practice: interpretive, collaborative, emancipatory approaches (Reason and Rowan, 1981; Sullivan, 1984; Young and Collin, 1992). These changes would therefore influence their relationships with their respondents and the kinds of research projects they undertook, with the possibility that their work would ultimately be seen as meaningful in the world of practitioners, clients and policy-makers.

What this chapter has proposed would greatly modify existing relationships between practitioners, researchers and theorists (Collin, 1996), and open the way to new approaches in the careers field. With a post-modern 'both/and' approach, rather than the 'either/or' of modernism, this would offer the field the opportunity to accept both theory and competencies, a development from which clients could only benefit.

BIBLIOGRAPHY

Argyris, C. and Schon, D.A. (1974) *Theory in Practice: Increasing Professional Effectiveness* (San Francisco, Jossey-Bass).

Arthur, M.B., Hall, D.T. and Lawrence, B.S. (1989) (eds) *Handbook of Career Theory* (Cambridge, Cambridge University Press).

Bimrose, J. and Bayne, R. (1995) Effective professionals engaged in reflective practice: a response to Kidd *et al., British Journal of Guidance and Counselling,* 23, pp. 395–9.

Brookfield, S.D. (1987) *Developing Critical Thinkers: Challenging Adults to Explore Alternative Ways of Thinking and Acting* (Milton Keynes, Open University Press).

Clarke, H. (1994) What are careers officers thinking of? How information cues are selected and used in careers interviews, *British Journal of Guidance and Counselling,* 22, pp. 247–9.

Collin, A. (1994) Fracture lines for career, *NICEC Careers Education and Guidance Bulletin,* 42, pp. 6–11.

Collin, A. (1996) Changing the relationships between researchers, theorists and practitioners: a response to the changing context of career, in: M. L. Savickas and W. B. Walsh (eds) *A Handbook of Career Counseling Theory and Practice* (Palo Alto, CA, CPP Books).

Collin, A and Young, R.A. (1988) Career development and hermeneutical inquiry, part II: undertaking hermeneutical research, *Canadian Journal of Counselling,* 22, pp. 191–201.

Collin, A. and Young, R.A. (1992) Constructing career through narrative and context, in: R.A. Young and A. Collin (eds) *Interpreting Career: Hermeneutical Studies of Lives in Context* (Westport, CT, Praeger).

Crosby, P. (1984) *Quality Without Tears* (New York, McGraw-Hill).

Ford, C. and Graham, B. (1994) The new qualification in careers guidance in higher education: a collaborative partnership, *British Journal of Guidance and Counselling,* 22, pp. 127–41.

Gilligan, C. (1982) *In a Different Voice: Psychological Theory and Women's Development* (Cambridge, MA, Harvard University Press).

Hammer, M. and Champy, J. (1993) *Reengineering the Corporation: a Manifesto for Business Revolution* (New York, Harper Business).

Harmon, L.W. (1994) Frustrations, daydreams, and realities of theoretical convergence, in: M.L. Savickas and R.W. Lent (eds) *Convergence in Career Development Theories: Implications for Science and Practice* (Palo Alto, CA, CPP Books).

Harre, R. (1981) The positivist-empiricist approach and its alternative, in: P. Reason and J. Rowan (eds) *Human Inquiry: a Sourcebook of New Paradigm Research* (Chichester, Wiley).

Irving, J.A. and Williams, D.I. (1995) Critical thinking and reflective practice in counselling, *British Journal of Guidance and Counselling*, 23, pp. 107–14.

Kanter, R.M. (1989) Careers and the wealth of nations: a macro-perspective on the structure and implications of career forms, in: M.B. Arthur, D.T. Hall and B.S. Lawrence (eds) *Handbook of Career Theory* (Cambridge, Cambridge University Press).

Kelly, G.A. (1955) *The Psychology of Personal Constructs* (New York, Norton).

Kidd, J.M., Killeen, J., Jarvis, J. and Offer, M. (1994) Is guidance an applied science?: the role of theory in the careers guidance interview, *British Journal of Guidance and Counselling*, 22, pp. 385–403.

Killeen, J. and Kidd, J.M. (1995) A rejoinder to Bimrose and Bayne, *British Journal of Guidance and Counselling*, 23, pp. 401–8.

Killeen, J. and Watts, A.G. (1983) The place of research in careers guidance, *Careers Bulletin*, Spring, pp. 15–17.

Krumboltz, J.D. (1994) Improving career development theory from a social learning perspective, in: M.L. Savickas and R.W. Lent (eds), *Convergence in Career Development Theories: Implications for Science and Practice* (Palo Alto, CA, CPP Books).

Kvale, S. (ed) (1992) *Psychology and Postmodernism* (London, Sage).

Lewin, K. (1951) *Field Theory in Social Science* (Chicago, University of Chicago Press).

McChesney, P. (1995) Yes, but how? Development and evaluation of careers education in higher education by careers advisers, *British Journal of Guidance and Counselling*, 23, pp. 327–45.

McNair, S. (1992) New maps for old: guidance and the reform of vocational qualifications, *British Journal of Guidance and Counselling*, 20, pp. 129–49.

McNiff, J. (1988) *Action Research: Principles and Practice* (Basingstoke, Macmillan).

Parker, I. and Shotter, J. (1990) Introduction, in: I. Parker and J. Shotter (eds) *Deconstructing Social Psychology* (London, Routledge).

Pedler, M., Burgoyne, J. and Boydell, T. (1991) *The Learning Company: a Strategy for Sustainable Development* (London, McGraw-Hill).

Pepper, S.C. (1942) *World Hypotheses: a Study in Evidence* (Berkeley, CA, University of California Press).

Polanyi, M. (1966) *The Tacit Dimension* (London, Routledge & Kegan Paul).

Polkinghorne, D.E. (1984) Further extensions of methodological diversity for counseling psychology, *Journal of Counseling Psychology*, 31, pp. 416–29.

Polkinghorne, D.E. (1990) Action theory approaches to career research, in: R.A. Young and W.A. Borgen (eds) *Methodological Approaches to the Study of Career* (New York, Praeger).

Polkinghorne, D.E. (1992) Postmodern epistemology of practice, in: S. Kvale (ed.) *Psychology and Postmodernism* (London, Sage).

Pryor, R.G.L. (1991) Policy challenges confronting careers guidance: introduction, *British Journal of Guidance and Counselling*, 19, pp. 225–9.

Reason, P. and Rowan, J. (eds) (1981) *Human Inquiry: a Sourcebook of New Paradigm Research* (Chichester, Wiley).

Savickas, M.L. (1994a) Convergence prompts theory renovation, research unification, and practice coherence, in: M. L. Savickas and R.W. Lent (eds) *Convergence in Career Development Theories: Implications for Science and Practice* (Palo Alto, CA, CPP Books).

Savickas, M.L. (1994b) Fracture lines in career counselling, *NICEC Careers Education and Guidance Bulletin*, 42, pp. 18–21.

Savickas, M.L. (1995) Current theoretical issues in vocational psychology: convergence, divergence, and schism, in: W.B. Walsh and S.H. Osipow (eds) *Handbook of Vocational Psychology* (2nd edn 1995) (Hillsdale, N.J. Erlbaum).

Savickas, M.L. and Lent, R.W. (1994) (eds) *Convergence in Career Development Theories: Implications for Science and Practice* (Palo Alto, CA, CPP Books).

Savickas, M.L. and Walsh, W.B. (1996) (eds) *A Handbook of Career Counseling Theory and Practice* (Palo Alto, CA, APP, Books).

Schon, D.A. (1983) *The Reflective Practitioner: How Professionals Think in Action* (New York, Basic Books).

Sternberg, R.J. (1985) *Beyond IQ: a Triarchic Theory of Human Intelligence* (Cambridge, Cambridge University Press).

Sullivan, E.V. (1984) *A Critical Psychology: Interpretation of the Personal World* (New York, Plenum).

Thomas, A. (1993) *Controversies in Management* (London, Routledge).

Walsh, W.B. and Chartrand, J.M. (1994) Emerging directions in person-environment fit, in: M.L. Savickas and R.W. Lent (eds) *Convergence in Career Development Theories: Implications for Science and Practice* (Palo Alto, CA, CPP Books).

Watson, C. (1994) Improving the quality of careers guidance: towards an understanding of the development of personal models, *British Journal of Guidance and Counselling*, 22, pp. 357–72.

Watts, A.G. (1991) The impact of the 'new right': policy challenges confronting careers guidance in England and Wales, *British Journal of Guidance and Counselling*, 19, pp. 230–45.

Weick, K.E. and Berlinger, L.R. (1989) Career improvisation in self-designing organizations, in: M.B. Arthur, D.T. Hall and B.S. Lawrence (eds) *Handbook of Career Theory* (Cambridge, Cambridge University Press).

Young, R.A. and Collin, A. (1988) Career development and hermeneutical inquiry, part I: the framework for a hermeneutical approach, *Canadian Journal of Counselling*, 22, pp. 153–61.

Young, R.A. and Collin, A. (eds) (1992) *Interpreting Career: Hermeneutical Studies of Lives in Context* (Westport, CT, Praeger).

Young, R.A. and Valach, L. (1996) Interpretation and action in career counseling, in: M.L. Savickas and W.B. Walsh (eds) *A Handbook of Career Counseling, Theory and Practice* (Palo Alto, CA, CPP Books).

Chapter 7

The challenge of change
Developing educational guidance for adults[†]

Unit for the Development of Adult Continuing Education

INTRODUCTION

All of us, as we move through adult life, undertake a great variety of learning tasks. We learn skills for enjoyment, for employment and to cope with unemployment; we learn to manage our finances and our relationships with other people; we learn to be parents and to support dependent parents. We undertake many of these learning tasks informally, by trial and error, with advice from friends and neighbours, by reading books and magazines or from radio or television. Probably most of our learning is undertaken in this informal way, but more formal opportunities are also available. These include a wide range of education and training courses, organised face to face or on a 'distance' basis, together with a variety of forms of 'open' learning or guided independent study. Such opportunities may be offered by educational institutions, employers, voluntary bodies, community groups and the media. They may be narrowly aimed at teaching particular skills or knowledge (electronic assembly, lip-reading or needlework) or more broadly at personal development (literature or parent education). Opportunities may be full- or part-time, local or remote, regular or occasional. They may be open to anyone, or to those with particular qualifications, or those employed in a particular organisation. Access to opportunities may be restricted or assisted by location, timing, the availability of child care or special equipment, or cost, including the availability of support, from employers, awards, grants or benefits.

While this variety of opportunities and agencies may reflect a flexible and creative service of education and training, offering a broad range of choice, it can be extremely difficult, even for experienced professionals, to find the right opportunity to meet a particular need, even when the opportunity already

[†] This chapter is an edited version of a report, *The Challenge of Change: Developing Educational Guidance for Adults* (1986) published by the Unit for the Development of Adult Continuing Education.[1]

exists. The problem is greater when a need can only be met by the reshaping of an existing course, or the creation of a new one. While many education and training agencies are willing to respond to new needs, designing learning opportunities for particular individuals or groups, most adults are unaware of this and many lack the necessary skills and knowledge to negotiate such changes successfully, whether this involves adjusting a timetable, organising child-care facilities, or fundamental curriculum change. All these problems are at their greatest for those who have had least contact with learning, at school and afterwards; who are most vulnerable to the impact of social and economic change and for whom education or training are therefore of special importance.

THE PURPOSE

There is a very widespread agreement that, if we are to meet the challenge of change in the next decades, we need a better educated and more adaptable adult population, who see themselves as successful and effective learners, and who see learning as a normal part of adult life, helping them to develop and adapt to new circumstances. If this is our aim the range and variety of opportunities described above offers us a great resource, but the difficulties which people experience in using that resource are often formidable. We have a great richness and range of opportunities available (or potentially available), and a substantial body of people willing to learn, separated by a great gulf of ignorance. It is this gulf which educational guidance seeks to bridge.

The primary purpose of educational guidance is to improve the match between learning opportunities and the needs and interests of learners and potential learners. This will include needs related to work (both paid and unpaid) and to personal development. Guidance can help clients, individually or in groups, to clarify their learning needs and find appropriate ways of meeting them. It can also channel information about unmet, or inappropriately met, needs to the education and training providers, helping them to develop more relevant and accessible provision. Thus, by helping learners and providers, educational guidance contributes to the development of an effective, economical and relevant service of education and training, and helps to increase public confidence in the ability of the education and training services to meet real needs.

Finding appropriate learning opportunities does not necessarily imply enrolment on 'courses', since many adults learn independently, on a self help basis, without contact with formal education or training agencies. Many of these could be more effective learners with assistance from educational guidance and some of those currently enrolled on formal courses might, with appropriate guidance, be able to meet their needs more effectively by less formal, and expensive, means. If we wish to ensure that the maximum benefit is obtained from all the resources available for adult learning we need to develop a more effective provision of educational guidance. The development of such provision is the subject of this chapter.

KINDS OF GUIDANCE

All of us need guidance in the course of our daily lives. We seek and receive it from a variety of sources – friends, relatives and acquaintances as well as a range of professionals. We may seek guidance in circumstances as varied as divorce, the choice of a degree course or the purchase of a roll of wallpaper. The common factor is that in every case we are making a choice, and seeking a means to make that choice as wisely as possible. Decision-making is thus at the centre of all guidance. The business of the 'guide' is to help the client both to make the most appropriate decision in the immediate situation and to develop the skills to make such decisions wisely in future. The client may need information, advice, counselling or assessment, and in some cases may need more direct support with enabling or advocacy.

Three kinds of guidance are relevant therefore:

- *Personal guidance* which embraces both educational and vocational guidance, and is concerned with choices about a wide range of personal issues, including identity, roles and relationships.
- *Vocational guidance* involving choices about the way in which individuals contribute to the community through paid work or other activities. Vocational decisions are usually seen as choices about paid employment, but social change is rapidly breaking down long-established assumptions about the place of paid employment in the lives of individuals. Vocational choices may therefore also involve unpaid work (including domestic, caring and voluntary roles).
- *Educational guidance* involving educational choices, concerned with learning needs and interests and ways of meeting them. This is the principal subject of this chapter.

These three kinds of guidance interlock in complex ways. Many adults who present themselves for 'educational' guidance have 'vocational' motives, either immediately in view, or in some tentative, long-term perspective. Many also have 'personal' ones, hoping that education will change their lives and the kind of people they are. On the other hand, many 'vocational' and 'personal' objectives can only be approached through 'educational' routes (and these are often surprisingly circuitous). However, it should be noted that there are areas of educational guidance for which there is little or no 'vocational' element (working with retired clients is one obvious example) and there are some areas of 'vocational' guidance (though a declining number) which have no immediate educational implications.

THE PLACE OF THE INDIVIDUAL

Whatever the motivation, and however much persuasion is applied by other people, the final choices will always be made by individuals.

The long-term interests of society require the development of a climate where learning is regarded as something natural and appropriate for all adults, and where those adults can recognise and find ways of meeting their learning needs easily and effectively as they arise. Educational guidance must, therefore, concentrate on individual clients, helping them to make informed choices, based on a sound assessment of their own experience, skills, knowledge, motives and opportunities.

This emphasis on the development of the individual does not stem from an idealised view of society or the individual, but from a practical recognition that all learning depends on motivation. While other people and agencies, including employers, government agencies and others, may wish to encourage individuals to undertake particular kinds of learning, nothing will be achieved without motivation, which depends on the learner understanding what is to be learned and its relevance to his or her needs and interests. There is a further reason for focusing attention on the individual. While other agencies may commit resources to education and training, the individual invests time, energy and often money in undertaking learning and has to live with the consequences over a much longer period than employers or governments plan for. The individual has, therefore, the greatest interest in making wise decisions and the greatest need for professional advice in doing so.

GUIDANCE AND TEACHING

While educational guidance has often been seen as a 'gateway' to education and training, it is important to recognise that learning and guidance are intimately connected. One of the principal objectives of any successful teacher or trainer is to help learners to understand their own learning, and to plan and approach it in the most effective way. While this is, and always has been, central to the teacher's role, it is also a guidance role. Guidance is that essential component of education and training which focuses on the individual's personal relationship with what is to be learned. The guidance worker, whether 'internal' or 'external', starts with a recognition that different people have different needs, knowledge, experience, motives and opportunities, and that these differences affect the ways in which they learn and the choices which they make. Educational guidance helps them identify what they need to learn and how to do so effectively. The same skills are required, whether they are applied by an 'external' guidance worker, helping a 'client' to plan a learning programme in advance or by an 'internal' one helping a 'student' or 'trainee' to approach a part of the learning task.

GUIDANCE AND THE CURRICULUM

While educational guidance concentrates on the individual and his or her needs, these will not be effectively met unless those providing learning opportunities are able and willing to change their provision to meet new and changing requirements. There is, therefore, a close relationship between educational guidance and curriculum development.

All agencies offering learning opportunities to adults need constantly to review the relevance of what they provide to the needs of potential and current learners. This involves a consideration of what is offered, the forms and style of its delivery, and how information about it is presented to potential learners. Both internal and external guidance workers therefore have a role to play in the design and implementation of education and training programmes, helping in the identification of needs and in the planning of ways to meet them, in the light of their special knowledge of what potential and current learners are seeking, and the ways in which they learn, or fail to learn. This involves major policy and curricular issues for education and training agencies and it is essential that they should be fully involved, at all levels, in the development of educational guidance provision.

THE PROCESS

While the agencies and institutions which deliver educational guidance will vary between areas and communities, the range of needs to be met are the same. A comprehensive service of educational guidance for adults will be able to assist all adults to:

- *Evaluate* their own personal, educational, and vocational development, possibly assisted by a guidance worker and/or formal assessment techniques;
- *Identify* their learning needs and choose the most appropriate ways of meeting them, bearing in mind constraints of personal circumstances, costs, and availability of opportunities;
- *Pursue and complete* a programme of learning as effectively as possible (this might include learning through a formal course, an open learning programme, a self-help group or self-directed private study);
- *Review and assess* the learning achieved and identify future goals.

Educational guidance is a process, rather than a single event, and the same individual will need different kinds of guidance at different times. It may be appropriate:

- *when an individual is first contemplating learning* and is seeking the most appropriate opportunity;

- *when first embarking on learning* (enrolling on a course, choosing a learning package, etc.), from staff knowledgeable about particular courses, materials or programmes;
- *during the course of study,* from tutorial staff, student counsellors or careers advisers;
- *on finishing a piece of learning* (whether or not it was successfully completed), in order to review what has been achieved and set new goals.

Educational guidance agencies also have a part to play in encouraging adults who have not previously considered it to engage in education and training.

> It is important to acknowledge that individuals may be part of networks and groups, and that the clarification of some educational needs has to be done in a group context, particularly where there is a history of indifference/antagonism to formal education. Advice and Guidance services may only gain trust by demonstrating to existing groups a commitment to their concerns, or by helping to develop new groups with resources to meet their own needs. Social learning is as important a part of the clarification of needs as individual guidance. We need to develop a clearer understanding of the relationship between the two.
>
> (EGSA Worker)[2]

THE ACTIVITIES

In this chapter the term 'educational guidance' is used to embrace a range of activities, which may be provided by a variety of agencies. In practice, these activities merge into one another but it is important to recognise the differences between them, since some agencies will choose, for reasons of policy or resource constraint to offer only a limited range. When such boundaries are drawn it is important that both staff and clients understand what is, and is not, being offered. While such a limitation may be appropriate in particular circumstances the choice should be made explicitly and not by default, and in full recognition that a client's needs are unlikely to be met by a single activity.

Although many agencies will only undertake some of these activities, a comprehensive service of educational guidance will include all of them.

Informing

Providing information about learning opportunities and related support facilities available, without any discussion of the relative merits of options for particular clients. Since most published educational information is produced for promotional purposes 'pure' information is rare.

Advising

Helping clients to interpret information and choose the most appropriate option. To benefit from advice clients must already have a fairly clear idea of what their needs are.

Counselling

Working with clients to help them to discover, clarify, assess and understand their learning needs and the various ways of meeting them. Clients requiring counselling are likely to be unclear about their needs and require time to explore their feelings about the options; counselling is therefore more likely to involve a series of contacts with a single client.

Assessing

Helping clients, by formal or informal means, to obtain an adequate understanding of their personal, educational and vocational development, in order to enable them to make sound judgements about the appropriateness of particular learning opportunities.

Enabling

Supporting the client in dealing with the agencies providing education or training, or in meeting the demands of particular courses. This may involve simple advice on completing application forms, advice on ways of negotiating changes in course content or arrangements, or assistance to independent learners. A further kind of enabling is provided through 'Access' and 'Wider Opportunities' courses which may offer both group guidance and the teaching of study skills.

Advocating

Negotiating directly with institutions or agencies on behalf of individuals or groups for whom there may be additional barriers to access or to learning (e.g. negotiating exceptional entry arrangements or modifications to courses).

Feeding back

Gathering and collating information on unmet, or inappropriately met, needs, and encouraging providers of learning opportunities to respond by developing their provision. This may involve practical changes (e.g. changing the presentation of course information or changing timetables) or curricular ones (e.g. designing new courses for new client groups, or changing the way in which existing courses are taught to make them more appropriate for adult learners).

In practice the seven activities are closely interrelated. Thus, for example, the choice of what information to present to a client, and how to do so, itself involves an 'assessment' of that client, whether or not this is consciously done. In the same way, the confidence building role of the 'enabler' often depends upon counselling skills.

Without an adequate base of information none of the activities are possible, but a service which seeks only to provide information cannot, in any adequate way, meet the guidance needs of its clients.

> information, in educational guidance, is not neutral. It is not as simple as passing information from education providers to the enquirer for him/her to make choices. Advice and counselling workers have a responsibility to assess and if necessary challenge the information and publicity given out by course providers. They have to make judgements about different courses and institutions, based on the past experiences of their enquirers. Of course they must be aware of the dangers of passing on their own prejudices, nevertheless they cannot evade this responsibility.
>
> (EGSA Worker)

EDUCATIONAL GUIDANCE WORKERS

Educational guidance is carried out by a variety of people, working in a variety of agencies. In this chapter the term 'educational guidance worker' is used to describe all such staff, whether paid or unpaid, and regardless of the agency within which they work. The term relates to the roles undertaken, rather than to the employing agency.

While some workers are employed exclusively in educational guidance, for many others this will only constitute a part of their work (as, for example, training or careers officers, librarians or advice workers in voluntary agencies). Many will only undertake a limited range of guidance activities, and some will only work with particular client groups.

THE AGENCIES[3]

Many agencies are involved in educational guidance. Some offer, or would wish to offer, the full range of educational guidance activities to any adult. Others, on the other hand, are more specialised, offering guidance only to some groups; or only in relation to some kinds of opportunity. Still others will provide only a limited range of guidance activities. This variety, in so far as it reflects genuine variation in local needs and circumstances, is both inevitable and desirable and this chapter therefore proposes the creation of networks for educational guidance which will bring all the various agencies into a closer collaboration without impinging on their legitimately different interests, skills and expertise.

It is possible to identify a number of key agencies which must inevitably be involved in the provision of educational guidance for adults. All are already engaged to some extent in this work (although not all offer the full range of guidance activities), and this should continue to be the case.

ACCESS

If educational guidance is to extend adult access to education then guidance itself must be accessible. This implies that basic information about where and how guidance is available must be very widely distributed, and that it will be necessary to develop an extensive range of 'contact points', where simple information is on display, or where appropriate individuals know how to make contact with guidance agencies. The use of a nationally recognised symbol for educational guidance could play a useful part in this.

At a number of points educational guidance will be directly available on a full- or part-time basis to clients who drop in or attend by appointment. These we have called 'Guidance Points', and they will form the first point of contact between a potential learner and a guidance worker. Guidance points will be provided by a variety of agencies, and within the area of a Local Authority might include:

- the *High Street* premises of an independent educational guidance service for adults (EGSA) offering the full range of activities six days a week;
- an *employer* offering employees, on site, a full range of guidance about employment-related learning;
- a *library* offering information, advice and support to independent learners;
- a *college* offering information, advice, counselling and enabling to its own students or potential students;
- a *Jobcentre* offering only information and advice about MSC[4]-funded courses;
- a *careers service* offering education and training information through its Careers library;
- a *voluntary organisation* working with physically disabled adults, offering the full range of activities to their own clients on a home visiting basis;
- a *community centre*, or a *Citizens Advice Bureau*, where an educational guidance service offers a *weekly advice* session;

- a *community information bus*, visiting outlying or rural communities on a regular basis with educational guidance staff;
- a *local radio station* providing advice through a 'phone in' service, either on or off air.

This list is intended as an illustration of some possibilities – many other kinds of guidance points already exist, and others will no doubt be created in the future. It seems certain that, at some stage, some form of computer-assisted systems will be developed, and will add dramatically to the number of people who can be reached by some form of guidance.

All these are points where clients can go to find guidance. In addition, guidance workers will go out to provide guidance to groups in a variety of locations.

> We are much concerned with the difficulties in organising a service to meet rural need, where the population is dispersed in small settlements with inadequate transport . . . The priority of actual provision in rural areas means that counselling can often not arrive at identifying an educational opportunity, but its absence. The feedback role from educational guidance in the rural situation may therefore often be different, and in some ways more difficult.
>
> (Organiser of part-time EGSA)

A LOCAL EDUCATIONAL GUIDANCE NETWORK

If educational guidance for adults were concerned only with formal course provision in the public sector, and if the learning needs of adults were homogeneous and predictable, it would be possible to propose the creation of a single new agency to provide a universal service of educational guidance. There are, however, almost as many different learning needs as there are adults, and more than half the formal learning opportunities available to adults are provided outside the public sector. Some are extremely difficult to find, or only of relevance to a very limited clientele. If the educational guidance needs of adults are to be met effectively it will be necessary to call upon a wide range of different skills and knowledge, some of which are very specialised. It would be uneconomic for a single agency to try to develop a universal expertise when other agencies are already well established and are in touch with the particular client groups concerned. Clients, for their part, will seek guidance from the agencies which they know and trust, whether or not the particular agency is best equipped to deal with the issue. Only if that agency in its turn knows and trusts other agencies with relevant expertise will the client be likely to receive the best service possible.

It follows that if the diverse skills and knowledge available are to be used to the maximum benefit of learners and potential learners, some form of network will be needed to link the various agencies which already provide a range of educational guidance in most parts of England and Wales (albeit sometimes on a very limited scale). An educational guidance network is such a group of agencies and individuals providing educational guidance in a given area. By formalising their relationships they can more readily assess how far the full range of educational guidance needs are being met, and whether, by a sharing of expertise or information they could improve the range or quality of the service which they jointly offer.

On an informal basis many such networks already exist, although they most commonly rest on personal contacts and on structures designed for other purposes. While informal relationships are essential to guidance they cannot provide a reliable basis for a permanent service, since they depend on chance encounters and on the commitment of particular individuals. Only in very exceptional cases can they produce the full range of skills and knowledge which potential learners may need to call on, and they cannot ensure that all the relevant agencies are fully involved. The development of a stable, effective, comprehensive and coherent service of educational guidance therefore calls for the creation of more formal networking arrangements.

An educational guidance network should seek to provide a comprehensive service, both by offering the full range of guidance activities and by offering them to all adults in its area. This does not, of course, imply that any single agency will necessarily be, or seek to be, comprehensive, although some EGSAs should wish to achieve this. Specialisation is both proper and consistent with the concept of networking, since a network is by definition a gathering of agencies with complementary skills and knowledge, where clients can be confident that any guidance point will be able to put them in touch with the agency best equipped to deal with their particular circumstances or needs. For their part, agencies can concentrate on what they do best and are freed from the necessity to try to hold all information and possess all professional skills. Thus, by collaborating, the partners can ensure that their special skills and knowledge are most effectively used both to meet existing, known needs and to tackle new, or unmet, ones.

> The role of teachers and . . . volunteer tutors in basic education as providers of advice and guidance is likely to be particularly crucial. Many adults receiving help with basic education will rely on someone they are familiar with and trust to provide advice and guidance on learning opportunities, rather than seek, or be prepared to accept, advice and guidance from a perhaps more knowledgeable, yet distant, specialist. A 'barefoot doctor' approach will perhaps be the most effective method of

ensuring that such adults receive advice and guidance, initially alongside information about more comprehensive services available locally, and encouragement to use them.

(Adult Literacy and Basic Skills Unit)[5]

THE OBJECTIVES OF A NETWORK[6]

While different agencies will play different parts they will need to agree a common policy for the network as a whole. A comprehensive service will need, at least, to ensure a provision of guidance which embraces all seven of the guidance activities, and is:

- *Client centred*
  The primary concern of the network should be the learning needs, wishes and interests of the adult population of its area, and its organisation and management should reflect this.
- *Confidential*
  Information received or recorded about clients, their personal circumstances and learning needs should be treated as confidential, and should not be conveyed to third parties without agreement.
- *Open to all adults*
  Different agencies will have different approaches to the definition of an 'adult', but for the purpose of the network this should embrace all those who have completed their initial education, at whatever age. We recognise that, within the network there will be agencies, like the careers service, whose brief extends into initial education, and that they will continue to work with this broader age range. We believe, however, that the concern of an 'adult' network must be to ensure that the needs of adults, as defined above, are met.
- *Accessible to all adults*
  This implies a service both physically accessible in terms of location, opening hours and outreach, and psychologically accessible to those who may be reluctant to approach formal institutions.
- *Freely available to all adults*
  Since guidance exists to make learning more accessible, especially to those whose previous experience of it has been least positive, a charge for guidance would be yet another barrier to access. Despite this we recognise that some agencies do charge some clients for personal, educational or vocational guidance, and this is likely to continue. If access is to remain genuinely open the norm should be that the service is free to clients, and it should be perceived as such by the public (as is the public library service, although many libraries charge for some parts of their service).

- *Independent in its advice*
  The network should seek to ensure that all guidance given is based on the needs of the client, and not distorted by the needs of the education or training providers or members of the network.
- *Publicised widely*
  A service which is not known about is not accessible. Many agencies currently avoid publicity as a means of preventing overload on staff or resources. This is likely to lead to a service biased in favour of particular client groups, either those most able to seek guidance, or those seen as the highest priority by particular workers. In either case the result is not a comprehensive and accessible service.
- *Able to contribute to the development of learning opportunities*
  A guidance agency will be unable to meet the needs of many of its clients if it can only offer access to those learning opportunities which already exist. It needs to be able to feed back information and ideas to education providers as it identifies changing or unmet needs. This will call for close working relations between guidance workers and the providers of education and training at appropriately senior levels.

In addition to meeting these criteria, an educational guidance network will need to be supported by a comprehensive base of information on learning opportunities available to adults, including opportunities available outside the immediate area. It will also be important that the network has access to information about employment opportunities and trends and about grants, benefits and other support facilities and regulations which affect the accessibility of education for many adults.

NOTES

1 *The Challenge of Change: Developing Educational Guidance for Adults* was a report published by the Unit for the Development of Adult Continuing Education (UDACE) in 1986. The report, which is now out of print, contained both discussion of the nature of educational guidance and structural proposals for its development. The report has been influential in framing our understanding of guidance, although the structural proposals made by UDACE have been overtaken by changes in the organisation of further and higher education and training.

In this chapter an attempt has been made to separate discussion of the purpose, place and nature of guidance from the context in which *The Challenge of Change* placed it. What appears here is taken from three chapters of the original report. There are relatively few changes to Chapters 2 and 3 of the original as these contain the development of the main ideas and the activities of guidance. The final section on access and networks is taken from Chapter 5 and is subject to considerable amendment. This section contains important discussion of the principles of guidance though these are developed as '*The objectives of a network*'.

The Challenge of Change was produced by UDACE after a process of consultation. At various points in the text, quotes from respondents were inserted to illustrate issues.

2 Many of the early services were developed by Educational Guidance Services for Adults (EGSAs). An EGSA worker was a guidance worker.

3 In this section the original report listed the sorts of agencies then involved in educational guidance with brief descriptions of their roles. These included EGSAs, Libraries, Careers Services, Local Education Authorities, Training Providers, Employers, Educational Institutions, Trade Unions and Voluntary Organisations.

4 Manpower Services Commission, which later became the Training Agency and is now a part of the Department for Education and Employment.

5 This is now the Basic Skills Agency.

6 These objectives have, in the period since 1986, been used in a variety of ways to develop the principles of guidance and to develop Codes of Professional Conduct. Perhaps the most surprising feature of the list is that there is no reference to equality of opportunity.

Chapter 8

School counsellors and guidance networks

Roles revisited[†]

*Judi Miller, Robert Manthei
and Alison Gilmore*

Guidance counsellors were first appointed to selected schools in New Zealand in the early 1960s to cope with specific social problems in those schools. Their role was one of rescuer and troubleshooter (Wadsworth, 1970). A Department of Education policy statement in 1968 changed the overall focus to one where counsellors would offer educational, vocational and personal guidance to all students. It was also recommended that counsellors should teach for 20 to 40 per cent of their time. Interestingly, early data from one counsellor (Wadsworth, 1970) indicated that 38 per cent of students presented with vocational concerns and 31 per cent for each of educational and personal concerns, a fairly even spread across the three recommended areas of focus.

In 1971 *Guidance in Secondary Schools* (Department of Education, 1971), widely known as the Working Party Report, appeared. This was an important early policy document outlining the schools' organisation of guidance services. It also included data from a national survey of all secondary school principals. Several trends in guidance were identified:

1   Most schools already had 'networks' of guidance personnel, including form teachers, deans, principals, deputy principals and senior managers, counsellors and careers advisors.
2   Most of the counsellors' time involved counselling, both individuals and groups.
3   Up to 33 per cent of the counsellors did some classroom teaching.
4   Almost every school had at least one careers advisor. Numerically this was the largest category of guidance worker.

As a result of its findings and deliberations, the Working Party made several recommendations regarding the role and functions of guidance services:

[†] This chapter is an edited version of an article in the *New Zealand Journal of Educational Studies*, 1993, 28(2): 105–24.

1   That guidance counsellors be renamed guidance teachers.
2   That guidance teachers should be seen as teachers and should continue to teach, but not necessarily in examinable subjects.
3   That careers advisors be phased out and replaced with guidance teachers.
4   That although guidance teachers have responsibility for educational, vocational and personal/social guidance, 60 per cent of their guidance time should be in educational and vocational counselling (the Working Party felt that too much time was spent counselling pupils with special personal and social problems).
5   That there be an occupational orientation included at all levels in the school.
6   That a wide range of staff be involved in guidance, each with different types of responsibilities (this concept became widely known as the 'guidance network').
7   That guidance teachers become consultants to the rest of the staff in day-to-day contacts with pupils.

In the years since the Working Party Report (Department of Education, 1971) there has appeared a number of surveys that have described the work and roles of guidance counsellors.

In summary, several observations about the developing role and functions of guidance counsellors seem warranted:

1   The Working Party's recommendation that guidance counsellors be renamed guidance teachers was rejected by the counsellors (Renwick, 1981; Wadsworth, 1981).
2   As recently as 1986 counsellors were still struggling with problems of role over load, role conflict and role definition (Manthei, 1987). These have been persistent problems that have been identified over many years by several researchers.
3   In spite of the Working Party's recommendation in 1971 and Strang's (1974) early data, vocational and careers work has not occupied a large amount of the counsellor's time. Nevertheless, most schools have developed extensive, reality-based work exploration and transition programmes that operate at all levels of the school.
4   Guidance networks have been developed in most schools to the point where a wide range of staff are involved and have some guidance time allocation. Some formal recognition of the training needs of guidance personnel other than counsellors was evidenced by the training package *On Being a Dean* (Department of Education, 1987). However, there has been scant research on the specific responsibilities and duties of the various staff involved.
5   Guidance counsellors, usually identified today as school counsellors, have developed several new foci in their work. Personal/social counselling

with students has always been a high priority activity, but there are indications that many counsellors are also developing skills in new areas of work, like family counselling.

It has been several years since research on guidance networks or the school counsellor's role has appeared in the literature. In the interim there have been substantial changes to the structure of secondary education, beginning with the Picot report (Taskforce, 1988) and *Tomorrow's Schools* (Minister of Education, 1988). These changes have not only affected classroom teachers, but also members of school guidance networks. The aim of this study, therefore, was to obtain a clearer picture of the present roles of guidance personnel and to identify developments in those roles since the mid-1980s. Answers to four questions were sought:

1   How much guidance time were members of a school's guidance network officially allocated?
2   How much time were such personnel actually spending on guidance activities?
3   What specific guidance activities did various members of guidance networks say they performed?
4   Whom did they regard as having the major responsibility for seeing that those activities were done?

PROCEDURE

A questionnaire survey was used to determine the roles of guidance personnel in schools in the greater Christchurch area.

Sample

The participants comprised members of the guidance networks in schools within a radius of 32 kilometres of Christchurch (twenty three schools met this criterion). All staff involved in guidance work were asked to respond, for example: principals, deputy principals/senior mistresses, counsellors, career advisors, deans, tutors, transition tutors, guidance teachers, special needs teachers, and a form teacher at each level. Two hundred and two completed questionnaires were received from twenty-two schools.

Questionnaire

A list of counsellors' guidance activities was compiled from several sources. In 1990/91 ten counsellor trainees each spent at least two half days observing school guidance staff in their work and interviewed them about their roles and functions. A composite list of guidance activities was drawn up. To this list were added activities that were derived from literature on the role of guidance counsellors. Several school counsellors, all of whom were co-ordinators of their schools' guidance networks, were then asked to check for activities that might have been omitted. Activities on the resulting list were then grouped into six main categories, five having to do with guidance work and one comprising general administrative work: A, Counselling Students; B, Counselling Teachers; C, Counselling Parents; D, Testing; E, Other Guidance Tasks; and F, General Administration. The face validity of these categories was checked with three school counsellors. A working definition of counselling was provided as a guide to respondents in completing the questionnaire: 'a process concerned with assisting people achieve their personal or educational goals or function more effectively'.

A questionnaire was constructed around these categories. Respondents were asked the following:

1   To report the number of hours officially allocated to them for guidance work.
2   To estimate the percentage of their guidance time that was spent on activities in the six categories.
3   To indicate which guidance activities they performed.
4   To indicate which person they considered had the main or substantial responsibility for carrying out each activity.
5   To comment on their roles and their functions.

After consulting with several school counsellors and pilot testing at three schools, a final version of the questionnaire was constructed and distributed to the participating schools. Analysis of the questionnaire was straightforward. Objective questions were analysed by computer and the written comments were transcribed and categorised according to theme. Also, through discussion with several counsellors, reactions to the findings were obtained.

RESULTS AND DISCUSSION

Allocated guidance time versus actual guidance time

Guidance personnel were asked to state how much of their time was officially designated 'guidance time'. They were also asked to estimate what percentage of their total work time was spent doing counselling and other guidance-related work.

Seven of the nine groups of staff exceeded their allocated time, but with three exceptions (careers advisors, deans and tutors) these discrepancies were minor. Obviously, different schools apportion time to guidance personnel very differently; what is also of note is the fact that different groups of personnel seem to use their apportioned time differently. There are substantial correlations between allocated and actual guidance time for only four groups. These groups – deans, tutors, transition tutors and guidance teachers – have time schedules that are relatively inflexible. For the other five groups the demands of the job are such that following a daily time schedule is unrealistic. These groups' schedules are typically more flexible and these staff are 'available' to take on additional, unplanned-for tasks (this explanation has been confirmed in discussions with several counsellors).

Distribution of guidance time

Respondents were asked to estimate the percentage of their guidance time that was spent on activities in each of the five guidance categories: A, Counselling students; B, Counselling teachers; C, Counselling parents; D, Testing; E, 'Other Guidance tasks. Results show that Category A, Counselling students is a frequent activity. Average times spent by each group indicate that almost 50 per cent of all allocated guidance time is spent on this group of activities (principals spend the least amount of time but even they average 23 per cent). When time spent on guidance tasks is translated into a percentage of each group's total working time, it is clear that counselling students is the guidance activity on which the most time is spent, but for five groups it occupies less than 15 per cent of their total working time.

The important point to be made here is that in spite of the size of each group's allocated time (ranging from 0 to 100 per cent of total time), each tends, on average, to spend about half of that time on counselling students. Is that really efficient or justifiable? Do those who claim to be doing counselling have sufficient training to do such work? Are the definitions of counselling held by the groups the same? In spite of having provided a definition of counselling in the questionnaire, we suspect not. However, since the respondents' training and experience as counsellors varied considerably, this is not so surprising.

In response to these data several counsellors have suggested that the 'large' amount of student counselling being done by all groups of staff reflects several trends: there is a greater need for counselling in the schools and consequently more staff are wanting to use 'counselling skills' in their work; the counsellor's work has been 'demystified' and is thought to be more accessible to those with even minimal training; efforts to make the guidance network concept work have resulted in more staff seeing themselves as being responsible for pastoral care; as community counselling services diminish, more is expected from schools. These trends suggest that counselling is not only a high frequency, needed activity, but also a valued activity.

Category A: Counselling students

Tasks done

Questionnaire items included: personal problems, vocational careers, educational issues, family matters, group counselling, crisis counselling. Virtually all counsellors said they spent some time on each of these activities. Other groups also saw this work as a legitimate part of their guidance role.

Time spent

Time spent doing this work was about 50 per cent of total guidance time for all groups. Such time ranged from an average of 23 per cent for principals to a high of 70 per cent for careers advisors. Counsellors averaged 59 per cent of their time. It was disturbing to see that the range of time spent for counsellors was 25 per cent to 85 per cent. Why were some counsellors spending as little as 25 per cent of their time on 'counselling students' tasks? Because of their specific job responsibilities and training for such work, it could be argued that they should be spending a greater proportion of their time on these activities. In response to these data, several counsellors suggested that those spending as little as 25 per cent of their time counselling may have been 'caught up' in other activities; they might also have made conscious decisions to share this work around other guidance staff, especially in schools where there is more than one counsellor.

Why were some DP/SMs, form teachers, deans and transition tutors spending all of their guidance time on these activities? Is this really a good use of their limited guidance time? Furthermore, do they have the necessary training to do this work? Previous writers have alluded to the conflict between teachers who have always regarded 'pastoral care' as part of their traditional role and counsellors who claim to have special training and time to do such work (Brammer, 1985; Renwick, 1981), and teachers' envy of the counsellors' job satisfactions (Small, 1982). Perhaps teachers and others want to retain their traditional pastoral roles and share in the satisfactions of such work.

Responsibility

From those sampled, counsellors were clearly seen as having major responsibility for personal, family, group and crisis counselling. On each of these items at least 80 per cent of all respondents named the counsellor as the person who has 'the main or substantial responsibility for carrying out each of the activities listed'.

Category B: Counselling teachers

Tasks done

Key questionnaire items included discussions of students with teachers and administrators; counselling teachers regarding personal problems, teaching matters, professional or career issues, family matters; and observing teachers in class. Virtually every guidance staff member discussed students with other teachers and administrators. However, it was clear that principals, DP/SMs and counsellors were far more likely to be involved in the remaining activities than the other personnel.

The fact that three such disparate groups were so involved in the counselling of teachers raises several questions. Would each group, principals, DP/SMs and counsellors, have similar notions of what constituted counselling? Are teachers free to choose the person to whom they want to talk? Who initiates this counselling with teachers (for example, counselling having to do with teaching matters or professional/career issues)? Future research needs to survey teachers about their experiences of, and opinions about, such 'counselling'.

Time spent

Average time spent on these activities, whether a percentage of guidance time only or total time, was far less than that for counselling students for every group except principals. The range of average guidance time spent was 4 per cent (careers advisors and guidance teachers) to 41 per cent (principals). Counsellors averaged 9 per cent of their guidance time on these activities, with a range of 0 to 20 per cent. Why would some counsellors be spending no time on activities having to do with counselling teachers? Such activities are generally accepted as part of their role (Brammer, 1985; Hermansson, 1981).

Responsibility

It seems appropriate that counsellors were seen by other guidance staff to have major responsibility for counselling teachers about personal and family matters (named by 59 per cent of all respondents). Responsibility for the other tasks was less clear cut with the exception of professional/careers matters where principals were named by 50 per cent of respondents as having major responsibility.

Category C: Counselling parents

Tasks done

This category included activities that involved contact with parents and families. Items included crisis, family and marital counselling, home visits and conducting parent interviews. Over 90 per cent of all counsellors said they did all of these tasks except for marital counselling (41 per cent). These findings seem a reasonable reflection of the school counsellor's role in this area. The much lower number of counsellors doing marital counselling highlights the debate about whether marital counselling is a legitimate school counsellor activity (see, for example, Abbott, 1984; Manthei, 1984; Muller, 1990).

Time spent

The average amount of guidance time spent on counselling parents over all groups tends to be less than the time spent counselling teachers. It is clear that these activities comprise a relatively small proportion of guidance and total time. The range of average guidance time spent counselling parents was from 3 per cent (careers advisors) to 18 per cent for principals. Individual counsellors spent from 5 per cent to 25 per cent of their guidance on these activities.

Responsibility

Counsellors were clearly seen as having major responsibility for crisis counselling (named by 91 per cent of respondents), home visits (76 per cent) and family counselling (88 per cent). They were also seen as having responsibility for parent interviews (49 per cent) and marital counselling (52 per cent). All respondents were clear that the counsellor was the one who had major responsibility for these tasks, even though these activities did not comprise a large proportion of a school's guidance work.

Category D: Testing

Tasks done

Tasks in this area included administering tests to new students, administering specialist tests, interpreting test results for teachers, parents, students and/or outside agencies. At least 70 per cent of all counsellors said they did each of these tasks. The results indicate that most counsellors are clear that testing activities are a legitimate part of their role.

Time spent

The time allocated to such tasks, however, was minimal. Counsellors spend only 2 per cent of their guidance time on these activities. Tutors and transition tutors spend larger amounts of their guidance time on testing, but even their proportions amount to only 6 per cent and 9 per cent respectively.

Responsibility

It was very clear that counsellors were the persons designated as having main responsibility for each of the testing tasks. Counsellors were named by 53 per cent to 82 per cent of respondents on the four items.

Thus, even though testing took up very little time, there was clear agreement that counsellors should do such work and were accorded responsibility for it. On the one hand this seems to argue for the continuance of a mandatory test and assessment course in any recognised training programme for school counsellors. It might also be argued that because it is such a low frequency activity, some other guidance person with relevant training in the area should assume responsibility, thus freeing counsellors to work elsewhere.

Category E: Other guidance tasks

Tasks done

Examples of tasks in this area included chairing guidance meetings, liaison with outside agencies, receiving and giving supervision, visiting contributing schools, etc. Three tasks out of the list of twenty four seemed specific to counselling and were in areas which one could argue every counsellor should have some involvement: supervising other counsellors, trainees or teachers (83 per cent of all counsellors said they performed this task); participating in the school's suspension process (87 per cent were involved); interviewing truants (78 per cent undertook this). It was also clear that counsellors do a wide range of general guidance tasks. On twenty of the twenty four items in this section of the questionnaire at least 70 per cent of the counsellors said they performed the task.

The results in this section confirm the very wide range of 'other' activities in which counsellors are involved and suggest, perhaps, that their roles are too diverse and that their specialised skills and training are being wasted, or at least under-utilised.

Time spent

The percentage of guidance time allocated to these activities is the second highest category for counsellors (17 per cent). Guidance time is usually flexible and initially, at least, unstructured. This may leave counsellors and guidance teachers vulnerable to requests to carry out tasks that staff with time-tabled classes are unable to do. In effect, they become extra administrative help, 'floating trouble-shooters'.

Responsibility

Another interesting aspect of these 'other' activities is that counsellors are seen as having major responsibility for twenty of the twenty four tasks. The exceptions are: the suspension process (most counsellors participate but principals are seen as responsible); interviewing truant students (deans responsible); organising third-form orientation programme (deans responsible); organising careers day (careers advisors responsible). These four exceptions seem to be appropriately handled by other than counsellors. However, counsellors' wide responsibility for the other twenty tasks reinforces the idea that they have too much to do and that their efforts may be spread too thinly around the school.

Category F: General tasks

Tasks done

Tasks in this area had little or nothing to do with guidance per se. Examples included leading assemblies, processing enrolments, attending to visitors to the school, etc. In a list of twenty eight general tasks only two were said to be done by at least 75 per cent of all counsellors: integrate new students into the school (78 per cent); attend other than guidance committee meetings (87 per cent).

Responsibility

Counsellors are seen to have administrative responsibility for only one of the general guidance tasks: organising and conducting parent education programmes. Most of the others are said to be the responsibility of principals (7 tasks), DP/SMs (9 tasks) or deans (5 tasks).

While their involvement in these 'general' tasks is not as extensive as in guidance work, many counsellors obviously contribute to work in this area. We would suggest that schools should review this work and redeploy their own counsellors to more appropriate duties where possible.

Additional information

There were 134 respondents who wrote 152 comments in the questionnaire. These responses substantiate and provide further insight into the data presented in the earlier sections. The following themes were evident.

Role clarity/ambiguity: counsellors

In the previous section, the number of times counsellors were nominated as having major responsibility for a task was taken to be a good indicator that their role was reasonably clear. This was supported by the fact that in their comments counsellors did not often mention role ambiguity. Comments from other members of the guidance networks also supported the finding that counsellors have a clear role in the school. There were fifteen comments from six schools about this. For example, one transition tutor had a clear notion of the counsellor's essential role:

> I believe all staff co-operate with the Guidance Department and our counsellor co-ordinates activities and information extremely well.

A dean in another school had a similarly clear perception:

> The counsellor becomes a vital resource in the school . . . to help students whose needs cannot be met quickly or simply by essentially untrained staff.

Value of counselling

Comments by six counsellors supported the view that their role as counsellor was valued by the school. For one counsellor the school administration had structured the timetable to increase counselling time. The counsellor stated:

> I value the fact that I am freed of a lot of course selection and careers work so that I can focus my efforts on problem-solving counselling.

These comments support our earlier suggestion that because it is a high frequency activity for which there is a perceived need, counselling is also seen as a valued activity; in fact, everyone in the guidance network does it. Thus, one deputy principal commented, 'I enjoy the counselling side of my job', and one dean felt it was important to preserve a counselling role:

> Sometimes I feel that when a student approaches me for help I should hand on the problem to someone else to avoid any misunderstanding but if the student has sought my help I am reluctant to do this.

There were, however, two counsellors who were concerned that counselling was not valued in the school. One stated:

> Counsellors are still seen I feel in a somewhat negative light by many students/parents/teachers.

and in a different school, a counsellor was concerned that because other staff members perceived that they too had counselling skills, the counsellor's special expertise had been diminished:

> I have been and am very happy to raise the awareness and skills of all staff but one of the results has been the devaluing of the very skilled aspects of the counselling.

Network concerns

The question of role definition in the guidance network was remarked on by three respondents. For example, one tutor stated:

> The counselling role in the school could be better defined. Our work brief sets out the lists of tasks that are required but does little to cover the role responsibilities with respect to counselling.

Other comments where changes to the guidance network were suggested concerned ineffective communication procedures. Six comments were made across five schools about this. For example one form teacher stated:

> Confidentiality is a problem I know but sometimes the class teachers can modify their handling of kids if we were made aware that kids have problems.

More common, however, were comments from guidance personnel, other than counsellors, about the efficient functioning of the guidance network. These comments suggest that although some guidance networks are effective mechanisms for administering pastoral care in schools they are not without problems. Each school needs some means by which these issues can be addressed. All of this assumes that schools will have sufficient resources for this task.

Work satisfaction

It appeared that where there was a well-structured network, guidance personnel were more satisfied with their work. For example, a careers advisor commented:

> I work with a great team and this makes my job enjoyable, manageable and challenging.

It also appeared that clarity of roles and perceived value of duties contributed to satisfaction with work. The counsellors had clear role definitions and were engaged in an activity that was valued. In spite of feeling pressured, vulnerable and frustrated by current economic pressures, they retained a positive attitude to their work. Many mentioned strategies that they were considering to be more effective in their work, for example, being more pro-active, working more with families or engaging in staff training. One counsellor considered recent structural changes as an opportunity to make some changes:

> The school and staff involved in the network have a strong commitment to guidance and counselling but time and resources are a limited factor. The future is scary but perhaps it is time to rethink and restructure the provision of guidance in schools and to consider innovative ways rather than following the traditional lines.

Demand for counselling services

There is an obvious need for schools to address ways in which the guidance networks can accommodate an increase in the demand for counselling services. This 'need', we believe, is another indication of the growing value attached to counselling in most schools. Of the nineteen comments from counsellors, over half pertained to their need to have more time to provide counselling. For example one counsellor commented:

> I am largely free to define my own work areas, but the stress comes from the quantity of the work so there is a feeling of never having enough time.

There were three comments across two schools where concern was expressed that very needy students were demanding so much guidance time that students with minor needs were being overlooked. For example, one deputy principal commented:

> I think that we're all doing as much of it as we can. The big problem is that there is so much need and so limited resources that at times the services get 'drowned'. This means that many *needy students* (but less critical) miss out. This is the thing I would most like to change.

Economic pressure

Comments about increased demands for services were most often linked with the current economic situation. These comments concerned the growing demands on all guidance personnel due to the increasing social and economic pressures in the community. Given that the timing of the survey coincided with the 1991 budget in which schools were required to restructure their guidance and counselling resources, such comments were not unexpected. The important point here is that the concern about how to address the problem of shrinking resources was felt across the whole guidance network. One deputy principal commented:

> There is increasing pressure on many of our students caused by home/ family difficulties, (some related to economic issues). The effect is . . . our counsellors are consistently handling serious cases. The demands and stresses have increased and show no sign of diminishing. Budget announcements hold little hope for maintaining, let alone increasing, our counselling resource. So . . . we do the best we can and accept that we can't do all that we would like.

Discussions with school counsellors have highlighted the trickle-down effects of government policy interventions. These were previously dealt with by agencies outside schools. Counsellors are now dealing with serious problems such as suicide, sexual abuse, depression and break-down in families, and deans, form teachers and senior administrators are undertaking basic pastoral counselling and guidance, that is, the provision of an effective educational and developmental environment in the school (Hamblin, 1978). Again this raises questions about the guidance policy in each school. How much counselling does the community expect to be done in a school? How much counselling does a school expect to be done by its counsellor and what roles should be adopted by the other members of the guidance network?

CONCLUSIONS

For counsellors in Christchurch schools the present data suggest that there has been some increase in the clarity of their role. Furthermore, their colleagues seem reasonably clear about the counsellor's responsibilities for 'other' guidance tasks. At the same time, however, one consequence of the development of guidance networks has been an overlapping of work with other guidance personnel, a situation that Munro (1990) describes as a diminution of counsellors' power as their skills have been shared with and employed by others. In spite of this overlap, important differences between counsellors and other guidance personnel exist. Most school counsellors have had the benefit of university-based training and many receive regular clinical supervision; deans and others, on the other hand, are largely untrained and unsupervised in their guidance work.

There are suggestions in the present study that counsellors are still doing too much, that their responsibilities are spread too widely. For example, counsellors are seen to have major responsibility for a large number of tasks and this may reduce their effectiveness in areas for which they are specially trained. In addition, most New Zealand counsellors work in schools with a counsellor/student ratio of 1:500 or more, far in excess of that recommended by the American School Counselor Association: 1:100 (ideal) up to a maximum of 1:300 (Borders and Drury, 1992).

Counselling students, it seems, has become a high priority activity in Christchurch schools. Most guidance staff report spending 50 per cent or more of their guidance time in such work. While one might question whether all groups of guidance workers share a common definition of 'counselling', the diversity of people claiming to spend so much of their guidance time engaged in it suggests that it is both an area of need and a valued activity.

Finally, if the notion of an effective guidance network is to continue in practice, it seems necessary at this point for schools to begin to rationalise the roles of the myriad staff who play a part. There is too much overlap amongst them. Personnel other than counsellors seem now to be at the point counsellors themselves were at in the early 1980s (McDiarmid, 1981): somewhat confused about their ambiguous roles.

REFERENCES

Abbott, B. (1984). Why work with families? *New Zealand Counselling and Guidance Association Journal,* 6, 79–82

Borders, L.D. and Drury, S.M. (1992). Comprehensive school counseling programs: A review for policymakers and practitioners. *Journal of Counseling and Development,* 70, 487–501.

Brammer, L.M. (1985). *The New Zealand School Guidance Counsellors: Their Training and Work.* Bulletin No. 19, Wellington: New Zealand Council for Educational Research.

Department of Education. (1971). *Guidance in Secondary Schools: Report of a Working Party.* Wellington.

Department of Education. (1987). *On Being a Dean. Parts I and II.* Christchurch: Southern Regional Office.

Hamblin, D.H. (1978). *The Teacher and Pastoral Care.* Oxford: Basil Blackwell.

Hermansson, G. (1981). Counselling: A valid activity. In Hermansson, G.L. (ed.), *Guidance in New Zealand Secondary Schools: Issues and Programmes.* Palmerston North: New Zealand Counselling and Guidance Association.

McDiarmid, J.K. (1981). The guidance counsellor's role: Consensus and conflict. *PPTA Journal, Term 3,* 28–30.

Manthei, B. (1984). Doing brief family counselling in schools. *New Zealand Counselling and Guidance Association Journal,* 6, 83–90.

Manthei, R.J. (1987). School counsellors and job-related stress. *New Zealand Journal of Educational Studies,* 22, 189–200.

Minister of Education. (1988). *Tomorrow's Schools.* Wellington: Government Printer.

Muller, A. (1990). Family therapy or family counselling: Issues for counsellors. In

Small, J.J. and Ambrose, T. (eds), *Counselling and Guidance Towards the Nineties.* Massey University: New Zealand Counselling and Guidance Association.

Munro, E.A. (1990). Records and reminiscences. In J. Small and T. Ambrose (eds) *Counselling and Guidance Towards the Nineties.* Massey University: New Zealand Counselling and Guidance Association.

Renwick, W.L. (1981). Review of guidance counselling, 1981. Speech of the Director-General of Education to the New Zealand Counselling and Guidance Association Conference, Wellington.

Small, J.J. (1982). An appraisal of guidance counsellors. *New Zealand Counselling and Guidance Association Journal,* 4, 52–74.

Strang, J.M. (1974). *Guidance Counselling in New Zealand.* Unpublished M.A. Thesis, University of Otago.

Taskforce to review education administration. (1988). *Administering for Excellence* (Picot Report). Wellington: Government Printer.

Wadsworth, E.J. (1970). The role of the school counsellor. *New Zealand Social Worker,* 6, 13–21.

Wadsworth, E.J. (1981). School counselling – limitations of the change agent role. *New Zealand Counselling and Guidance Association Journal,* 3, 20–25.

Part III

Management and policy discourses

Chapter 9

Counselling in a secondary setting – developing policy and practice[†]

Colleen McLaughlin

INTRODUCTION

In this chapter I propose to explore how secondary schools and colleges can work towards the development of a policy on counselling and guidance.

BACKGROUND TO COUNSELLING IN SECONDARY SCHOOLS

If one looks at the development of counselling in secondary settings the model is largely one based on problem-solving work with individuals or groups. This reflects the developments in training and thinking. In the 1970s the predominance of the Rogerian or 'client-centred' model can be seen. There were counselling training courses for those wishing to become counsellors in schools, where counsellors did exist. Their existence was not always unproblematic (see Richardson, 1974) but many schools employed them. In the early 1980s many factors impinged to change the situation. First, there were cuts in education spending and counsellors came to be seen as a luxury; in many local authorities counselling posts were the first to be cut. Second, there was an increase in the emphasis on counselling skills for *all* teachers, influenced by the work of people such as Egan (1986). This was in contrast to the emphasis on the Rogerian model. Third, there was an increasing interest and debate on the use of coun-selling in applied settings, that is in settings where counselling was not the primary task of those engaging in it. Fourth, there was an increase in the development of programmes of work for students which aimed to give the concepts of counselling and guidance to the students. These programmes were often called guidance programmes or personal and social education

[†] This chapter is an edited version of a chapter in Bovair, K. and McLaughlin, C. (eds) (1993) *Counselling in Schools: A Reader*, London: David Fulton.

courses and they developed the teacher's role from a reactive to an educative one.

Since then, there have been further developments in the area of counselling. Many initiatives have drawn on counselling skills, such as records of achievement and teacher appraisal. In such initiatives the skills are very similar but their intentions are different, for largely the skills are being drawn on to enhance communication. Other developments have drawn on counselling psychology and theory. For example, there has also been much work in the pastoral field on bullying and child abuse. The initiatives in this area emphasise the importance of respect for students and their feelings. These developments have been accompanied by an increasing awareness of what the emotional world of schooling looks and feels like to students. An example is the acknowledgement that behaviours such as teasing and bullying have an adverse effect on students' mental health and development.

So there is much work occurring in the area of guidance and counselling. However, the development of different models and the accumulation of new functions, for example the educative added to the problem-solving, has led to much confusion or lack of time to sort out how these different elements work together and what the differences between the contributions are. The HMI survey of guidance reflects this position (DES, 1990). The survey concentrated on students aged thirteen to nineteen in twenty six maintained secondary schools and sixth-form colleges: the schools included the full range of size, setting and location. The survey showed that 'schools and colleges had a variety of approaches to guidance'. The report acknowledged that a range of activities contributes to appropriate provision in this area and that many schools are contributing well. The best responses were characterised by:

- clarity and precision;
- evidence of a coherent underlying policy;
- an integrated approach (bringing together personal and social education, pastoral work, the role of subject teaching, relationships with parents and outside agencies, ethos, teaching and learning styles);
- a recognition that the quality of guidance was influenced by the school–student–home partnership;
- a relating of guidance provision to students' needs and perceptions;
- evidence of a link between intentions and practice.

The conceptions of guidance were wide ranging and not necessarily mutually exclusive. They included:

- non-directive guidance in response to students seeking help;
- guidance that sought to direct students along a particular path;

- crisis and problem-solving guidance;
- guidance built into the curriculum;
- guidance provided to meet institutional perceptions that government and employers thought guidance was important in providing efficient matching of talents and motivation to jobs;
- guidance perceived as a specialist function of those with relevant training.

These conceptions covered 'both formal and informal arrangements and many existed, quite reasonably, side by side in the same institution; however, there were cases where there was some inconsistency in the various practices adopted. This could usually be related to the absence of explicit aims, of clearly identified elements of guidance provision and of evaluation of outcomes.' (DES, 1990). All these issues need to be considered in the development of a clear policy and integrated practice.

AIMS OF COUNSELLING IN SECONDARY SCHOOLS AND COLLEGES

Section 1 of the 1988 Education Reform Act states that schools have a statutory responsibility to develop a curriculum which 'promotes the spiritual, moral, cultural, mental and physical development of students at the school and of society; and prepares such students for the opportunities, responsibilities and experiences of adult life'. Guidance plays a part in helping schools to fulfil this commitment. The aim is to contribute as fully and as positively as possible to the mental health of the students in the school community and to do this in different ways: through the curriculum, through the community of the school and through one-to-one and group work.

Counselling and guidance have a developmental function as well as a reactive one. Early in the development of counselling in schools the task was seen as involving teachers in working one-to-one with students and viewed as developmental in nature. The objectives of counselling were related to:

- fostering self acceptance in students and not changing or remediating personality;
- developing control from within or fostering an internal locus of control;
- helping students to learn strategies and coping skills for situations which were difficult or important in terms of their impact on future life.

(Hamblin, 1974)

These aims have not changed but there was a realisation that in a school context the work could play a more educative role. Marland (1980) summed it up when he talked of the art of giving individual guidance without having to give it individually. It is interesting to see how many of the key figures in counselling progressed to writing in the widest sense about schools and their impact on individuals (Glasser, 1975; Rogers, 1983).

Schools have a responsibility to develop students personally and socially, so there is an *educative* function. However, personal and social development does not take place in isolation. Our personal development and sense of identity are learned in our interactions with others. We learn who we are in the context of a community and those in it. Therefore, there is also the responsibility to explore the impact of the school or college on the personal and social development of the students there. This *reflective* or evaluative function involves exploring the possible impact of and contribution to personal and social development of practices in the classroom and other aspects of the school community. This generally incorporates interactions between teachers and students as well as between students and students. It also includes wider issues of teaching and learning styles, classroom and school climate. In addition, there is the *welfare* function: the responsibility to plan for and react to issues which impact on students' welfare and development. This is the area where counselling has traditionally been seen to play a part. It is helpful to distinguish these different aims but there is also the need to co-ordinate them and see the links between them.

THE EDUCATIVE ELEMENT

The educative element includes guidance in the curriculum as well as the wider field of affective education or education for the emotions. In terms of guidance in the curriculum, the framework of personal, vocational and educational guidance is now a well accepted one. It is often hard to distinguish between them. The curriculum is related to the different needs and ages of students. It should also reflect the particular needs of students in relation to their community and context. It includes giving students the personal and social skills without which they may require problem-based counselling – for example, helping students acquire the skills of listening and responding appropriately to others, or developing the ability to express feelings and opinions. It also contains elements which are in response to guidance needs perceived as arising from particular themes in groups or individuals. This may include working on topics such as friendship or negotiation, as well as the experience and development of the ability to work in a group.

We also know that the time of vulnerability for many students is at periods of transition (Hamblin, 1974; DES, 1990). Hamblin called these 'critical incidents'. They are critical because they are occasions when students can affiliate to the school or become alienated. At these times, such as entry to school, transfer to new courses or transfer to new institutions, students need support and this support needs to be of an organised form and have a curricular element. In providing effective guidance there is a need to plan a programme which is coherent and not merely a collection of one-off events. Guidance is most effective when it is continual and cumulative (Wall, 1977; McPhail, 1972). The same themes will recur and yet will differ according to the age and stage the students have reached.

So far I have commented on what could be called the 'content' of guidance curriculum. However, there are other elements of the educative function. These are to do with the way in which such guidance programmes or elements are delivered, as well as the context and processes of the learning. Guidance teaching requires an awareness of the appropriate methods in this field, for example the ability to help students think for themselves, or the ability to work with groups rather than individuals. HMI (DES, 1990) identified three areas of weakness here. First, 'not all teachers involved being at ease with various aspects of content and approaches'; second, 'over-reliance on commercially reproduced schemes and duplicated work-sheets so that students were not encouraged to think for themselves'; and third, 'failure to achieve appropriate balance between content and related personal, vocational and educational issues'. Many teachers still do not have the opportunities to develop a range of teaching styles.

The educative element also has implications for the context of the classroom. The creation of an appropriate classroom climate and the establishment of procedures is as important as the content and teaching format. There are many complex issues here. In a recent study of girls' development, Mikel Brown and Gilligan (1992) show that during adolescence girls lose the ability to express their real feelings and opinions. They describe this as a loss of voice. They argue that girls do this to avoid endangering relationships and that it has long-term consequences for the development of women. As a result they argue for the need to encourage adolescent girls to express difference and disagreement. This would suggest that procedures in the classroom, such as the negotiation of ground rules and rules for constructive controversy, are important. The Elton Report (DES, 1989) on discipline in schools has also emphasised the importance of students' negotiating rules and procedures, as well as having opportunities for the expression of opinion. The classroom context, the procedures and the nature of the interactions all impact on student self-image and self-esteem. These are important elements in motivation as well as important elements in the school's contribution to personal and social development.

Other processes, such as the development of self assessment and the formation of action plans, facilitate the personal development of students. In the one-to-one dialogues with students, teachers are required to use skills drawn from counselling. It is important to distinguish between drawing on counselling skills to make communication effective and conducting a counselling interview. The ethical constraints, the boundaries of the talk and the student's choosing of that dialogue are all important differences between the two activities.

In summary it can be said that in terms of policy formation at this level the tasks are to co-ordinate the curriculum content and delivery; to examine the context of the learning; and to ensure that teacher development in these areas is addressed.

THE REFLECTIVE ELEMENT

I stated earlier that the reflective function was related to an exploration of the impact of the school on the personal and social development, as well as the mental health, of the students. This is to argue that the role of counselling is to promote healthy institutions as well as healthy individuals. Research has shown that schools can have a substantial impact on children's psychological development both in the present and in the future (Rutter, 1991).

Recently we have seen a development in approach to many issues which reflects this position of developing schools as healthy environments personally, socially and academically. Previously the disciplinary role of the school was largely to do with the reaction to incidents of bad behaviour, although there were of course attempts to foster positive behaviour. The Elton Report (DES, 1989) argued for the promotion of positive behaviour. It was a much more proactive and wide-ranging approach, one which acknowledged the role of *all* in the school community and which shifted the emphasis to a concentration on developing positive behaviour rather than focusing on problem behaviours. Similarly, in the area of counselling and guidance I would want to argue for a more proactive and wide-ranging approach. This should reflect the promotion of positive strategies to developing mental health rather than a focus on reacting to problem situations, although I am not arguing for the exclusion of the latter. It is an argument for reflection on aspects of school or college life which may not come under the heading of the formal curriculum.

Initiatives in child abuse and bullying, allied to an emphasis on children's rights, have alerted us to what the experience of young people is. The voices of young people are being heard more clearly and the nature of their experience is being acknowledged more fully. In reaction to this, teachers and others (Besag, 1989) have argued for intervention by teachers and the co-ordination of approaches in the curriculum as well as in response to incidents. The task here then is to explore the school as a community and examine its impact on students and teachers. It will involve teachers in actively inviting students to give feedback on the functioning and health of the school and its practices. This may engage teachers in debates about teacher–student interactions and the values underpinning them – a difficult and controversial area for many to engage in.

The health of the institution also involves exploration of areas which are the responsibility of management. The health of the adults is also up for scrutiny here. Surveys on teacher stress and discussions in this field have led many to argue for counselling for staff. It may be the case that there is a need for such services but there is also a danger here that adoption of the one-to-one problem-solving model will be to the exclusion of debating wider issues such as support for staff in their professional roles and work (see Lodge, McLaughlin and Best, 1992).

THE WELFARE ELEMENT

The welfare aspect of counselling and guidance is the area most focused on and developed in writing about counselling in school settings. Hamblin (1974) described the school's role as that of being 'a guidance community'. The objectives in this area are:

- to aid students in decision-making and problem-solving;
- to support students in a constructive manner at times of difficulty;
- to monitor and detect students who are at risk or under pressure;
- to react in appropriate fashion; and
- to co-ordinate work within and outside the school.

The area will include a range of activities mentioned earlier: for example, counselling when it is sought by students; more focused guidance activities such as that involved in decision-making of a predictable kind; counselling to react to crisis, problems and transitions; and more specialist counselling. It will also involve liaising with outside agencies and parents.

These activities require many different skills and abilities. They also require practitioners to be able to distinguish between these different activities. Heron (1990) argues that there are six possible types of intervention between practitioner and client. By an intervention he means 'an identifiable piece of verbal and/or nonverbal behaviour that is part of the practitioner's service to the client' (p. 3). The six categories are subdivided into two main types – authoritative and facilitative. These are shown in Figure 9.1.

The first three categories are called authoritative because they are rather more hierarchical – the practitioner is taking responsibility for and on behalf of the client. The second three are called facilitative because they are rather less hierarchical – the practitioner is seeking to enable clients to become more autonomous and take more responsibility for themselves.

This is helpful to our work in schools and as a framework for teacher development. It can also highlight some of the problems of work in schools. I have detected some confusion about the role and type of interventions

1. **AUTHORITATIVE**
   Prescriptive
   A prescriptive intervention seeks to direct the behaviour of the client, usually behaviour that is outside the practitioner–client relationship.
2. **Informative**
   An informative intervention seeks to impart knowledge, information, meaning to the client.
3. **Confronting**
   A confronting intervention seeks to raise the client's consciousness about some limiting attitude or behaviour of which they are relatively unaware.

   FACILITATIVE
4. **Cathartic**
   A cathartic intervention seeks to enable the client to discharge, to abreact painful emotion, primarily grief, fear and anger.
5. **Catalytic**
   A catalytic intervention seeks to elicit self-discovery, self-directed living, learning and problem-solving in the client.
6. **Supportive**
   A supportive intervention seeks to affirm the worth and value of the client's person, qualities, attitudes or actions.

Figure 9.1 The six categories of counselling intervention (Heron, 1990)

that are described in schools as counselling interventions. For example, wanting to change someone's behaviour because it causes problems for the school or is seen as unacceptable by a particular teacher is not necessarily a prescriptive counselling intervention. Hamblin (1974) has described vividly the misuses of counselling in schools. He has argued that counselling is not about personality change; it is not solely for those perceived as 'deviant' and 'disadvantaged'; it is not an opportunity to exercise subtle control or manipulation; nor is it probing into the student's private world. HMI (DES, 1990) comments on the lack of clarity between discipline and counselling, saying that 'staff and students often perceived a clash between guidance and the need to enforce discipline'.

There is a need to establish some principles which help to distinguish counselling from other activities in schools. The first is that counselling is something which the student must be aware is occurring and which must in some way be chosen. I am not implying that this requires that counselling can only be student initiated but rather that it should be invitational in nature. For example, the teacher might say, 'Would you like to talk about this?' There is an assumption inbuilt into counselling that the student can change – it is an essentially optimistic, but not unrealistic, activity.

The student's needs are paramount in counselling rather than the needs of the school or the teacher, although the student may need to know the views and perceptions of others. The counselling should aim generally to empower the student and to develop a sense of control and autonomy. The relationship in which the counselling takes place should be:

- respectful (including an acknowledgement of and respect for the views and experiences of others different from ourselves);
- genuine on the part of the teacher; and
- aim to demonstrate empathy.

In addition, the counselling should include the full range of counselling interventions and be practically helpful to the student.

Some of the issues being debated here are to do with a specialist level of work and it would be helpful to distinguish between the different levels of work in schools and colleges. Hamblin (1974) distinguished three levels of work in schools:

1   *The immediate level*
    This level of work is for all teachers in the school and involves the use of first-level counselling skills and an awareness of what counselling is. Counselling skills will be used to facilitate good communication as well as to acknowledge the emotional dimension of learning and living. Reasonable demands would be made on students and teachers. Teachers would be able to work in the emotional domain, adapting to individuals and groups in the light of what is known, and providing reinforcement and support. Teachers would also be involved in detecting signs of stress and tension in students and communicating this to others if that is appropriate. Hamblin (1974) calls this an exploratory and screening function.

2   *The intermediate level*
    Here Hamblin argues that the school or college is concerned to provide continuity of care, concern and relationships. It is to do with the co-ordination of efforts and resources, including those outside of the school setting. It is also to do with the establishment and operation of systems which act as early warnings of students who may need counselling and guidance. This means that systems of communication need to be established, monitored and reviewed. The HMI survey (DES, 1990) commented on aspects of provision at this level. It highlighted the importance of good record-keeping, 'including recording interviews held with students, by whom, when, for what purpose and with what result'. Part of the co-ordination of resources includes knowing what training and expertise exists amongst the staff.

3   *The specialist level*
This level demands training for the task and this expertise may reside within the school or outside of it. It also involves the identification of students who may require this level of help. It may involve specialists in the running of groups as well as working with individuals.

In the formation of policy the levels of work and the training needs of the teachers need to be determined. The provision needs to be evaluated and managed. There are many professional and practical issues which need to be debated alongside matters of who does what and how.

ETHICAL AND PROFESSIONAL ISSUES

Part of the ethical requirements of schools is to monitor and evaluate the nature of the provision. In the HMI survey (DES, 1990) it was clear that this was not a common activity. Only two institutions 'had a systematic approach to evaluating the planning, processes and outcomes of the personal, educational and vocational guidance offered to students'. There is also a responsibility to ensure that staff are equipped to provide adequate counselling and guidance and this involves looking at the training and development needs of the staff.

Confidentiality is another ethical matter which the school or college needs to debate. There is rarely a clear statement on this issue and students often receive very mixed messages on this. The school setting is a complex one to work in regarding this issue. There is a desire to protect student privacy and at the same time there are legal requirements which prevent the promising of total confidentiality to students in certain areas of work, for example child abuse. What is important is that both staff and students are aware of the limits of confidentiality in various settings and types of interview, as well as being aware of what happens to information shared with teachers and other professionals.

Staff working in this area also need professional support and a forum to debate some of the difficult professional and moral decisions which may occur.

MANAGEMENT ISSUES

Apart from managing the development of policy on ethical and professional support there are many other management issues. The provision of private spaces for counselling and guidance work is important. HMI (DES, 1990) comment that 'effective guidance was promoted where the physical environment was such as to encourage good relationships and a positive ethos, and where special accommodation for a range of guidance activities was readily available and of a good standard'. The allocation of time is also important. HMI (*ibid.*) noted big variations between institutions. They concluded, 'Institutions may like to consider reviewing the time allocated for guidance, on the basis of a closer identification of need.'

They also found that 'responsibilities for planning the use of guidance resources were usually too widely dispersed to allow for effective management'. The issue of managing staffing, training and development of staff, and co-ordinating the communication between them, is central to the management task. I have identified many of the management issues in the course of this chapter and they can be summarised as:

- a need to clarify the purposes of counselling and guidance, acknowledging the different purposes and different levels of work;
- a need to evaluate that provision, including the student voice in that process;
- a need to draw up and communicate policy in this area.

REFERENCES

Besag, V. (1989) *Bullies and Victims in Schools*. Buckingham: Open University Press.

DES (1989) *Discipline in Schools*. The Elton Report. London: HMSO.

DES (1990) *HMI Survey of Guidance 13–19 in Schools and Sixth Form Colleges*. London: DES.

Egan, G. (1986) *The Skilled Helper* (3rd edn). Monterey: Brooks Cole.

Glasser, W. (1975) *Schools without Failure*, New York and London: Harper and Row.

Hamblin, D. (1974) *The Teacher and Counselling*. Oxford: Blackwell.

Heron, J. (1990) *Helping the Client*. London: Sage.

Lodge, C., McLaughlin, C. and Best, R. (1992) 'Organizing pastoral support for teachers: some comments and a model', in *Pastoral Care in Education*, 10, 2: 7–12.

McPhail, P. (1972) *Moral Education in the Secondary School*. London: Longman.

Marland, M. (1980) 'The pastoral curriculum', in Best, R. (1980) *Perspectives on Pastoral Care*. London: Heinemann.

Mikel Brown, L. and Gilligan, C. (1992) *Meeting at the Crossroads – Women's Psychology and Girls' Development*. London: Harvard University Press.

Richardson, E. (1974) *The Teacher, the School and the Task of Management*. London: Heinemann.

Rogers, C. (1983) *Freedom to Learn for the Eighties*. Ohio: Charles Merrill.

Rutter, M. (1991) 'Pathways from childhood to adult life: the role of schooling', in *Pastoral Care in Education*, 9, 3: 3–10.

Wall, W.D. (1977) *Constructive Education for Adolescents*. London: Unesco.

Chapter 10

Managing guidance in Further Education

Jackie Sadler and Kate Atkinson

DEFINING THE SECTOR

At its broadest, the Further Education (FE) sector in the UK is taken to include most post-16 learning not undertaken in schools and higher education institutions: although learning offered in both these sectors (for example GCSEs, HNDs, etc.) is also undertaken in the FE sector. This chapter will focus on the guidance being delivered within the FE sector, including sixth-form colleges. This spans a broad curriculum, including academic and vocational programmes to the 16–19 year cohorts; to an increasing number of adults of all ages; and at all levels of attainment. Over two-thirds of those studying within the sector are now mature students. The term guidance is taken to include the range of activities which support individuals in making decisions on learning and work.

Learning accredited by the sector occurs in a wide range of locations. These include institutions specialising in specific vocational areas, such as horticulture; those serving particular client groups, such as students with learning difficulties or physical disabilities; programmes offered on employers premises (such as through employee-development programmes and NVQs/ SVQs); and home study (through open and flexible learning). Community-based franchised provision has expanded in recent years and, despite some concerns about accountability, developments aimed at broadening participation are likely to reinforce this trend. The modularisation of the curriculum also offers learners more frequent choices about learning options than hitherto with a concomitant need to ensure academic coherence.

Those responsible for delivering guidance in the sector are part of this diversity and have to embrace and respond to it. This chapter will address how colleges are attempting to do this and examine the main issues arising from their work. It draws substantially upon research undertaken for two projects by the Further Education Unit (FEU) and its successor body the Further Education Development Agency (FEDA). The first of these (FEU, 1994) was based upon a national survey of colleges and local action research projects. It sought to identify delivery structures and support institutions in enhancing their provision. In particular, colleges chose to focus on developing quality frameworks and improving threshold services. The second project (Sadler and Reisenberger, 1997), funded by the Department for Education and Employment, investigated the careers education and guidance offer to students on programme and in preparation for exit.

THE CONTEXT

Following the Education Act of 1944, local authorities assumed responsibility for further education colleges, which they retained until 1992, when the institutions in the sector achieved independence, assuming corporate status. The 1992 Further and Higher Education Act resulted in the introduction of market principles into the sector at a time when the contribution of guidance to successful recruitment, achievement and progression was beginning to be more widely recognised. At the same time, concern at the cost of non-completion in the sector was highlighted by the Audit Commission (1993). Identified funding allocations, linked to the provision of guidance and assessment, were introduced within the Further Education Funding Council's (FEFC) funding methodology in 1993. This raised awareness in colleges of the requirement for guidance and supported the case for enhancement of provision. There was a financial 'carrot and stick' to ensure that students received appropriate pre-entry guidance and that decisions were verified at induction. In *some* institutions, information and guidance services were restructured and moved to a more central location. Guidance became more visible. Different models emerged, often with development focusing particularly on the pre-entry and entry stages (FEU, 1994). None the less, the autonomy enjoyed at institutional level meant that the allocation of resources for guidance activities, particularly on-programme and at exit, remained largely within the discretion of the senior management team, competing with a range of other priorities.

Since incorporation, the sector has witnessed widespread restructuring, including institutional mergers requiring frequent reviews and the streamlining of pre-existing systems and organisational structures, including those relating to the guidance provision. Many are also delivering on multiple sites. Incorporation also introduced the concept of the marketplace into the sector. Performance-related funding, linked to the achievement of growth targets, coupled with demanding efficiency gains within a convergence process, aimed at reducing inherited imbalances in funding levels. These contributed to the creation of fierce levels of competition between post-16 institutions as they sought to increase their market share. In some institutions, the impartiality of the guidance provided was severely threatened as little distinction was drawn between *marketing* and *guidance*. In some cases, the two functions shared common management. Colleges found that some schools refused them access to their students who were denied information about the full range of opportunities open to them. Concern at such practices prompted the inclusion of a clause (No. 44) in the 1997 Education Act, requiring schools and colleges to allow careers advisers reasonable access to students in order to provide guidance. In addition, the white paper, *Learning to Compete*, sought more broadly to establish an entitlement for young people to career planning.

Throughout England and Wales, colleges also participated actively as redeeming agencies in the former Employment Department's Gateways to Learning (1993–6) and Skill Choice programmes. These offered guidance and assessment to targeted groups of adults and were funded by Training and Enterprise Councils (TECs), usually through vouchers or credits. This drew more college staff into local adult guidance networks, often initiated originally by the Local Education Authorities and subsequently facilitated by representatives from the TECs. Despite the often ephemeral nature of such initiatives, they stimulated developments in adult guidance within the sector, helping to develop a wider understanding of the needs of the target groups served, and of the application of quality assurance and standards to guidance provision.

In recent years, careers education and guidance has become an integral part of many high profile reports on FE (Tomlinson, 1996; Kennedy, 1997a; Fryer, 1997). The Tomlinson report on Inclusive Learning (1996) promotes steps towards a learner-centred system on the premise that it is the professional staff who have the responsibility to develop the milieu that facilitates learning. This is clearly concomitant with a person-centred guidance process. The latter enables the students to gain skills and information to make the best decisions and develop individual learning plans based on preferred learning and assessment styles. Although Tomlinson has a focus on students with learning difficulties and disabilities, the concept is based on a requirement for a whole-college approach to developing a flexible learning culture that meets the needs of all individual learners. The report includes an audit instrument against which institutions can establish a baseline and map progress. Kennedy (1997b: 5) stressed that 'a coherent system of information, advice and guidance is essential to widen participation'. Central to this recommendation is the creation of an individualised 'new learner pathway', (ibid.), particularly for adults, who have failed to achieve in education and training. '*Guidance*, support and recognition of life experiences' (ibid.) are seen as essential to the success of the learning pathways, and it is proposed that there should be a national entitlement to information, advice and guidance. Similarly, the nine main characteristics of good practice identified for widening participation, includes 'good quality information and guidance' which is 'readily available and impartial' (Kennedy 1997a: 84). Fryer (1997: 8) states that advice and guidance are essential if lifelong learning is to be successful. In addition, many other factors are also influencing the trend to widen participation:

- the impetus to reach the National Targets for Education and Training;
- policy priorities such as the introduction of flexibility into the benefits system to reward those who seek to 'improve themselves';
- initiatives targeted at the disaffected (for example Welfare to Work and the New Deal), attracting larger numbers of the longer-term unemployed, lone parents and less-well qualified young people into FE.

Such external influences on the work of colleges is embedding the concept of guidance across the institution. However, it is not easy to ensure quality and consistency, especially in large and multi-site colleges. Whilst concern at falling retention rates, due in part to inadequate selection and inappropriate admissions, is leading to the enhancement of guidance provision in some cases, the picture remains very variable. Moreover, the journey from the periphery to the core of institutional provision has not been without set backs: in particular the prevalence of financial constraints and cut backs have affected some of the best established guidance provision.

Since incorporation, a number of factors have contributed to a tendency in the sector to provide for existing learners rather than to reach out to non-participants. The funding methodology, which has rewarded retention and achievement, has not encouraged colleges to recruit students with low levels of attainment in learning, or those who may be at risk of 'failure'. Institutions have sought to increase their own share of the existing market rather than deploy the necessary additional resources to attract and support those who have chosen to reject formal learning at the first opportunity.

Changes to the FEFC's inspection framework – and anticipated amendments to the funding arrangements in the sector to ensure that poorly-qualified students from deprived areas are 'unit-rich' – will ensure that widening participation is accorded some priority within institutions. To ensure achievement, some of these additional resources will unequivocally need to be directed to providing additional, probably accredited, guidance and support for these students.

GUIDANCE ACROSS THE STAGES

It is easier to describe the complexity of the guidance process in colleges with reference to the four stages at which they occur:

1 *Pre-entry* Including linked activities between colleges and schools as well as processes associated with admissions and selection procedures.
2 *Entry* The funding arrangements require colleges to be able to demonstrate that students have received appropriate guidance at entry. Audit evidence has to be available to demonstrate that students are satisfied with this, resulting in a learner agreement. Colleges are only

compensated for the costs of pre-entry guidance where learners are actually recruited onto programmes. This has tended to mitigate against the provision of impartial advice, often covertly rather than overtly.

3   *On-programme* This will encompass a wide range of activities offered within the curriculum and outside, such as: the accreditation of prior learning; recording achievement and action planning; careers-related assignments; individual and group work with tutors and college or careers service 'specialists'; work experience and work shadowing; use of information resources and information technology packages; cross-college workshops (i.e. to develop transition skills, such as interview techniques); outside speakers, visits to HE institutions, etc. A wide range of staff will be involved.

4   *Exit* This may be more appropriately referred to as pre-exit and post-exit guidance, since:

a   for many students, particularly those on one-year programmes, guidance to support progression should commence early in their studies, not least to broaden the focus of those unable to proceed immediately in level;

b   institutions often offer post-results guidance with college or careers service staff being available at specific times.

The FEFC (1997) Good Practice report on Careers Education and Guidance noted that whilst some innovatory practice exists, there is a lack of adequate information and guidance available to students with disabilities and learning difficulties and for speakers of other languages. Colleges need to develop individual packages and induction processes to enable *all* students to take an active part in their own assessment and diagnosis of need, whilst making informed decisions about learning and personal development. The appropriateness of group interventions, which do not reflect or allow for individual needs, is also being called into question.

DELIVERY MODELS

In many cases responsibility for guidance activities is shared between academic and specialist staff, often working within a Student Services unit. Some development has been driven by short-term funding, which may have been lost when funding ceases and no succession strategy implemented. In other cases, an influential individual has initiated improvements, which may disappear if s/he moves on, unless formalised and integrated into college structures or procedures.

The allocation of funding units to pre-entry guidance in 1993 tended to encourage colleges to review and enhance their provision at this stage. In some institutions, high-profile centralised units emerged with specialist staff, qualified in guidance to undertake admissions and pre-entry/entry processes. As guidance specialists, the staff could often provide better-informed, more impartial advice than faculty-based admissions staff, particularly for potential entrants to non-vocational programmes or those unsure of career goals. The development of this pre-entry provision also facilitated the enhancement of systems to capture and feed back relevant data at this stage for strategic and curricular planning. However, links to curriculum-based, on-programme and pre-exit guidance may be weak if not specifically built into this model. There is a danger that policy may focus on the initial stages without adequate reference across the full spectrum stages.

In the past, smaller institutions, such as sixth-form colleges, have tended to adopt more informal approaches based on personal contact and with a strong emphasis on pastoral care, focusing on delivery through tutorial programmes. Whilst this approach was often more coherent, policy and systems tended to be less well developed and the provision was designed to cater solely for young people between 16 and 18, the traditional clientele. A wide range of often committed staff, including senior managers and tutors, was involved in delivery, but often without the support of a professionally qualified full-time careers adviser. Tutors were also usually responsible for both admissions and most on-programme guidance, often with an option of referral to a senior tutor, counsellor or part-time careers co-ordinator. Accessibility to specialist advice was, often limited therefore, to self referral to the linked careers officer. In such cases, adequate procedures needed to be in operation, supported by appropriate staff development, which recognised the need for staff to be aware of their own limitations in relation to the guidance they offered, and to facilitate referral to any internal and external specialists. The advantages of this model included the level of tutorial support available to students, delivery by tutors aware of curriculum developments and the relatively high profile of guidance in an institution where senior managers were actively involved in the processes.

Many sixth-form colleges have diversified their curriculum and sought to recruit adult learners as a response to the growth targets set in the 1990s. Informal approaches have become less appropriate and unmanageable as numbers have increased. By 1996, a third of sixth-form colleges were offering vocational adult programmes. Some employed adult co-ordinators, who may have responsibility for adult guidance. Institutions marketing learning programmes to new groups need to review their guidance offer to ensure that it is appropriate and staff are trained to meet their needs. By 1996, 87 per cent of sixth-form colleges also indicated that they had a written policy on guidance, and 31 out of 46 were employing at least one full-time guidance specialist, most likely a Head or Co-ordinator of Careers.

Some larger institutions have also sought to develop guidance provision through the tutorial programme, using curriculum-based activities such as recording of achievement and action-planning processes linked to the production of National Records of Achievement. However, whilst this may provide a more structured process linking to the curriculum, tutors may not be able to offer the specialist guidance required by students at transition points. Ensuring consistency and coherence in delivery are major obstacles to assuring quality, particularly where careers education is delivered by tutors with varying priorities and levels of commitment, whose main concern is to maximise achievement within the time allocated to deliver their programmes. The potential of careers education to increase student motivation is not always recognised by tutors. In recent years, some institutions have started to address this problem, primarily by:

- improving support to tutors (i.e. through enhanced staff development, preparing tutor packs), and ensuring centralised planning with flexibility for tutor modification;
- developing 'super-tutors' or careers specialists to deliver careers education, thus removing responsibility from untrained personal tutors.

In some cases, guidance specialists have worked with academic staff to define their role and responsibilities, develop common careers education programmes, and produced materials for use in tutorials.

Where responsibility for guidance activities is allocated to different, relatively autonomous sections and tutors in faculties across the college, there is a danger that these will not function effectively as a coherent unity, particularly without shared line management or an over-arching policy. The 'dispersed function' arrangement may ensure delivery across the stages, but guidance is likely to have a lower profile within the institution, there may be duplication of effort and some confusion over responsibilities experienced by staff and students. The institution may not be able to respond as effectively or quickly to new guidance-related initiatives. Mergers within the sector may tend initially to exacerbate difficulties, as models may differ, and new policies and systems have to be agreed. However, they also offer the opportunity to introduce greater coherence into systems and structures.

Effective guidance requires communication and collaboration between all those involved in the planning and delivery of aspects of the provision. There has been a danger that the association of guidance with a particular stage in the programme has produced a provision which is unbalanced in relation to the whole of the learner pathway. For the learner, an individual record of achievement can be a mechanism for linking the guidance processes between the stages, bringing coherence and progression to personal development.

DEVELOPING A WHOLE-COLLEGE APPROACH

In the past guidance has tended to be seen in the sector as a bolt-on activity or additional provision. Over more recent years, guidance has been promoted as an embedded process, focusing on individual needs and responding to the sector's preoccupation with retention and achievement. Colleges are complex institutions and the guidance process impacts on all systems, and indeed may provide the linkages between many. Achieving coherence requires an understanding of the range of guidance-related activities taking place within the institution, and where appropriate outside, how these inter-link at each stage of the learner pathway and how the learning from them can be captured.

A school-leaver may expect that the work undertaken to develop his or her record of achievement is valued, used in decision-making at entry, and built upon once on-programme. She may hope also that a careers education programme in the FE college would take account of related activities taking place in the early years in schools. A learner could reasonably expect action planning in the curriculum to interface with career action planning, so that the two processes compliment each other. Yet research (Sadler and Reisenberger 1997) indicated that the introduction of (curriculum-based) action-planning and recording achievement was having little impact on the work of careers services.

Data collected by other functions also may inform the planning and delivery of careers education and guidance. Student tracking in institutions is undertaken using the ISR (Individual Student Record), which follows students' progress through the institution and beyond. The data provided on the ISR can be exploited for a range of purposes by a variety of staff. In addition to assessing the value-added for each learner and contributing to reports on student destinations, an analysis of the data may help target guidance interventions more effectively. Appropriate exchanges of information on student destinations between the careers service and colleges, working within the requirements of the Data Protection Act, can assist both organisations to meet their objectives. Staff on vocational programmes may be very knowledgeable about the labour market and opportunities in their own specialisms, but unless this is captured and held centrally, it will be inaccessible to learners outside their programmes. Useful insights into industry and work practices may be gained on work experience, which would also justify cross-college dissemination and inclusion in careers education programmes.

A whole-college approach to guidance is a complex concept which confirms the importance of guidance and the commitment of the institution to put learners first. The development of an inclusive, flexible organisation requires a number of inter-related critical success factors to be addressed: supportive leadership; shared concept of the delivery model;

shared understanding of learner needs; and effective delivery systems and processes. To achieve these, staff development, cross-college access and consistency of delivery and adequate monitoring systems are all required. The benefits to the college of such an approach to guidance appear to include improvements in retention. Benefits to the students include an integrated programme with the focus on achievement and the development of the individual learner within a supportive culture.

A shared philosophy is fundamental to the success of a whole-college approach. This might include for example, commitment to guidance as a learner-centred decision process which enables students to develop the skills required for lifelong learning, recording their achievement and developing their career path. Once a philosophy is established policies and systems can follow. Policy needs to be linked to strategic and operational planning. An audit framework, within which 'non-specialists' in programme areas can work together with the recording of guidance activity, is essential to be able to provide evidence that appropriate guidance interventions are happening. The audit trail needs to start from pre-entry, through induction and pre-exit.

COLLABORATION WITH CAREERS SERVICE PROVIDERS

Since 1993, careers services have been responsible for providing similar services to full-time students in Further Education as those available to sixth-formers in schools. Following the Trade Union Reform and Employment Rights Act of 1993, this responsibility was extended to part-time students on programmes preparing them for work. Individual arrangements were negotiated locally and the Act required that they were documented in Service Level Agreements (SLAs). In some cases, individual SLAs were agreed at faculty level or for particular groups such as Students with Learning Difficulties or Disabilities (SLDD). Colleges and careers services were subsequently expected to produce partnership agreements building on the SLAs to focus on the production of a strategy which establishes priorities for careers education and guidance for each institution.

SLAs and partnership agreements have offered clarity of definition and responsibility, and focused on service performance. Such negotiation processes should also assist in reaching a mutually shared understanding of what constitutes 'success' or 'failure'. The range of activity in which the careers service can support an institution is relatively broad, and includes for example, assisting in policy development, informing the curriculum, supporting careers information and dealing with destination data (Department of Employment, 1993). However, formalising arrangements may bring an inherent danger of a minimalist approach to the work. In this respect 'contract cultures' can become counter-productive, particularly if the targets are too narrowly focused or inadequate account is taken of the range of expertise and skills the careers service provider can offer. Greater flexibility has been introduced where careers services have offered a menu of activities from which colleges can select according to their own priorities.

The FEDA research (Sadler and Reisenberger, 1997) indicated that the activities on which *college staff* expected the careers service to take a lead were providing job vacancies and the labour market information. However, careers service providers considered that they themselves had the main responsibility for guidance interventions once students had commenced their programmes. At the same time, the FEFC (1997) found a considerable number of colleges failing to prepare students adequately to enter employment. Institutions needed to work more closely with careers services to ensure that their knowledge of the labour market informed careers education programmes, tutorial programmes and cross-college workshops on topics relating to job search. In the past, most young people studying within the sector tended to progress either to Higher Education or into employment. In the future, careers education programmes need to be devised to take cognisance of part-time employment for those studying and of the need for recurrent and lifelong learning, whatever the initial destination of leavers.

If the range of potential contributions from careers service staff working in FE has sometimes been unrecognised and unexploited by the sector, evidence suggests that they themselves have not been encouraged to engage fully within institutions. The 1996 survey (Sadler and Reisenberger, 1997) indicated that only just over half of careers services were inducting staff working in FE colleges. They reported problems with internal communications and the complexity of institutions as major obstacles to working effectively within the sector.

The survey also revealed the inequitable distribution of careers service resources for statutory clients between schools and colleges, partly because careers services were more confident of meeting targets in school sixth-forms where pupils were more accessible. This is confirmed elsewhere (NFER, 1996). Also, the need to adhere to targets may reduce the range of activities undertaken by careers advisers. Contracting may have encouraged a target-driven, monolithic approach to careers service provision in both schools and colleges, with a single guidance intervention at the transitionary point between learning and work – or unemployment. Anecdotal evidence has also revealed the tensions inherent in resolving the conflicting need to meet predetermined targets and activities whilst being responsive to individual 'customers' and accommodating their idiosyncratic demands. Pressures to meet targets may encourage colleges to collude with their careers service providers and allow them to undertake interventions and processes, such as career action planning, which may not be the most appropriate for particular cohorts or individuals at that time. Subsequent reviews of careers service requirements and targets should allow increased flexibility and decrease pressures to subject students to unnecessary interventions.

The 1997 Education Act placed new legal duties on colleges to work with the careers service, particularly in ensuring that:

- students receive impartial and comprehensive careers information; and
- careers services have reasonable access to students within its statutory client group.

Guidance issued by the 'Choice and Careers' division of the Department for Education and Employment (DFEE, 1997) encourages institutions to work more closely together to develop policy and deliver a joint programme of careers education and guidance.

DEVELOPING CAREERS EDUCATION

A number of factors have combined to encourage the delivery of guidance as an integrated element of the curriculum in the institutional context, including:

- the flexibility offered by increased use of information technology;
- funding pressures;
- the modularisation and unitisation of the curriculum;
- increased potential for accreditation, particularly through Open College Networks.

Whilst careers education is most likely to be provided for students via tutorial programmes or careers education programmes, it may also be provided through specific modules, cross-college workshops and work experience. The complexity of these arrangements often results in elements of careers education being delivered by many different (and potentially untrained) staff, which can result, at best, in lack of continuity for individuals and, at worst, in conflicting advice.

One of the by-products of the introduction of a competence-based approach to a national qualifications framework has been the strengthening of the connections between careers education and the curriculum. In particular, some GNVQ units require students to undertake careers-related assignments, many of which increase opportunity awareness. These also offer possibilities to introduce students to careers information resources and to link in appropriate group and individual guidance interventions.

Accreditation of guidance processes, such as induction and recording achievement is growing and may:

- encourage learners to adopt a more serious attitude towards career planning;
- provide a more structured and systematic approach to planning careers education.

Specific units on career planning and work experience are also under development. Kennedy (1997b) also proposed the allocation of funding for the accreditation of learner support and guidance in the new Learning Pathway. However, reaching decisions about learning and work is ultimately an individual experience, often undertaken during a number of small steps over a period of time and the requirement to undertake a 'total package' at a given time may not match individual needs.

Where careers education programmes have been developed these have most commonly reflected the DOTS model (Decision-making, Opportunity awareness, Transition skills, Self-awareness) developed in the 1970s. In the past, some programmes have suffered from an over-emphasis on opportunity awareness to the neglect of the other skills, particularly decision-making. Some institutions, for example, centred their careers education around a programme of outside speakers from a number of occupational areas. If, in the future, a quarter of the workforce will be part-time or temporary workers, greater emphasis needs to be placed by institutions on developing transition (e.g. self presentation, etc.) and decision-making skills. An essential outcome from initial learning is that students will have developed what has been termed 'metacognitive learning' – they will have learned how to learn and will thus be able to approach change with equanimity, also taking greater responsibility for future career development.

ASSURING QUALITY

Staff development is key to enhancing the quality of careers education and guidance in many institutions. Although an increasing number of colleges are recruiting their own professionally qualified staff (Sadler and Reisenberger, 1997), information, advice and guidance is often delivered or mediated through tutors. Awareness-raising about guidance is not adequate for these staff.

Only 71 per cent of the sector surveyed in 1996 (Sadler and Reisenberger, 1997) had written policies on careers education and guidance. The quality of these statements is very variable and the FEFC (1997) has found some evidence that they are not always implemented. Some policy statements identify the principles within which the staff should work often reflecting those accepted more broadly within the field. However, in only just over half of cases did policy statements specify that staff should work to agreed quality standards and a quarter of institutions did not include guidance within their internal policy for quality assurance.

Potential conflicts of interest relating to an institution's position as both provider of guidance and of learning opportunities have generated more debate within the guidance community about the principle of *impartiality* than any of the others. The rights of students to impartial guidance is enshrined in colleges' Student Charters, which they are legally required to produce. However, in some cases inadequate consideration has been given as to how this might be translated into an entitlement and implemented. In 1996, only 41 per cent of colleges addressed how impartiality was to be ensured within their policy. In the case of sixth-form colleges, this dropped to 33 per cent. Also, fewer than a quarter of respondents to the FEDA survey attempted to evaluate either the value-added that guidance brings (for example, in relation to retention) or the cost-effectiveness of the provision. Quantitative data alone from surveys of student satisfaction often takes no cognisance of the plethora of variables which influence the perceptions of learners and will often not be detailed enough to deliver meaningful results, enabling corrective action to be taken. The planning and development of guidance provision in institutions may be impeded by the lack of monitoring, particularly of usage of facilities. The FEFC (1997: 13) concluded that: 'the majority of colleges give inadequate attention to careers education and guidance in their strategic plans and monitoring procedures'.

ENSURING EQUITY IN GUIDANCE DELIVERY

The growth targets of the early 1990s contributed to a fundamental shift in the profile of learners in FE, as the proportion of adult learners mainly studying part-time, in the sector increased steadily. Results from the research (Sadler and Reisenberger, 1997) indicated that the variation in the student population was having a major impact on the work of both college and careers service staff. However, the systems in place were initially established in the main to support full-time learning for young people. These have had to undergo root and branch reviews to accommodate older learners. Many Student Services units have been pro-active in addressing these needs, for example, by establishing specialist posts for adults, advising on the financial implications of study, developing procedures for accrediting prior learning and reviewing childcare provision. However, as identified in the inspectorate's good practice report (FEFC, 1997), staff development needs are not always being met, particularly amongst subject specialists, who have been used to giving information to young people, not guidance to adults. Responsiveness to the needs of mature students needs to permeate the whole institution.

The FEDA survey (Sadler and Reisenberger, 1997) found that, whilst 81 per cent of the further education and specialist colleges with a written policy on guidance specify entitlements for both full- and part-time students, only 56 per cent of sixth-form colleges do so, reflecting their lower level of involvement with this learner group. Where written policies do exist, the need to provide guidance at all stages for part-time students has tended to lead to entitlement statements being drafted, based around the specific programme being followed and the number of learning hours. At entry, colleges have had to address the requirement to provide adequate guidance to all learners, including those who may be only enrolling for a few hours per week, leading to a diversity of practice in the sector in relation to the depth of guidance offered. There may be concerns at the extent of involvement of non-qualified staff.

Whilst mature students studying full-time, and those on programmes preparing for entry to Higher Education are likely to find that guidance is incorporated into their programmes, the vast majority on part-time programmes will often need to self refer to access the assistance they require. This depends on the individual's ability to identify when they need guidance and to take the initiative. Where programmes run in the evening, information and guidance facilities may not be open. Not surprisingly then that take-up of provision is lower amongst part-time students.

The tendency of careers service providers to prioritise work with young people on full-time programmes has reduced adult access to qualified staff, unless the institution employs its own. One approach to enhancing guidance for excluded groups is through the provision of cross-college workshops and events. However, these need to be adequately publicised and not just at induction, when progression is not a priority for new entrants. Saliency is crucial in this respect: systems need to ensure that customised information reaches learners at the point they are ready to act upon it.

CONCLUSION

Emphasis on moving from welfare into work will require colleges to harness all the resources available to them to effect successful transitions into employment, particularly when learners may be studying at institutions on programmes of just one year. Whole-college approaches which ensure that the range of expertise and information available to the institution, both internally and externally is captured and used effectively, are likely to be more successful. Some institutions will need to review their networking arrangements and forge closer links with community-based agencies supporting adults, both those assisting entry into employment and those offering a more general service.

In some cases, guidance provision may need to adapt to provide more individual support to the new learners entering colleges as participation widens. Minimum pre-packaged, pre-entry guidance is unlikely to suffice for those who have experienced long periods of unemployment or social exclusion. Many may require longer term guidance and mentoring support prior to and post exit to effect a successful entry into the labour market. Practitioners working in colleges, both those employed by the institution itself and those employed by linked careers services, may need to access appropriate staff development opportunities to enhance understanding of these new learners, their cultures, life experiences and aspirations.

The importance attached to community-based initiatives in reducing social exclusion, including, for example, the development of locally-based learning centres with outreach facilities, also offers challenges to those managing the delivery of guidance in FE to secure resources and develop provision. Flexibility and responsiveness have increasingly become the by-word of the FE sector. Whilst much remains to be done, individuals are beginning to determine and follow their own customised learning pathways. The relaunched national record of achievement may provide one tool for introducing greater coherence into episodic learning throughout life and assist individuals to manage their personal development more effectively and more autonomously.

BIBLIOGRAPHY

Audit Commission (1993) *Unfinished Business*, London: Audit Commission.

Department for Education and Employment (1997) *Working with the Careers Service – A Guide for Colleges*, Sheffield: DfEE.

Department of Employment (1993) *Requirements and Guidance for Providers*, Sheffield: DE.

Fryer, R.H. (1997) *Learning for the Twenty-First Century: First Report of the National Advisory Group for Continuing Education and Lifelong Learning*, London: NAGCEL.

Further Education Funding Council (1997) *Careers Education and Guidance, Good Practice Report from the Inspectorate*, Coventry: FEFC.

Further Education Unit (1994) *Managing the Delivery of Guidance in Colleges*, London: FEU.

Kennedy, H. (1997a) *Learning Works: Widening Participation in Further Education*, Coventry: FEFC.

Kennedy, H. (1997b) *Pathways to Success: The Widening Participation Committee Emerging Conclusions*, Coventry: FEFC.

NFER (1996) *An evaluation of the performance of Pathfinder Careers Services*, National Foundation for Educational Research, Slough: NFER.

Sadler, J. and Reisenberger, A. (1997) *On Course for Next Steps: Careers Education and Guidance for Students in FE*, London: The Further Education Development Agency.

Tomlinson, J. (1996) *Inclusive Learning: Report of the Learning Difficulties and/or Disabilities Committee*, Coventry: FEFC.

Chapter 11

Models of student guidance in a changing 14–19 education and training system[†]

A. G. Watts and Michael Young

INTRODUCTION

The role of guidance is receiving ever-greater attention, in relation both to educational change and to lifelong career development. The notion of more individually driven 'careers for all', linked to continuous learning throughout life, is being viewed as the means of achieving the 'skills revolution' Britain requires if it is to achieve competitive advantage in the global economy (CBI, 1989), as well as sustaining social cohesion within flexible labour markets (Watts, 1996). Effective guidance within compulsory education is seen as critical to laying effective foundations for lifelong career development; continuing access to guidance is viewed as essential for supporting the process of such development.

The role of guidance in relation to the curriculum and qualifications structures for the 14–19 age-group is central to these debates. Such structures lie at the transition point between compulsory schooling, based on a standard curriculum entitlement and diverse individualized routes through specialized learning and work structures. The ways in which they reconcile the competing 'forward' pressure for continued entitlement and the 'backward' pressure for diversification will affect the kind of guidance that is offered and how its provision is structured.

This chapter will start by clarifying the nature of guidance and its relationship to the curriculum. It will then explore the current structures of guidance provision, its relationship to the present three-track qualifications structure at 16–19, and the impact of 'learning markets'. Finally, it will explore the role of guidance in relation to the three possible models for the future: rigid qualification tracks, a flexible common framework and a unified system.

[†] This chapter is an edited version of a chapter in Hodgson, A. and Spours, K. (eds) (1997) *Dearing and Beyond: 14–19 Qualifications, Frameworks and Systems*, London: Kogan Page.

THE NATURE OF GUIDANCE AND ITS RELATIONSHIP TO THE CURRICULUM

Guidance can be defined as a range of processes designed to enable individuals to make informed choices and transitions related to their personal, educational and career development. Different commentators and different guidance systems attach varying weight to the three adjectives 'personal', 'educational' and 'career'. Some see career as subsuming educational; some view personal as embracing both educational and career; some are very concerned to maintain the boundaries between the three. At the level of the individual student, the boundaries become difficult or impossible to maintain. But they are useful in conceptual terms, and they are often important in defining the terms of reference of particular guidance services. The main focus of this chapter is on educational and career guidance but it also recognizes that these need to be viewed as part of a broader guidance process that includes wider aspects of personal development.

The 'range of processes' which guidance encompasses was influentially defined by the Unit for the Development of Adult Continuing Education (1986) as comprising seven activities: informing, advising, counselling, assessing, enabling, advocating and feeding back. Because this definition comes from an adult guidance background, it tends to view guidance as lying outside the curriculum. When the Standing Conference of Associations for Guidance in Educational Settings (SCAGES, 1993) sought to broaden the definition to embrace the role of guidance within schools and colleges, it extended this definition to include the institutional role of guidance and also what Marland (1980) termed the 'pastoral curriculum', which is based on a concern 'to help all the individuals without always giving individual help' (p.153): in other words, 'to transpose the aims of guidance into the aims of a curriculum' (Law, 1996: 214). SCAGES (1993) accordingly added 'teaching', 'managing' and 'innovating/systems change' to the list. 'Teaching' here is defined as 'providing a planned and systematic progression of learner-centred experiences to enable learners to acquire knowledge, skills and competences related to making personal, educational and career decisions and transitions' (p.37).

The difficulties which SCAGES experienced in extending the definition in this way underline the problems of reconciling the individual-centred concept of guidance with organizational structures in general and the curriculum in particular. It is useful in this respect to distinguish three possible models of the relationship between guidance and the curriculum: the 'boundary' model, the 'enclosed' model and the 'systemic' model (Watts, 1990). These are shown in Figure 11.1.

Under the boundary model, guidance is viewed as being separate from the central learning functions of educational institutions, but as enabling these functions to operate effectively. Thus guidance might be seen as

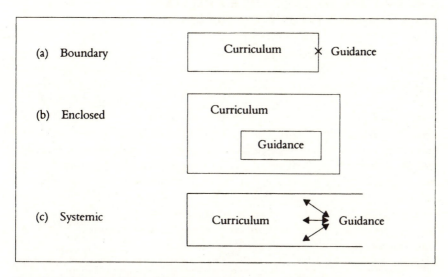

Figure 11.1 Three models of guidance in relation to the curriculum

dealing with personal problems which impede learning, or as responding to individual problems that stem from the learning process – like the need for career redirection. In effect, guidance patrols the boundaries between the curriculum and the personal life of the learner, so permitting the design of the curriculum to be based on other criteria and other organizing principles – in particular, the nature of knowledge and the perceived needs of society. From this boundary position, those entrusted with guidance can seek to feed back issues related to the personal experience of learners, so that these can be taken into account in the curriculum-development process: this role is much more strongly developed in adult continuing education (Oakeshott, 1990) than in initial education.

Under the enclosed model, guidance is seen as being a distinctive part of the learning functions of the institution. This can be seen in schools, for instance, in the development of programmes of personal and social education (PSE) which have a clearly bounded place within the curriculum. Usually such programmes are given a limited amount of time and do not deal in the hard currency used by the rest of the curriculum – notably, examination passes. They accordingly tend to attract lower status and perceived legitimacy from staff and students alike (Whitty *et al.*, 1994).

Under the systemic model, guidance is viewed as a concept which permeates the curriculum and makes it subject to negotiation with the individual learner. Within this model, guidance can become so closely interwoven with the learning process that it may lose its boundaries altogether. It may for example be viewed not as a specialist function, but as an integral part of

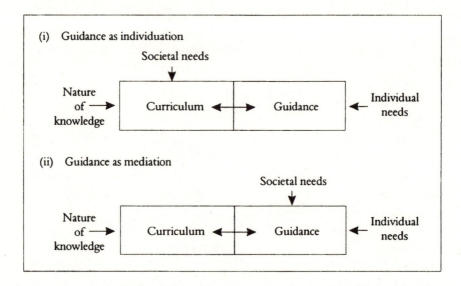

(i)   Guidance as individuation

Societal needs

Nature of knowledge → Curriculum ←→ Guidance ← Individual needs

(ii)   Guidance as mediation

Societal needs

Nature of knowledge → Curriculum ←→ Guidance ← Individual needs

Figure 11.2 Guidance and societal needs

the role of the teacher. This is shown diagrammatically in Figure 11.1(c), which also attempts to show how such a concept breaks open the walls of the curriculum, making it all continuously subject to adaptation to the learner's needs.

Guidance, however, is arguably not concerned with meeting the individual's needs in some kind of social vacuum. Many would agree with the view advanced by Morris (1955) in his seminal paper on guidance as a concept in educational philosophy: that its essence is as a process of mediation between individual needs and societal needs. We will conveniently ignore for present purposes the problematic nature of the concept of 'needs', its relationship to 'wants', and the issue of who is to define such needs and on what basis. In these simple terms, however, the concept of mediation poses an important issue. It has been suggested above that the design of the curriculum itself tends to be based upon the perceived needs of society as well as upon the nature of knowledge: such a view leaves guidance as serving what tends to be seen as a second-order role of 'individuation' – in other words, relating it to individuals' needs. In principle, however, the mediation model (Figure 11.2) opens up the possibility that societal needs could be infused into the curriculum through the role of guidance. There are strong hints of this, as we shall see later, in the concept of 'learning credits': the underlying notion here is that societal needs will be met in significant measure through the learning choices of individuals, supported by guidance provision which ensures that these choices are informed by labour-market demand. Such a notion places guidance in a position of much greater significance in terms of public policy.

CURRENT STRUCTURES OF GUIDANCE PROVISION

The nature of guidance provision in schools and colleges is varied and its limits are not easy to define with precision. In schools pre-16, for example, careers education and guidance is conventionally described as comprising five components: a planned programme of careers education within the curriculum; continuing access to individual guidance as part of the pastoral-care system and from the Careers Service; access to information resources on educational and vocational opportunities; active experiences of the working world through work-experience programmes and the like and the processes of recording achievement and action planning (NCC, 1990; SCAA, 1995). Some of these – notably access to individual guidance and to information – are compatible with the boundary model as outlined above. Careers education within the curriculum, on the other hand, can encompass specific programmes in careers education *per se* (narrow enclosed model), inclusion of careers education in PSE programmes (broader enclosed model) and infusion of elements of careers education across the curriculum (systemic model). Similarly, work-experience programmes can be separated from the rest of the curriculum (narrow enclosed model), attached to the careers or PSE programme (broader enclosed model) or linked to the curriculum as a whole (systemic model) (Miller *et al.*, 1991). Again, the processes of recording achievement and action planning can be viewed as part of the pastoral-care structure (boundary model) or as integrated into the curriculum itself (systemic model) (Watts, 1992).

In schools with sixth-forms, and in sixth-form colleges developed from a school tradition, many of these practices are sustained or adapted post-16. In colleges of further education and tertiary colleges they tend to assume a different shape, linked to the vocational tradition of the colleges, their complex structures and the mixing of school-leavers and adult students (Hawthorn, 1996). Traditionally, further education was the educational sector in which guidance was least well established. It was assumed that students were on set courses leading towards predetermined vocational targets, and therefore had no further need of guidance. Now, however, the growth of modularization and of more broadly based course structures has meant that guidance is required on a continuing basis to help students to build up and review their learning programmes. As a result, further education is the sector in which guidance has become most strongly institutionalized. The funding procedures, inspection guidelines and audit requirements developed by the Further Education Funding Council attach considerable importance to guidance on entry to, during and on exit from learning programmes. The reification of guidance for accountability purposes, together with the heavy emphasis on guidance on entry to learning programmes, has tended to lean provision towards the boundary model; on the other hand, the potential for application of the systemic model would seem greater than in schools.

Organizationally, current structures of guidance provision within schools and colleges fall into three categories. The first is specialist services based outside the institution. The Careers Service has a statutory remit to provide a neutral guidance service, free of charge, for individuals in full-time education and on part-time courses concerned with preparation for employment (other than in higher education), and also for young people who have left education or full-time training up to two years earlier. It thus covers virtually all individuals in the 14–19 age-group. The process of competitive tendering introduced following the Trade Union Reform and Employment Rights Act 1993 removed the service from the mandatory control of Local Education Authorities. In most cases the contracts have been awarded to companies formed through partnerships between LEAs and Training and Enterprise Councils, though the creation of a quasi-market has also resulted in some elements of 'expansionism' (such companies winning contracts in areas other than their own) and of 'new entrants' (contracts being won by private companies). The position of careers services, and their present subjection to rigid activity targets imposed by central government, means that they are largely confined to the boundary model. On the other hand, research by Morris *et al.* (1995) has demonstrated that the most effective practice is based on a 'community guidance' model in which careers services are able to play flexible roles in relation to guidance structures within the institution, including contributions to programmes based on the enclosed and systemic models.

The second category is specialist services based inside the institution. This includes, in schools, the role of careers coordinator. In almost all cases, however, careers coordinators are only weakly professionalized: their career guidance role takes up only part of their time, alongside subject-teaching responsibilities and few of them have received accredited training for their guidance responsibilities (Andrews *et al.*, 1995). In colleges there is more likely to be a central student services unit which coordinates and manages the whole guidance process from admission to exit from the institution: this may include an admissions tutor, a careers officer, a careers coordinator and a welfare officer (FEFC/OFSTED, 1994). Such services tend also to operate a boundary model, but have stronger opportunities than the Careers Service for making specialist contributions to the curriculum (enclosed model) or for supporting teachers and lecturers in their guidance roles (potentially, systemic model).

The third category is guidance as part of the role of teachers and lecturers, integrated into the teaching and learning process. Most teachers and lecturers combine their teaching roles with roles as tutors. Particularly post-16, guidance provision tends to centre on tutorial systems, where tutors meet groups of students on a regular basis (FEFC/OFSTED, 1994): such provision is based on the enclosed model. The doubling of roles should in principle make it easier for guidance to influence their teaching roles, so leading towards the systemic model. As we shall shortly see, however, some curricular structures lend themselves more readily to such influence than do others.

THE ROLE OF GUIDANCE WITHIN THE TRIPLE-TRACK STRUCTURE

The current (1997) system of qualifications post-16 is a triple-track system based on academic qualifications (A/AS-levels), broad vocational qualifications (GNVQs), and occupationally specific qualifications (NVQs plus others). The tracks tend to be distinct and are based on different principles of curriculum and assessment. They are also strongly insulated: combining elements of different tracks or moving between tracks is difficult and tends to be discouraged. The extension of Part 1 GNVQs to the 14–16 curriculum is producing some element of differentiation at this level too, though in this case students normally combine the GNVQ elements with GCSEs, so the tracking is less rigid.

Within a strongly tracked structure, a key role of guidance is to help students in making the critical choices between the tracks. As a result of the National Curriculum, curricular differentiation at 14–16 is more limited than it used to be. Accordingly – prior to the advent of Part 1 GNVQs – most schools have not considered such differentiation sufficient to require formal careers education and guidance provision in Year 9 (Morris, 1996). The choices made at 16, however, are critical ones, and tend to dominate 14–16 guidance programmes.

The effectiveness of current guidance programmes in relation to choices at 16 is open to question. A survey by OFSTED (1996) found that students were generally well aware of the range of longer-established A- and AS-levels available to them; their knowledge of GNVQs was, however, generally poor. Moreover, in about a quarter of schools with sixth-forms there were unresolved tensions as to how far students should be encouraged to see for themselves what was on offer in other local institutions. This evidence reinforced long-standing criticisms of the tendency of some schools with sixth-forms to bias guidance at 16 in order to encourage students to stay on (with the financial advantages this brings to the school) rather than to move on to learning opportunities elsewhere (HMI, 1992).

Guidance in relation to choices between tracks is based on the boundary model. In relation to ongoing guidance post-16, the role of guidance tends to differ strongly from track to track, because each track's different curriculum structures vary in their capacity to accommodate guidance elements.

Within the academic A/AS-level track, guidance tends to be largely based on the enclosed model. While all schools and colleges provide opportunities for students to transfer from one subject to another during the first half-term of such courses, it is much more difficult to do so thereafter (FEFC/OFSTED, 1994). The introduction of modular A/AS-levels could produce some degree of greater flexibility, though even here the rules of combination are usually very restrictive. The content of syllabuses tends to be strongly theoretical and knowledge-based, and to pay limited attention to vocational relevance: few A/AS-level courses, for example, include examination requirements for work experience or work-related assignments (FEFC/OFSTED, 1994). Accordingly, attention to guidance tends to be concentrated in group tutorial periods.

In the broad vocational track the more integrated curriculum design of GNVQs, together with the vocational focus and the emphasis on negotiated learning, lean strongly toward the systemic model. Careers education is likely to be embedded within the mainstream curriculum (FEDA, 1996). Separate careers education and guidance units are being developed, but based on the same model of performance criteria, range statements and evidence indicators as are used for other units. Work experience is common and fully integrated into the curriculum structure, as are recording of progress and action planning. In the occupationally specific track, the diversity of learning programmes, and the separation of learning from assessment within NVQs in particular, makes it more difficult to generalize about the role of guidance. The specificity of the occupational destinations tends to exclude guidance from the curriculum and confine it to a boundary role. Many individuals working towards such qualifications are work-based rather than college-based; for those who are college-based, work experience is designed for 'preparatory' rather than 'exploratory' purposes (Miller *et al.*, 1991). There is none the less evidence that many young people within this track tend to sample various types of work-based learning and to follow varied pathways before 'settling down' (Payne, 1995).

An important role of guidance 16–19, however it is structured, is to help young people to the next stage of their progression in learning and work. This includes, for some, progression into higher education. With the erosion of student grants, such guidance increasingly needs to take account of financial issues. It seems likely that the roles of career guidance and financial guidance will become ever more closely intertwined (Collin and Watts, 1996) – with important implications for the skills and knowledge required of guidance practitioners.

THE IMPACT OF 'LEARNING MARKETS'

The current position of guidance in relation to education and training provision 14–19 has been elevated – and complicated – by the government's policy of introducing market competition in learning provision, with the student viewed as 'customer'. This is relevant in three respects: current market competition between institutions; emergent internal markets within institutions; and the concept of learning credits.

One effect of market competition between institutions at 16 has already been mentioned: the pressures exerted by some schools to encourage students to stay on rather than to explore learning opportunities elsewhere. This has been in tension with other aspects of government policy, notably the promotion of new work-based options including Modern Apprenticeships. The way government has sought to resolve the dilemma is by looking to the Careers Service to provide the impartial guidance which it cannot depend upon from schools themselves. This has been the rationale for enhanced funding for the Careers Service's work within schools, plus proposals for legislation to secure students' access to its services (DTI, 1994; 1995).

The other effect of competition at 16+ has been on the guidance offered within colleges. The pressure of financial incentives on colleges to recruit students has meant that some colleges regard guidance provision on entry as a form of marketing. This is exacerbated by the fact that, under FEFC regulations, such provision is only funded if it leads to enrolment. The FEFC's hope is that funding penalties for non-completion of courses will outweigh the inducement to enrol, so encouraging colleges to protect the impartiality of the guidance they offer – the government is now proposing to apply a similar model of output-related funding to school sixth forms (Cabinet Office, 1996).

In both of these cases, there is an important distinction between two levels of impartiality. 'Reactive impartiality' is passive and minimalist: it may involve, for example, schools making available information on colleges only to those who seek it, and colleges providing information on courses in other institutions only in fields which they do not cover themselves. 'Proactive impartiality', on the other hand, involves making positive efforts to provide information and advice about the full range of opportunities, outside as well as inside the host institution. In the case of schools this might include an active programme of visits to local colleges or, in the case of colleges, information and advice about the pros and cons of all local courses in fields of interest to the individual. In general, the survey by FEFC/OFSTED (1994) found that:

> students had a better knowledge of the full range of provision available for 16 to 19 year olds in local institutions in areas where partnerships or consortia, involving local schools and further education

colleges, had been established; where cooperative arrangements existed between the different providers; or where local careers services provided material describing the provision.

(p.6)

The market-driven nature of recent government policy seems to have been designed to obstruct rather than support the development of such cooperative arrangements.

The second aspect of learning markets relevant to our concerns here is the emergent development of internal markets within institutions. Modularization is not necessarily designed to increase student choice: it is frequently more concerned with breaking down qualifications into smaller units of learning which can be assessed in a more immediate and transparent way, and the rules of combination often severely limit the range of choices which is permitted. Insofar as such choice is extended, however, and insofar as the allocation of funding within the institution is linked to recruitment of students on to particular modules, the result is the development of an internal market in which teaching units are competing with one another for student recruits. The role of impartiality accordingly arises here too. It is unrealistic to expect teacher/lecturers or tutors to provide fully impartial guidance in such situations, since they have an interest in the outcome of the students' decisions. If such guidance is to be available, therefore, internal markets of this kind tend to strengthen the case for specialist guidance services, whether based inside or outside the institution.

This suggests a further important distinction in relation to impartiality, based on its range: the distinction between 'comprehensive impartiality' relating to the full range of options open to individuals, and 'intra-institutional impartiality' relating more narrowly to the full range of options within the institution in question. In these terms, a possible three-level structure of provision might involve the Careers Service offering comprehensive impartiality, particularly on entry and on exit; central guidance services within the institution offering at least intra-institutional impartiality, both on entry and when a student wishes to transfer between learning programmes; and teachers/lecturers and tutors making no claim to impartiality but offering guidance and support on-programme. Some central guidance services within institutions might seek to offer comprehensive impartiality, particularly where this is based on a *concordat* with other local institutions.

The third aspect of learning markets is the concept of learning credits. The basic notion here is to direct public funding for learning at 16+ to the 'customers', i.e. the young people themselves, rather than to education and training providers. Young people are accordingly provided with a publicly funded voucher which enables them to 'buy' their learning programme. Strongly promoted by the CBI (1989), the application of the concept has so far been limited to work-based learning through a system of youth credits. The government has, however, confirmed its intention to extend the scheme to cover the full range of education and training post-16 (Cabinet Office, 1996).

Such a scheme is likely greatly to enhance the role of guidance. It in principle leaves individuals responsible for the decisions about what they are to learn, and expects providers to adapt their provision in response to such consumer demand. As noted earlier, the synchronization of learning provision with societal needs – including, in particular, the needs of the labour market – is accordingly mediated through the choices of individuals. This makes it essential to ensure that such choices are informed in relation to labour-market demand. Access to high-quality guidance is therefore widely recognized as critical to the success of any learning credits scheme (CBI, 1989; Coopers & Lybrand, 1995). Whether even this is likely to be adequate is open to question: Hodkinson and Sparkes (1993) found that the 'pragmatically rational' way in which young people reported making career decisions was very different from the 'technically rational' system of guidance built into the design of the original training credits scheme. But the onus to resolve such tensions falls on the guidance services themselves. In effect, guidance becomes, in policy terms, a 'market-maker': a way of making the labour market and the learning market work effectively, by ensuring that the supply-side actors within these markets have access to market information and are able to read market signals (Watts, 1995).

Some pressure groups have argued that the application of market principles should be extended still further, to the delivery of guidance itself. In particular, the CBI (1993) suggested that 'creating an effective and informed market in careers guidance provision is the best way to guarantee that the range of individuals' needs can be satisfied, that individual choices are maximised and that customers remain the focus' (p.22). The government has accepted this argument in relation to adults, but not young people. For the latter, application of market principles to guidance delivery has been limited to competitive tendering for Careers Service contracts, as outlined earlier, to deliver what is still in effect a local public-service monopoly. The notion of moving toward a multi-provider, market-led approach, based on guidance vouchers, was rejected by Coopers & Lybrand (1995) on the grounds that 'the potential for confusing young people through overlaying one market (for guidance) on top of another (for education and training) would be substantial and might run the risk of jeopardising the success of learning credits entirely' (p.55) (see also Watts, 1995).

ROLE OF GUIDANCE IN POSSIBLE FUTURE STRUCTURES

For the future, the role of guidance at 14–19 depends a great deal on what structure of qualifications and curriculum emerges as the dominant model. If rigid tracking continues, then the role is likely to remain much as at present. If, on the other hand, the notion of learning markets breaks down the rigidity of this model, moving towards a flexible common framework in which modularization is extended in response to individual choices, then guidance is likely to be cast largely in a boundary role, detached from the curriculum, in order to assure its impartiality. Coopers & Lybrand (1995) emphasized the importance of ensuring that guidance is delivered 'by agencies with no actual or even perceived interest in the outcome' (p.53). This does not negate possible additional roles for guidance, based on the enclosed or systemic models, but it tends to downplay their significance.

The third option is a unified system based on a series of alternative 'pathways' through a common framework of units and assessment strategies, with a common core. The argument for such a system is based on the concept of 'connective specialization', enabling specialists to share an overall sense of the relationship between their specialization and the curriculum as a whole (Young, 1993). Guidance can support such 'connectivity' by linking the curriculum as a whole to its value for career development (Law, 1996). Within such a structure, guidance based on the systemic model could accordingly form an integral element of the core. Thus, in the proposals for a British Baccalaureat (Finegold *et al.*, 1990), all students would do work/community-based modules: these could be extended to include guidance elements. Also the emphasis on core skills could provide a mechanism for infusing guidance elements into other modules, particularly if career management skills were added to the list of core skills. Alongside this, guidance based on the boundary model would be needed to support the choice of individual pathways. Guidance and counselling are accordingly included in the list of 'core processes' which it would be mandatory for institutions to provide in order to enhance personal progression and student learning.

The Dearing Report (1996) does not move significantly away from the current triple-track system. It does, however, emphasize that 'central to maximising achievement and reducing wastage is the provision of expert independent careers education and guidance to young people in their choice of pathways and goals' (p.127). It also stresses the importance of core skills, including 'self-management of learning programmes', which could readily be extended to cover career management skills more broadly. Moreover, its proposals for a relaunch of the National Record of Achievement emphasize the relevance of the requisite underlying processes to the development of such skills, including 'setting personal objectives, monitoring performance, reviewing work plans in the light of achievement, and reviewing both short-term objectives and long-term aspirations' (p.42). The radical implications of these proposals do not seem fully recognized in the Dearing Report as a whole. If, however, they are seriously followed through, they provide a base on which development towards a strong role for guidance within a unified system could be built.

CONCLUSION

The functions of guidance in relation to education and training systems can be seen in three ways. One is 'remedial', helping to make good the confused nature of the system itself by enabling individuals to find their way through it. There are strong elements of this within the current system which, despite the rigidity of the three tracks, is in many respects a complex and confusing structure. The second is 'operational', enabling a coherent system to run effectively. Within a cohesive framework system based on modularization, for example, guidance would be the essential means of enabling students to build learning programmes linked to their career aspirations. The third is 'augmentative', enhancing the learning which the system is designed to foster. Where guidance is viewed in these latter terms, enabling learners to develop the skills and competences to manage their lifelong career development, it is most likely to be seen not just as a desirable support to the curriculum, but as an integral part of the curriculum itself. A unified system would seem to provide the best prospect of making guidance based on such a view available to all young people up to the age of 19.

REFERENCES

Andrews, D., Barnes, A. and Law, B. (1995) *Staff Development for Careers Work*, NICEC Project Report, Cambridge: CRAC/Hobsons.

Cabinet Office (1996) *Competitiveness: Creating the Enterprise Centre of Europe*, Cmnd. 3300, London: HMSO.

Collin, A. and Watts, A.G. (1996) 'The Death and Transfiguration of Career – and of Career Guidance?', *British Journal of Guidance and Counselling*, 24, 3, 385–98.

Confederation of British Industry (1989) *Towards a Skills Revolution*, London: CBI.

Confederation of British Industry (1993) *A Credit to Your Career*, London: CBI.

Coopers & Lybrand (1995) *Learning Credits Consultancy Study: Final Report*, London: Coopers & Lybrand (mimeo).

Dearing, Sir Ron (1996) *Review of Qualifications for 16–19 Year Olds*, London: SCAA.

Department of Trade and Industry (1994) *Competitiveness: Helping Business to Win*, Cmnd. 2563, London: HMSO.

Department of Trade and Industry (1995) *Competitiveness: Forging Ahead*, Cmnd. 2867, London: HMSO.

Finegold, D., Keep, E., Miliband, D., Raffe, D., Spours, K. and Young, M. (1990) *A British Baccalaureate: Ending the Division Between Education and Training*, London: IPPR.

Further Education Development Agency (1996) *Careers Education and Guidance for Students in Transition from Further Education*, London: FEDA.

Further Education Funding Council/OFSTED (1994) *Guidance 16–19*, Coventry: FEFC/OFSTED.

Hawthorn, R. (1996) 'Careers Work in Further and Adult Education', in Watts, A.G., Law, B., Killeen, J., Kidd, J.M. and Hawthorn, R., *Rethinking Careers Education and Guidance: Theory, Policy and Practice*, London: Routledge.

Her Majesty's Inspectorate (1992) *Survey of Guidance 13–19 in Schools and Sixth Form Colleges*, London: Department of Education and Science.

Hodkinson, P. and Sparkes, A.C. (1993) 'Young People's Career Choices and Careers Guidance Action Planning: a Case-Study of Training Credits in Action', *British Journal of Guidance and Counselling*, 21, 3, 246–61.

Law, B. (1996) 'Careers Education in a Curriculum', in Watts, A.G., Law, B., Killeen, J., Kidd, J.M. and Hawthorn, R., *Rethinking Careers Education and Guidance: Theory, Policy and Practice*, London: Routledge.

Marland, M. (1980) 'The Pastoral Curriculum', in Best, R., Jarvis, C. and Ribbins, P. (eds) *Perspectives in Pastoral Care*, Oxford: Heinemann.

Miller, A., Watts, A.G. and Jamieson, I. (1991) *Rethinking Work Experience*, London: Falmer Press.

Morris, B. (1955) 'Guidance as a Concept in Educational Philosophy', in *The Yearbook of Education 1955*, London: Evans.

Morris, M. (1996) *Careers Education and Guidance Provision for 13 and 14 Year Olds*, QADU/RD10, London: Department for Education and Employment.

Morris, M., Simkin, C. and Stoney, S. (1995) *The Role of the Careers Service in Careers Education and Guidance in Schools*, QADU/RD7a, Sheffield: Employment Department.

National Curriculum Council (1990) *Curriculum Guidance 6: Careers Education and Guidance*, York: Longman for the NCC.

Oakeshott, M. (1990) *Educational Change and Curriculum Change*, London: Further Education Unit/Unit for the Development of Adult Continuing Education.

OFSTED (1996) *A Survey of Careers Education and Guidance in Schools*, London: HMSO.

Payne, J. (1995) *Routes Beyond Compulsory Schooling*, Youth Cohort Report No. 31, Sheffield: Employment Department.

School Curriculum and Assessment Authority (1995) *Looking Forward: Careers Education and Guidance in the Curriculum*, London: SCAA.

Standing Conference of Associations for Guidance in Educational Settings (1993) 'Statement of Principles and Definitions', in Ball, C. (ed.) *Guidance Matters*, London: RSA.

Unit for the Development of Adult Continuing Education (1986) *The Challenge of Change*, Leicester: UDACE.

Watts, A.G. (1990) 'The Role of Guidance in Educational Change', in Watts, A.G. (ed.) *Guidance and Educational Change*, Cambridge: CRAC/Hobsons.

Watts, A.G. (1992) 'Individual Action Planning: Issues and Strategies', *British Journal of Education and Work*, 5, 1, 47–63.

Watts, A.G. (1995) 'Applying Market Principles to the Delivery of Careers Guidance Services: a Critical Review', *British Journal of Guidance and Counselling*, 23, 1, 69–81.

Watts, A.G. (1996) *Careerquake*, London: Demos.

Whitty, G., Rowe, G. and Aggleton, P. (1994) 'Subjects and Themes in the Secondary-School Curriculum', *Research Papers in Education*, 9, 2, 159–81.

Young, M. (1993) 'A Curriculum for the 21st Century? Towards a New Basis for Overcoming Academic/Vocational Divisions', *British Journal of Educational Studies*, 40, 3.

Chapter 12

The measurement of quality in guidance

Ruth Hawthorn

WHAT ARE WE MEASURING?

Tomorrow afternoon you are going to see someone at the local college who has offered to help you plan your return to work over the next few years. You have never had this kind of help before. How on earth will you know if it is any good?

It is not easy to judge the quality of educational or career guidance, and in this chapter we will look at some of the reasons for this. We don't seek guidance often in our lives, and because the circumstances are likely to be different each time, it may be quite inappropriate to compare the different types. In thinking about how one might set standards, there is a temptation to look at how we judge more familiar services, such as those of a travel agent or a doctor. In these cases, although still difficult, we know how to weigh up the strengths and weaknesses of the service: there is a common-sense touch-stone for more formal measures. We don't necessarily expect a doctor to make us well immediately. But we do expect certain skills from doctors themselves, and if our doctor's surgery was not linked to other local health services (health visitors, hospitals) we would be suspicious. We would expect the doctor's own team to include a nurse and we'd be unhappy if the premises were dirty. There are some parallels in guidance: at the very least, there is no commonly accepted notion of what the outcome of good guidance should be (some people do expect to come away from it with a job, just as some people expect to come away from a doctor feeling well, but they are both likely to be disappointed). A lot of it is to do with the skills of the professional. But what exactly are those skills, and what about the office in which they work?

People working in the field have strong views about professionalism (for their own kind of guidance at least), and what would be appropriate in a guidance service. The competences of guidance staff are now minutely defined (Advice, Guidance, Counselling and Psychotherapy Lead Body, 1995). Most guidance quality systems cover staff numbers and qualifications, information bases, premises, equipment, and referral networks in some detail (Hawthorn, 1995), but few people in the general population have any idea of this. One study of how guidance is perceived by the general public revealed that they thought it was what you got at the Jobcentre (PA Cambridge Consultants, 1993), an idea far removed from that proposed by professional associations for adult guidance workers or Careers Service professionals (Institute of Careers Guidance and the National Association for Educational Guidance for Adults, 1992). The formal responsibility for measuring quality in guidance has been taken by the professionals who offer it, or the larger bodies (public and private) which finance it. The difficulty with this has been that the funding bodies often find it difficult to define what quality is in this context and the professionals have had rather different views.

Another difficulty has been that even where guidance providers have been subjected to quality assurance systems, some clients still complain about the help they have received. For someone using the service, their psychological state, their age and experience, the pressures on them from other parts of their life, are all going to affect the usefulness of the kind of help offered. It is difficult to predict what is going to feel helpful when that moment of need arises; the combination of skills and resources that seem useless to someone on one day may be just what is needed on the next. There is a complex relationship between client satisfaction and a good service. It is possible for a user to go away dissatisfied from a service that is as good as could be reasonably expected, and this makes it difficult to know how to make the best use of their negative feedback. It can encourage a regrettable complacency on the part of the provider: if there is nothing you can do about it, perhaps you can ignore it. There is a subtle difference between the attitude of a commercial organisation that wants to know about a customer complaint because if it can respond it may help increase its share of the market, and a public service with fixed resources. But a guidance service that really wants to improve what it is able to offer should be just as interested in the views of its dissatisfied clients.

Public expectations are determined by successive policy responses to needs within quite different sectors. There is no overall plan. A single individual may have had help at school from a careers teacher, form tutor or the Careers Service. If they then went into further education, they might have had help from admissions staff, lecturers or careers staff internal or external – or if they'd gone on a youth training programme, from an adviser, training officer or employer. If they'd gone on into mainstream higher education, they would have experienced something similar to the FE pattern. If they'd got a job they might have got guidance from their personnel or human resource development manager, or if they had been unemployed, from their claimant adviser at the Jobcentre or on a week's Restart course. They might have got a voucher from their local Training and Enterprise Council for an hour's guidance from any one of a number of services. And in addition, they may have paid for advice from an independent firm of occupational psychologists. The diversity of these experiences reflects the different significance of career or educational choices in the context in question: education, employment-related or personal development. Each policy response at the level of direct provision reflects other social and economic structures and is specific to any one country and its history. Even within the UK, quite fundamental differences can be found in the four different countries (Burdin and Semple, 1995) with their own cultural expectations and provision surrounding education and training. Successive studies of European guidance services (for example Watts, 1992; Watts *et al.*, 1994) reveal great differences in provision and therefore in expectation of educational and careers guidance, making comparison between countries so complex as to be valid on broad dimensions (Watts, 1996), but not in the detail of delivery. Young people in France would not expect a careers service to be provided by their university, but when they did seek help they would expect their counsellor to have a degree in psychology, quite unlike that which might be expected in the UK.

The measurement of quality has various benefits, but the most important is surely in the attempt to improve it. Quality standards and charters, performance indicators, inspection, evaluation, codes of practice and professional guidelines all involve a process of definition and an atmosphere of monitoring and accountability that practitioners can find invasive and irksome, even destructive of the helping relationship which, as suggested above, has to be sensitive to highly individual needs. Measurement takes up time and resources and can even paradoxically distract managers and staff from improving their service. Bodies dispensing public funds seem to concentrate on bringing the less good up to some mechanistic middle level, without addressing the much more interesting question of what would make it really good. What is a reasonable balance between providing what has been agreed in public policy, and the need to allow professionals to get on with helping individuals and developing skills in the way their own observations suggest is wanted? There are approaches to quality management that aim for a more reasonable balance, but it has taken some time and experimentation to identify problems and possible solutions.

BACKGROUND

During the fifteen year period between 1980 and 1995, there was a great advance in awareness of guidance at a policy level, as well as a realisation that there could be benefits in closer links between the different sectors. All approaches to quality assurance involve some basic clarification of what guidance workers are trying to do. This is not necessarily to make sure that they are all doing the same thing, but to try to see roughly where there are similarities and where differences. During this period questions about definition and quality standards permeated discussions over collaboration, funding and public accountability, and training.

Guidance and counselling was developed in schools as well as in further and higher education before 1980, but a new impetus was given to discussions about collaboration in the development of adult guidance networks through the 1980s. This idea developed following discussions about the future of adult education (Advisory Council for Adult and Continuing Education, 1979), and was picked up by what was to become the National Association for Educational Guidance for Adults (NAEGA) (Butler, 1984) as well as the Unit for the Development of Adult Continuing Education (see for example UDACE, 1986). In networks of agencies with distinct and non-overlapping roles there is not so much of a problem about what each does and how well they do it, but where an entire service depends on the combined activities of different local bodies (colleges, universities, the Careers Service, community groups, the Citizens' Advice Bureaux and so on) it is essential that each respects the work of the others. One role of the Educational Guidance Service for Adults (EGSA) was seen to be to act as a 'broker', directing people to where they could get the particular help they needed. The EGSA would need its own models of good practice (successive UDACE reports throughout this period offered detailed suggestions of how that might look) and a system of quality assurance (for example Hawthorn, Alloway and Naftalin, 1988); but if it was going to refer a client to one or other of the services on the network, it would want some sort of assurance that the quality of help offered there was also reliable. UDACE suggested that providers should be asked to subscribe to certain principles but no method was suggested for enforcing this, or for measuring whether a service was, for example, confidential enough. When central government funding was made available to local guidance networks in the late 1980s, criteria were laid down for the quality of the network itself, that is, how well the referral system worked (Rivis, 1989). Those particular criteria were used to select projects for funding, but in general the emphasis during this period was on self-monitoring, and on accountability to professional standards. Many services were operating within larger organisations that had their own approach to quality management and in some cases these appeared actually to pull in the opposite direction from the principles of good guidance. (A familiar example was where FE college admissions staff were trying to meet college targets for increased enrolments and at the same time honour NAEGA principles of impartiality, a problem that has not gone away.)

During the second half of the 1980s, principles of quality assurance in manufacturing were transferred to the provision of services, including educational services. Colleges began to seek BS5750 status (a system of measured quality control perfectly appropriate to material objects which has application by analogy to professional services); the idea that it might more particularly be applied to guidance first appeared in a UDACE publication in 1991 (Rivis and Sadler, 1991). This coincided with the creation of Training and Enterprise Councils (Local Enterprise Councils in Scotland) as the conduit for public funding to training programmes for the unemployed, and they quickly saw how important guidance was within that process for adults as well as for young people. With the strong presence of employers on their Boards, and a commitment to the transfer of private sector management procedures to public sector services, it was understandable that TECs would want to quality-assure any services which were funded from their budgets. The Employment Department offered a series of annual funding programmes for guidance through TECs and LECs, and it too insisted that any provision financed in that way should be quality-assured within a framework laid down nationally (ED, 1993, and subsequent updatings).

Although some attention at this time was paid to the Total Quality Management model, which stresses the importance of staff taking responsibility for setting and meeting their own quality targets and in many ways is more appropriate to professional services, the model generally adopted was that of BS5750 (later ISO9000). Here the 'supplier's' procedures are analysed and then audited on behalf of the commissioning body (in this case the TEC). Many TECs and LECs employed consultants to develop guidance quality standards from which to conduct their audits, and in some cases these were modifications of the Employment Department's quality framework; in other cases they were drawn out of previous models of UDACE or Careers Service origin. These standards had to be applicable to many different providers, because in most cases TEC or LEC money was used to fund guidance interviews for clients in target groups chosen by them, but with the additional intention of stimulating a 'market' involving a range of agencies. It was hoped that the 'product' would be comparable, but also that the context would be different enough so as to include an element of choice, at that time an increasingly essential component, at least in theory, of any publicly-funded service.

Standards are essential to transparency, but they bring their own dilemmas. If the written standards are detailed enough to be applied by someone who is not themselves an expert, they are likely to be much too long and pedantic to be able to be applied by busy managers, or by clients. If they are simple enough to be usable, then they will be too broad to ensure a specific level of quality. It is generally agreed that an information base should be comprehensive, but immediately this needs to be qualified: comprehensive for which sorts of client group? Without a list of all the appropriate publications and electronic materials and sources (which apart from anything else would date rapidly), it is not easy for a non-specialist employee of a TEC, say, to judge the full requirements of a clientele that may include people with research degrees and those with learning difficulties, and people who have not worked for several years as well as people at the height of a successful career.

At the time that Britain was entrenching the ISO9000 approach into guidance work, other European countries were still debating first whether this kind of quality assurance was appropriate to sensitive interpersonal work of this kind, and second whether the European Framework for Quality Management (EFQM) might not be more appropriate. In this, the rigorous and objective approach of ISO9000 is softened by local target-setting of a kind similar to the workteam development approach of TQM (Mooijman and Stevens, 1995). Some British and multinational companies had adopted EFQM, but no actual examples of guidance services were cited.

Throughout both the period of the development of EGSAs, and the early stages of TEC- and LEC-provided guidance, even if the general public thought of guidance as being what was offered by the Jobcentre, among guidance providers the service that came closest to providing a common-sense touchstone was the local authority Careers Service. EGSAs may have used it as a way of describing what they did *not* do (Edwards, 1989), but the Careers Service had, since 1973, provided a unified service throughout the country, comparable in provision from one authority to another (Killeen and Kidd, 1996). It was an accepted and recognised partner in secondary and further education as well as the world of work: alongside offering advice to young people at the point of leaving school, it worked with teachers in school and young people in the labour market as well as their actual and potential employers. Staff trained by the careers service also worked in further and higher education, either as part of their LEA contracts or through direct employment. Because of these strong connections across education and employment, expectations of good practice have been influenced strongly by the Careers Service model. Most importantly, Careers Service staff were trained to a single qualification, the Diploma in Careers Guidance, and quality in the Careers Service itself was maintained by a national Careers Service Inspectorate to a single set of guidelines. When the Careers Service was privatised following the 1993 Trade Union Reform and Employment Rights Act, this centralised regulation of quality was continued through the publication of a single set of quality standards to serve as the basis for the contracting out of the service to a range of separate providers.

Other individual sectors of guidance were developing unified systems of quality control throughout this period. OFSTED inspection guidelines cover careers education and guidance in schools, and the Further Education Funding Council (FEFC) guidelines cover guidance and student support. FEFC funding criteria (FEFC, 1994) also lay down specific requirements for entry guidance which are in essence measures of quality. From the mid-1980s, the Regional Advisory Councils for Further Education were active in developing the quality of adult guidance. Nationally the Further Education

Unit, and more recently the Further Education Development Agency published a series of studies on ways of both improving guidance and student support (for example FEU, 1994; Sadler and Reisenberger, 1997), and the FEFC reports on good practice (FEFC, 1997). The publication of quality guidelines for guidance by the Higher Education Quality Council (HEQC, 1994) provided the closest which that sector, with each institution's sensitivity about its own autonomy, could come to quality standards. Where careers education and guidance activities were funded through specific government programmes, as with the Enterprise in Higher Education and the Guidance and Learner Autonomy projects, it was possible to set specific targets and performance indicators. As with funding programmes in other sectors, these standards do not last beyond the end of the funding, but hopefully their influence lingers on (Hawkins and Winter, 1997; McNair, 1996).

MEASURING THE WORK OF PROVIDING ORGANISATIONS

In 1994, the CBI and the RSA founded the National Advisory Council for Careers and Educational Guidance (NACCEG). It was made up of representatives from relevant professional associations and other national organisations with an interest in guidance, and its spectrum of guidance interest was broad. Early on it set itself the task of agreeing a single set of quality standards for all organisations that provided guidance. These standards were agreed after a period of negotiation, and published in 1997. While the standards themselves apply across the full range of providers, the kinds of provider were subdivided into 'service groups': they were combined in ways that reflected client target groups (adults or young people), whether or not guidance was offered specifically or embedded in other kinds of activity, and whether or not the provider had some sort of interest in the outcome of the guidance.

The preliminary study carried out for the Guidance Council on the way in which standards were deployed within guidance (Hawthorn, 1995) distinguished between quality systems driven by the needs of the funding body (such as the TECs or the government) to ensure that money was well spent; those that came from professional bodies (for example, codes of conduct produced by the National Association for Educational Guidance for Adults, by the Institute for Careers Guidance, or by the Association for Graduate Careers Advisory Services); and those that reflected the wishes of the clients. This last kind were reflected in the intent behind the student charters introduced in 1994 for further and higher education, and in the statements of entitlement that began to appear as part of TEC guidance schemes. None of these actually reflected a grass-roots demand from students or clients themselves, but what the funders and professionals said would be reasonable for them to expect from the provision in question. The Guidance Council hoped to encapsulate the client's wishes in its standards, and in its development of organisational standards the Council consulted groups who could be considered as users. It also published its own statement of the principles of guidance, and the range of services which someone might expect from guidance. These were agreed across the full membership of the Council and they therefore encompassed all possible professional views (NACCEG, 1996). They were intended as a 'plain English' guide for people who wanted to find out more about it: perhaps potential clients, or perhaps college principals and governors, or other employers, who might be considering investing in guidance provision. While not actually providing 'client-oriented' standards, they offered a baseline from which these might be drawn up.

Another development during this period, alongside the growing interest in *quality assurance* for state-funded services, was the increasingly insistent requirement to *evaluate* the effectiveness of any government spending programme. These are different exercises, but they can use similar measures. The first is intended to ensure that a continuing service will be provided at a standard which is reliably high, and the second to discover whether some innovation or additional service made a significant difference. One approach to the evaluation of guidance *per se* is to ask what individual clients gain from a guidance session. If you could devise a suitable test, you could apply it before and after guidance to a suitably large number of clients and measure the difference, and on the basis of that decide whether there had been enough of an improvement to justify spending the money. But an instrument of this kind could also, in principle, be used to measure whether the guidance offered by any individual agency or even an individual guidance worker was of an acceptable standard. In practice, the development of a measure like this presents serious difficulties, for the now familiar problem that clients have different needs and start from different levels of understanding, and that services offer different things. In addition, few clients are willing to be subjected to elaborate and pedantic tests at a time when they are more concerned about pressing decisions. However, the Employment Department did commission the development of a test that used something of this approach. It was devised as an evaluation tool, but it was adopted by some TECs as part of their quality-assurance effort (NFER, 1993).

MEASURING THE WORK OF GUIDANCE STAFF

Rather than measuring processes and products, it may make better sense to look at the skills of the practitioner. The principle of accrediting technical, and later professional, 'competence' of practitioners through the system of National and Scottish Vocational Qualifications (N/SVQs), was extended to guidance through the creation in 1992 of a Lead Body which encompassed a much broader range of professionals than those that made up the adult guidance network. Its aim was to produce a single set of standards of competence for practitioners across the spectrum even broader than that of the Guidance Council, covering staff who provide information, advice, guidance, counselling and psychotherapy.

Apart from the qualifications required by the Careers Service, at the time that the Lead Body began its work there was a multitude of different qualifications considered wholly or partly suitable for people engaged in this broad field of activity. The push, and funding, for the development of NVQ standards had come from the Employment Department, keen to establish some sort of unanimity in a highly fragmented and mutually suspicious professional patchwork, but in fact by the end of the 1980s there had anyway been movement within some professional bodies to standardise training, and to explore whether competence statements would be a way of making skills, and therefore training targets, more transparent. Adult guidance workers, careers advisers with young people, and guidance workers in higher education had all done preliminary feasibility studies in this area by the time the Lead Body began its work.

There was opposition to the introduction of NVQs into the field on at least three counts: that professional skills cannot be so simply defined and measured as less complex manufacturing skills; that NVQs can only be assessed in the workplace, which makes them inappropriate for initial training; and that basing qualifications on minimal levels of competence may contribute to an un-professional attitude that constant updating and development is not essential. The occupational standards were agreed in 1994, through a detailed process of clarifying and negotiating the terminology and expectations of all the relevant professional associations. While it did prove possible over time to agree a single set of standards, different groups within the overall body wished to determine for themselves what would constitute acceptable evidence that practitioners had achieved that standard. These different 'evidence routes' now form the basis for a range of separate N/SVQs at levels 2, 3 and 4. Although the new system of qualifications is time-consuming to acquire, the clarification of professional practice across the different guidance sectors has gone a long way towards addressing the problem of mutual suspicion between professional groups. Furthermore a standardised system can make it possible for staff to move between different kinds of guidance work (to the benefit of those individuals, but also of employers, students and clients).

With a distinction between practitioner standards and organisational standards, the capabilities of the individual practitioner can be measured more or less independently of the capabilities of the service within which they work. But one important dimension is left out. Both kinds of standard inevitably make reference to guidance networks, but neither provide measures of how effectively a network operates: in effect, from the point of view of someone seeking help, how well in any one area all their needs were covered by appropriate agencies, and as importantly, how well the referral system would work. As we saw, the issue was addressed in the late 1980s at the time of UK government funding for adult guidance networks, but is the one area that has not been picked up since. If a uniformly high-quality service is to be made available to everyone, wherever they live, the development of an effective quality-assurance system of this kind is essential.

CONCLUSION

There is a considerable momentum for quality measures in guidance, within learning programmes and in independent guidance services. Has it helped users of guidance to know good provision from bad? Has it actually improved the quality of provision?

The single theme that permeates the developments described above is the need to increase the transparency of guidance provision. The three different groups (funders, professionals, and clients) all need to understand what they should be giving and getting, and what the others should get and give. The competence statements of the N/SVQs and the development of the Guidance Council's quality standards attempt to clarify the work of professionals to their colleagues, and make the professionals' ideas about good practice intelligible to the body that funds them. Charters and statements of entitlement try to open such concepts to users. It is not clear whether these materials make any significant difference to public perceptions of guidance. They help professionals articulate for themselves exactly what it is they are trying to achieve, and that indirectly helps their clients, but the direct effect on the public is less apparent. If we are going to identify any gaps between what people want and what is provided, we need to seek client feedback, and more importantly, use it constructively. In one TEC area that operated a quality-assurance system of the ISO9000 type, in which inputs and processes were assessed by TEC staff, clients were interviewed by independent evaluators of clients six months after their guidance. The providers had met their quality standards, but the survey revealed that a quarter of their clients had either been badly disappointed by the help they had received, or had been satisfied by the help they had received but only because they were not aware of the help they should have received and were grateful for anything. Where the pressure on providers from their funding bodies is to demonstrate what a good service they provide, there is a temptation to look for ways of explaining away any complaints from their clients. Quality assurance systems for guidance should incorporate a systematic and independent inquiry into client satisfaction, with a genuine interest on the part of the providers in how they could improve their service.

As to whether standards have actually improved, there are few systematic evaluations of quality-assurance systems for guidance, and it would not be easy to carry one out. There have been so many changes in funding and management to all the services concerned that it would be hard to single out either positive or negative effects. But whatever the effects so far, the alternative, of not trying to define what is good practice, is surely unacceptable. The important thing is that the debate is now out in the open. Funders and professionals agree, at least in principle, that the views of the clients or students are a key component, and both, at least in principle, know that if a potential user asks for a statement of entitlement they should be able to provide one. If we want to know how to judge whether or not that college adviser is going to be any good, we could at least now ask for some sort of statement of what they are offering, what sort of qualifications the staff have, and to what quality standards they are working.

REFERENCES

Advice, Guidance, Counselling and Psychotherapy Lead Body (1995) *Occupational Standards*, Welwyn: AGC&PLB.

Advisory Council for Adult and Continuing Education (1979) *Links to Learning*, Leicester: ACACE.

Burdin, J. and Semple, S. (1995) *Guidance for Learning and Work: Report on an Anglo-Scottish Consultation*, Glasgow: University of Strathclyde.

Butler, L. (1984) *Educational Guidance: A New Service for Adult Learners*, (2nd edn) Milton Keynes: Open University.

Edwards, R. (1989) *Separating Educational and Vocational Guidance*, Occasional Publication No. 13, Canterbury: National Association for Educational Guidance for Adults.

Employment Department (1993) *Requirements and Guidance for Providers*, Sheffield: ED.

Further Education Funding Council (1994) *Recurrent Funding Methodology: Audit Evidence for Entry Units*, Circular 94/16. Coventry: FEFC.

Further Education Funding Council (1997) *Careers Education and Guidance: Good Practice Report*, Coventry: FEFC.

Further Education Unit (1994) *Managing the Delivery of Guidance in Colleges*, London: FEU.

Hawkins, P. and Winter, J. (1997) *Mastering Change: Learning the Lessons of the Enterprise in Higher Education Initiative*, Sheffield: Department for Education and Employment.

Hawthorn, R. (1995) *First Steps: Quality Standards for Guidance across all Sectors*, London: Royal Society of Arts.

Hawthorn, R., Alloway, J. and Naftalin, I. (1988) *Evaluating Educational Guidance for Adults*, Leicester: National Institute for Adult Continuing Education.

Higher Education Quality Council (1994) *Guidance on Quality Assurance*, London: HEQC.

Institute of Careers Guidance and the National Association for Educational Guidance for Adults (1992) *A Guidance Entitlement for Adults*, Stourbridge: ICG/NAEGA.

Killeen, J. and Kidd, J.M. (1996) 'The Careers Service', in Watts, A.G., Law, B., Killeen, J., Kidd, J.M. and Hawthorn, R., *Rethinking Careers Education and Guidance*, London: Routledge.

McNair, S. (ed.) (1996) *Guidance and Learner Autonomy Network News* (4th edn), Sheffield: Department for Education and Employment.

Mooijman, E. and Stevens, R. (1995) 'Quality Improvement and Quality Assurance in Knowledge Intensive Service Organisations', in Bartholomeus, Y., Brongers, E. and Soren, K., *The Quest for Quality: Towards Joint European Quality Norms*, Leeuwarden: LDC National Careers Guidance Information Centre.

The National Advisory Council for Careers and Educational Guidance (1996) *The Guidance Council's Code of Principles*, London; Royal Society of Arts.

National Foundation for Educational Research (1993) *Measure of Guidance Impact: Manual*, Slough: NFER.

PA Cambridge Consultants (1993) Research on the Labour Market Need for Advice and Guidance Services: Final Report, Cambridge: PACEC (mimeo).

Rivis, V. (1989) 'Monitoring and Evaluation', in *Delivering Educational Guidance for Adults*, Leicester: National Institute for Adult Continuing Education.

Rivis, V. and Sadler, J. (1991) *The Quest for Quality in Educational Guidance for Adults*, Leicester: National Institute for Adult Continuing Education.

Sadler, J. and Reisenberger, A. (1997) 'On Course for Next Steps: Careers Education and Guidance for Students in Further Education', *Developing FE*, Vol, 1, No. 5, London: Further Education Development Agency.

Unit for the Development of Adult Continuing Education (1986) *The Challenge of Change*, Leicester: National Institute for Adult Continuing Education.

Watts, A.G. (1992) *Occupational Profiles of Vocational Counsellors in the European Community*, Berlin: CEDEFOP.

Watts, A.G. (1996) 'International Perspectives', in Watts, A.G., Law, B., Killeen, J., Kidd, J.M. and Hawthorn, R., *Rethinking Careers Education and Guidance*, London: Routledge.

Watts, A.G., Guichard, J., Plant, P. and Rodriguez, M.L. (1994) *Educational and Vocational Guidance in the European Community*, Luxembourg: Office for Official Publications of the European Communities.

Watts, A.G. and Hawthorn, R. (1993) *Careers Education and the Curriculum in Higher Education*, Cambridge: Careers Research and Advisory Centre.

Part IV

Academic discourses

Chapter 13

The politics of careers education and guidance

A case for scrutiny[†]

Inge Bates

Much attention has been given by researchers and curriculum developers to the formulation of appropriate aims for careers education. Further work has focused on research into models for criteria for evaluation purposes. Both types of work imply an assumption that curriculum development and evaluation are in significant measure rational endeavours, guided by research and theorising. This assumption is not untypical in the curriculum planning field, where models for curriculum change have been elaborated and justified at length on the basis of philosophical, psychological, sociological and pedagogical arguments. Such approaches have been criticised by sociologists of education who, approaching from a variety of theoretical backgrounds, have argued the importance of viewing curricula as developed through conflict and shaped by social structures and social movements (for example Young, 1971; Goodson, 1983; Cooper, 1984; Whitty, 1987). The central purpose of this chapter is to introduce the latter perspectives into the study of definitions of careers education, drawing evidence from a socio-historical case study of policy-making and implementation. The processes of defining the subject were, it will be argued, highly conflictual, and shaped by social and political factors. Debates about the subject were not free-floating but nested in 'micro', 'meso' and, ultimately, 'macro' social and political structures which shaped the terms and outcomes of discussion. The chapter demonstrates the need to examine such structures in order to understand and intervene effectively in the development of careers education and guidance.

The chapter concentrates on the experience of the Schools Council Careers Project (1971–81). In what follows I shall summarise some debates about definitions of careers education at different stages of the journey from policy-making to practice. It should be stressed that I am not concerned here with the educational merits of any particular version of careers education

---

[†] This chapter is an edited version of an article in the *British Journal of Guidance and Counselling*, 1990, 18(1): 66–83.

identified in the course of discussion: my concern is rather to highlight the multiplicity of competing versions and examine their social and political *viability*, as an aspect of their success or failure.

The chapter draws on three stages of involvement in developing and researching careers education curricula. The first stage was as a participant actor involved as a team member in the Schools Council 'Careers' Project. The next stage involved research for a doctoral thesis, focusing on curriculum change in careers education (Bates, 1985a). This study examined the development of careers education, historically, within the project and within schools. The school-based research was based on an ethnographic study of one 'good' project trial school, referred to here as 'Lifeskills' School, and comparison with findings from the project's evaluation relating to some twenty trial schools. As a result of covering aspects of curriculum production both within the 'Careers' Project and within schools, the study as a whole was able to span several distinctly different types of contexts in which curricula are defined. This gave rise to interesting possibilities for comparison of the factors affecting the development of curricular definitions in the various settings. The third stage of work is a by-product of continued and more wide-ranging observation of the development of definitions of careers education both over time and in a variety of different professional contexts. These more recent observations have provided further evidence of the malleability of careers education, of the importance of conflict in processes of defining the subject and of the significance of social and political factors which affect these processes.

CAREERS EDUCATION FROM IDEOLOGY TO PRACTICE

As necessary background to the discussion which follows, a summary account is given below of the emergence of the 'developmental' model of careers education, its incorporation within a Schools Council curriculum project and its further re-interpretation in the school context, drawing on previous work (Bates, 1985a).

The emergence of the 'developmental' model

In the late 1960s a new careers education paradigm emerged in the academic and professional literature, sponsored initially by individuals and organisations active in the field of vocational guidance. The model drew academic credibility from newly emerging 'developmental' theories of occupational choice and for this reason came to be referred to as a 'developmental' approach. The 'developmental' theories were recognised even by critics as 'promising a much-needed shaft of light' into processes of occupational decision-making and as 'the most influential ideas in the careers work field in the last two decades' (Roberts, 1977). The chief implication for careers education and guidance arose from the emphasis in the 'developmental' theories on occupational choice as the outcome of a long-term process of vocational adjustment requiring parallel provision of careers education.

At the heart the 'developmental' paradigm celebrates the ideal of individual autonomy and development of potential through choice of job, or increasingly with the rise of unemployment, choice of role in life. This central premise was vigorously challenged by critics, particularly sociologists (for example Speakman, 1976; Willis, 1977; Roberts, 1977), arguing that in British society jobs are not chosen, particularly by working-class youth, but are entered as a result of the interplay between social influences on career expectations and opportunity structures. The most insistent critic was Roberts, who criticised not only the 'developmental' theories of occupational choice but the related model of guidance, arguing for an alternative emphasis on 'adjustment' and placement.

Despite these various characteristics, which might perhaps have been expected to handicap the progress of the 'developmental' paradigm – namely vagueness of formulation, academic vulnerability and political sensitivity – this model became the dominant version of careers education and guidance in Britain during the 1960s and 1970s at the level of subject ideology. It was frequently stipulated in the academic and professional literature as *the* definition of careers education. It also came to underpin the main careers education and guidance textbooks and has been an influence on the closely related paradigm of social and life skills. Most importantly, perhaps, as a mark of its official acceptability, the model provided the initial conceptual basis for the Schools Council 'Careers' Project.

The Schools Council 'Careers' Project

Academic and professional support, even a high degree of consensus within a subject community, are insufficient conditions for the successful take-off of new subjects or curricular emphases. Such developments ultimately require *official sponsorship*. This term is used here to refer to the initiating and legitimating activities of the relevant network of organisations and official bodies which, for a particular historical period and a particular dimension of the curriculum, are collectively able to empower curriculum change (Bates, 1985b). Official sponsorship of careers education was somewhat hesitant. It was possibly least ambiguous in the late 1960s and early 1970s when the Schools Council launched the 'Careers' project. However, in the course of the development of this project the definition of careers education re-emerged as a constant source of debate.

In the following analysis I shall suggest that, while the 'developmental' model provided broadly stable parameters for the definition of careers work throughout the life of the project, much discussion surrounded the question of socio-political aims (Watts and Herr, 1976). It was this issue which generated the most heated debate, often overwhelming other important questions: for example, questions of pedagogy, the form of teaching materials and teacher training.

The project was preceded by a Schools Council Working Party report (Schools Council, 1972) which provided basic guidelines for the 'Careers' Project. This report elaborates a definition of careers education in the course of a discussion of the transition from school to work and the implications for education generally. The subject areas proposed as coming within the aegis of careers education broadly reflect the 'developmental' approach, with frequent references to the teaching of self-awareness, knowledge of occupations and decision-making. Particular attention is given to the question of values in careers education, or its 'socio-political aims'. The impression is given that the authors are taking considerable pains to justify careers education in terms of what are assumed to be the liberal educational values of the teaching profession, while at the same time asserting the importance and legitimacy of a subordinate function for education in relation to the economy.

Overall the careers education values articulated in this report reflect what is termed here a 'liberal' position in contrast with the 'radical' position discussed below. For present purposes I am defining this as an educational ideology which assumes no fundamental conflict between the development and expression of individual potential and existing social order. Individual autonomy and the development of potential are viewed as central values. Society and the opportunity structure are assumed to be broadly compatible with human interests and aspirations. Insofar as social deficiencies are acknowledged, they are regarded as remediable, partly through the contribution which it is assumed the education system can make to the development of critical awareness and thus, indirectly, to social change.

The practical outcome of the Working Party was the setting up of the Schools Council 'Careers' Project, the purpose of which was to produce careers education teaching materials for the whole ability range in the 13–18 age group. What is of interest here are particular aspects of the project's debates about the definition of careers education. This definition was in fact contested throughout the project's life, sometimes implicitly in the course of discussion about specific examples of teaching material, sometimes explicitly when project staff directly addressed the question of formulation of careers education aims.

Distinctive to the project context, however, was the emergence of a 'radical' version of careers education with an emphasis on social change, which came to be contested by organisations with interests in the project. Stated baldly, one view of careers education developed within the project challenged the central assumptions of the 'liberal' position outlined above. Society and the range of job and other opportunities were regarded as more incompatible than compatible with the goal of encouraging the development and expression of human potential. This led to an emphasis on stimulating pupils to assess critically society and the occupational roles available and to act as an influence for social change, particularly in the world of work. This was reflected in pupil materials and project documents circulated to teachers.

The development of this emphasis in project documents and teaching material generated a further contest over the definition of careers education. Criticism in circles surrounding the project caused the Schools Council to set up a sub-committee to conduct an enquiry. The enquiry was 'to see whether the general criticisms had any factual basis and to work with the project during the final revision process'. The main sources of criticism were individual members of the project's Consultative Committee, some staff within the Schools Council, the Executive Committee of the National Association of Careers and Guidance Teachers and the project's prospective publisher. Their criticism centred around aspects of the project's 'radicalism' and were expressed particularly in terms of concern that the final teaching materials expressed a 'negative view of the world of work'. 'Negativism' became the theme of the enquiry, functioning to some extent it would seem as a code-word for 'radicalism'.

In focusing on 'negativism', critics of the project were also drawing on the currency of the 'Great Debate', part of which was constructed around an alleged problem of young people's 'negative' attitudes towards industry. The launching of the 'Great Debate' coincided with the enquiry into the 'Careers' Project and fuelled the concerns of individuals and organisations involved with the project, who were anxious not least about the implications of adverse publicity for the future of the Schools Council itself.

The Schools Council enquiry resulted in protracted and painful negotiations with the project team and eventually in considerable modification of the teaching materials as a condition of publication. The main emphasis in this revision was on the inclusion of additional materials or adaptation of existing materials to reflect a more 'positive' view of industry, thus effecting a shift to the right in the implicit socio-political aims. The range of materials ultimately published were a hybrid product, somewhat lacking in ideological coherence. This inconsistency was the visible residue of the multiple contests involved in processes of defining careers education. As a result, different socio-political perspectives came to be incorporated in the texts at different stages of production and these could not be ironed out on account of surrounding political and practical difficulties.

Careers education in school

In the school setting, my original interest had been in exploring what became of the project's radicalism. What actually emerged was that, within schools, the terms of the debate had changed. Discussion of the project's political values was displaced by an altogether different debate. Teacher constructs in relation to careers education were essentially bi-polar. On the one hand, they defined a traditional approach to careers work revolving around information and advice-giving. This was regarded as old-fashioned and unacceptable by teachers who supported the 'Careers' Project. On the other hand, there was the 'new' thinking, careers education as 'preparation for life', represented by the 'developmental' model. This approach was taken up enthusiastically by most 'Careers' Project users. From their perspective, the most important contest was between these two approaches. The 'developmental' model was loosely equated with a progressive educational position, and traditional careers work, with its overtones of fitting pupils into employment, was viewed as conservative. Data from the project's formative evaluation confirmed the findings of the ethnographic study in this respect. While each trial school was unique in the way in which it incorporated the project, discussion of the project's political values was a low priority on teacher agendas in comparison with the apparently more mundane question of how far careers education should concentrate on job information.

The 'Careers' Project was identified with the new current of thinking on careers work. It was regarded as simply one of a number of tributaries intermingling to form a broad trend towards defining careers education as 'preparation for life'. The different political nuances of the various strands was not of great consequence to teachers; what was important was their common emphasis on lifting careers education out of its uninspiring origins in job information. The particular significance of the 'Careers' Project was not its distinctively 'radical' slant, but that it represented an abundant source of lesson materials. This capacity was all the more valued since teacher priorities did not easily accommodate lesson preparation, course planning or even close reading of the materials.

The ethnographic study revealed much more detail of the social situation in which teacher debates were located. In 'Lifeskills' School, teachers were constantly encountering pressures to revert to a more traditional, job-information-based version of careers work, and were consequently highly preoccupied with the struggle to defend the new ground. Pressures came largely from two sources: other teachers and pupils. Many careers teachers locally had either not encountered the new careers education or had rejected it in favour of a more traditional approach. Within the careers department, one teacher expressed frequent doubts about his three colleagues' preferred philosophy. However, the existence of such sceptics did not prove a major obstacle. Rather their presence fuelled a 'vanguard' ethos in the department where members tended to see themselves as pioneers, 'streets ahead' of many of their contemporaries.

The second and much more influential source of pressure came from pupils. Both the ethnographic data and the project's evaluation provided overwhelming evidence that most pupils would have preferred a more narrow definition of careers education, revolving around local labour-market information: they constantly pressed the careers curriculum to meet their more mundane, socially structured concerns – jobs and pay, not the lofty goals of career choice or self-awareness. This analysis echoed the findings of a long line of research studies which have repeatedly pointed to the extent to which young people assess education in terms of vocational criteria (for example Morton-Williams and Finch, 1968; Pollock and Nicholson, 1981; OECD, 1983; Atkins, 1984). The conclusions are therefore not novel. What is interesting is that the study revealed the persistence of tension between teacher and pupil definitions of relevant subject matter in the context of a curricular movement (careers education), which came into being partly on the strength of its assumed capacity to contribute to the solution of this conflict.

In 'Lifeskills' School, pressures from pupils ultimately caused teachers to significantly modify their approach at the classroom level. In the course of the ethnographic study, they were moving increasingly towards the transmission of stratified job information and were re-setting groups. Thus teachers' practices, in contrast with their intentions, could be seen as complementing wider processes of social reproduction. This shift in emphasis was not fully acknowledged by teachers themselves. What emerged was a dichotomous definition of careers work since, in departmental meetings, they continued to promote careers education as 'preparation for life'. As was the case with the 'Careers' Project's published materials, discussed above, we again observe here loss of coherence and hybridisation of the definition of careers education as a result of surrounding political struggles.

The journey summarised

The particular story of careers education and guidance as related above runs as follows. In the late 1960s a more sophisticated version of careers work emerged in the academic and professional literature than had existed hitherto. It was based upon newly emerging 'developmental' theories of occupational choice. This 'developmental' model of careers education was highly individualistic and egalitarian in emphasis, revolving around the ideals of individual autonomy, occupational choice and the development of individual potential. It was also extremely broadly formulated and open to numerous political interpretations. Consequently, at an operational level, there was still all to play for. The model was contested in academic circles on the grounds that the underlying 'developmental' theories misrepresented processes of occupational entry: most young people, it was argued, must enter jobs which they do not actually 'choose' in a meaningful sense, as a result of the constraints of the 'opportunity structure' (Roberts, 1977). Despite these criticisms, the model attracted official sponsorship and became the starting point of the Schools Council 'Careers' Project. Within the project, the question of socio-political aims became the site of contest over the definition of the subject. At one stage in its history, the project gave careers education a 'radical' twist, arguing that careers workers should involve young people in social change. The 'radical' emphasis was criticised in official circles surrounding the project and thus resulted in a Schools Council enquiry. The enquiry led to modifications of the project's materials and adjustment of the anti-industry stance.

Meanwhile, in schools, the introduction of the 'Careers' Project generated quite different problems. Central amongst them was that it did not conform to a more conventional definition of careers work based on the provision of job information. Amongst teachers the 'developmental' model, in its broadest form, was taken up enthusiastically as ideology. The 'Careers' Project was viewed as a *means* of implementing this approach, as indeed was originally intended by the Schools Council. In the classroom teachers experienced massive pressures from pupils to revert to a traditional approach to careers work. As a result of the contest which ensued, teachers in the interests of survival modified their approach considerably in the classroom, but at the level of ideology, this departure was not fully acknowledged. The result was that teachers operated a dichotomous version of careers education and guidance: 'preparation for life' for educational publics; job information in the classroom.

TOWARDS AN ANALYSIS OF THE POLITICS OF CAREERS EDUCATION AND GUIDANCE

The above account has identified different types of debates surrounding the definition of careers education at particular points of one journey from policy to practice and different consequences in terms of the definition which became dominant in particular organisational settings. A central problem, whether examined from the perspective of sociology of the curriculum, curriculum evaluation or policy development in careers education, is to explain this variability. The argument I wish to propose as meriting further investigation is that these differences reflect aspects of the social and political malleability of careers education and, more broadly, the conflictive nature of curriculum change. The implication of this view is that gulfs between 'theory' and 'practice' cannot be adequately conceptualised within a curriculum evaluation paradigm. Rather the curriculum 'schizophrenia' observed needs to be explored in terms of repeated contests over the definition of the subject between the groups of actors concerned, resulting in different outcomes in different occupational and organizational settings. The variety of outcomes can partly be explained by the politics of particular struggles, but these were in turn influenced by the wider social and political context. The following discussion begins to sketch out the case for further investigation and an embryonic model for analysis.

It is essentially the vantage point of *comparison* which renders transparent the ideological malleability of careers education, and curricula more generally. This is most apparent when historical perspectives are employed; resonances between curricula and 'zeitgeist' then emerge which are difficult to ignore (see, for example, Bates, 1984). However, the cultural contrasts between spheres of activity and work locations within any particular historical period may also have significant effects on definitions of curricula. The identification of ways in which careers education was differently defined in different contexts creates a basis for exploring the extent to which such definitions were potentially transferable across contexts or were context-dependent.

The above account has identified at least four different instances of redefinition of careers education. For the purposes of further discussion it may be helpful to highlight these differences: in the context of official sponsorship, the dominant definition could be characterised as *de-vocationalised vocationalism*; in the project setting, we find the emergence of *radicalised vocationalism*; in the staffroom, there was a re-surfacing of *de-vocationalised vocationalism*; in classrooms, the dominant definition could be described as *re-vocationalised vocationalism*. The evidence of the above study points towards the conclusion that these definitions were not readily transferable across contexts, even with the assistance of improved structures of curriculum development and dissemination. The gaps between levels arose not because the various groups of actors failed to grasp the intentions and objectives of other groups, but because they had different priorities and their institutional and operational contexts gave rise to different possibilities and constraints in pursuing their goals. Insofar as 'failed' curriculum change was observed, it was not so much the result of *deficiencies* within the given structures, but rather the result of the *political efficiencies* of the various groups of actors in promoting their preferred definitions of the subject.

This initial analysis hinges on three central concepts: the contested nature of curriculum change; participants' (or actors') missions or goals; and the distribution of power resources. The significance of these terms will be briefly outlined before exploring their relevance in relation to the above material. Missions are defined here as professional goals, expressed in the form of ambitions for curriculum change. They act as group banners, serving to unite individuals with similar ideals more effectively for the purposes of curricular struggles. Missions may appear as freely chosen commitments but can be seen as fragments of wider ideologies, surfacing as curricular definitions. The distribution of power is central to understanding the outcome of curricular contests in any one sphere of action. Following Cooper (1984; 1986), power can be examined through scrutiny of power resources. However, developing further Cooper's model, the analysis of these resources needs to take account of the different types of armouries which could be found in different occupational and organisational contexts, for example within the Schools Council, within the curriculum project, within staffrooms and within classrooms.

The conflictual nature of curriculum change in careers education, together with the role of competing missions, are amply evidenced in the above case-study. At all points of the journey described, there were competing goals, or missions, relating to the definition of the subject. In the context of production of ideology, there were the aspirations of industrial-ists for a model of careers education which gave priority to the needs of employers. In contrast there was the 'developmental' model, promoted by academics and developers in the field of careers education and counselling, which centred on individual self-development. The relatively idealistic 'de-vocationalised vocationalism' which was elaborated in Schools Council Working Paper 40 reflects the tensions between the priorities of various groups involved at this level – for example, industrialists, academics and representatives of the teaching profession. Discourse in this document involves a complex rhetoric of accommodation, as the authors seek to promote the concept of careers education in terms of the liberal ideals of the teaching profession, while recognising the potentially conflicting prior-ities of employers.

At the level of the curriculum project and production of texts, this tension deepened and, as the accommodative rhetoric was briefly dispensed with, its utility for the purposes of lubricating social action was exposed. Within the project, the mission for a more 'radical' definition of careers education competed with a 'liberal' version preferred by some project team members. With the emergence of the 'radical' approach within the project's teaching materials, a contest within the Schools Council ensued. The project's spon-sors and those with interests in it, their concerns heightened by the 'Great Debate', sought to temper the project team's critique of the world of work and opportunity structure and to reinstate recognition of the needs of employers.

Moving closer to the classroom, the contest in the staffroom was between the 'developmental' model or 'de-vocationalised vocationalism' preferred by most teachers and the pupils' 'mission' which was for job information or 're-vocationalised vocationalism'. Teachers held their ground in the context of staffroom talk, but at the chalk-face pupils tended to win the day, resulting in an increasing emphasis on classroom delivery of stratified job information.

In summary, the course of defining careers education did not run smoothly at any stage of the proceedings nor would it appear that its progress would have been facilitated by improved models of transmission. Under the guise of discussion, exchanges of comments on texts, exchanges of correspondence, and negotiation with pupils, the definition was, essentially, fought over. At root, the contests were about social and political values in relation to careers education, about whose interests were to be served and in what ways. 'De-vocationalised vocationalism' involved deference to both individual and employer interests. The 'radical' vocationalism preferred within the project team involved an assumption of conflict between human and industrial needs and focused on long-term social change as a means of reconciling the two. 'Re-vocationalised vocationalism' in classrooms resulted from the determined resistance of pupils who asserted their more short-term interests in job information and job-getting skills.

In the course of these struggles, the outcomes – that is, the various definitions of careers education which became dominant within particular settings – appeared to be largely determined by the distribution of power between the groups of actors directly involved. For example, at the level of production of ideology, the success of the 'developmental' model can be seen as a reflection of the power resources accumulated by its sponsors, central amongst which was the fine tuning of the definition itself to the educational politics of the early 1970s as discussed above. There were no equivalent channels for promotion of alternative definitions of careers education: for example, the 'radical' definition of the 'Careers' Project or the 'adjustment emphasis' recommended by Roberts (1977). Nor in any case does it seem likely that, in the climate of the early 1970s, these definitions could have successfully mobilised the subject community: viewed in terms of what was, in official circles, typically deemed politically acceptable in this period, they leaned too far to the 'left' and 'right'.

Within the 'Careers' Project, the distribution of power resources again played a crucial role at two stages: in debates within the project team, and in the subsequent negotiation with the Schools Council. The different outcomes which resulted from inter-project contests and project v. Schools Council contests can partly be explained by the different types of power resources which could be employed in each setting. Within the project team, everyday work revolved around the production of a distinctive variety of teaching materials based on ingredients such as games, simulations, group-work activities, and fictional case-studies, all of which were originated by team members. This led to a complex micro-politics of writing and editing, one consequence of which was that ability in, together with opportunity for, writing lesson materials were crucial power resources. During the phase of the project's life which is the focus of this chapter, the more 'radical' team members were the main writers and editors of materials. In the course of disagreements about content and drafting of materials, their control of the means of production of texts facilitated their control over curricular meanings. Thus the materials slid towards an emphasis on their 'missions' rather than the common ground of the entire project.

With the setting up of the Schools Council enquiry, the project team were re-engaged with the wider context of educational politics at a national level, which were, moreover, now rapidly being re-defined as a result of the 'Great Debate'. In the course of the contest with the Schools Council, the capacity to influence actors' career interests emerged visibly as a power resource, being a factor in both sides' considerations. The Schools Council, particularly conscious of its vulnerability at this time, needed to avoid damaging publicity in order to protect its officers and preserve its reputation. For project team members it would have been extremely disadvantageous professionally for the materials on which they had worked for several years not to be published. Consequently, there were strong incentives for both parties to compromise, with the result that, while the 'radical' emphasis within the materials was muted, it was by no means completely eliminated. The result was the ideologically eclectic range of materials described above.

The contests observed within 'Lifeskills' School again, although less obviously, involved political struggles. The most striking contest was at the classroom level where teachers were confronted with frequent, insistent and explicit group demands for job information of a type which was realistic in terms of the occupational strata pupils were likely to enter. Most of the careers teachers were initially highly resistant to altering their approach to careers education along these lines. However, pupils were able to influence teachers through their possession of a crucial power resource, namely their capacity to threaten teacher survival in the classroom, which was at times mercilessly exploited. 'Mucking about', sometimes escalating to fights, was a constant feature of some groups' careers lessons: when asked about this, pupils typically complained, 'It's boring, they should tell us about the jobs we can get instead'. The classroom battles led to a 'group dread', ill-health, domestic tensions, and, in the case of one teacher, absenteeism. However, when teachers adapted lessons to a model based on transmission of job information and re-setted groups, a relative peace reigned. When we take into account their classroom circumstances, it is not difficult to explain why teachers gradually jettisoned their preferred 'de-vocationalised' model of careers education and 're-vocationalised' the careers curriculum at this level.

IMPLICATIONS FOR RESEARCH AND PRACTICE

In order to understand or facilitate the development of careers education and guidance, it is important to examine the processes through which curricula typically develop. In recent years there have been some significant attempts to analyse and theorise such processes sociologically, but the resulting perspectives have not been put to use in the field of careers education and guidance. This chapter has sought to make explicit the political dimensions of processes involved in defining careers education in a number of contexts. The analysis has implications for both research and practice.

The research implications can be seen as falling within three areas. In general, this case-study illustrates the importance, more generally, of socio-historical studies of curricula in order to understand their development. Second, and more particularly, it points towards the scope for a different breed of research in careers education, guidance and counselling, namely studies of policy development, as distinct from policy evaluation. A rich variety of possible cases suggest themselves: school departments, college departments, the various relevant professional associations, as well as national organisations. Some of the broad aims of such studies could be to illuminate: the variety of competing goals and priorities within these various spheres; social and political influences upon these; latent and explicit processes of negotiation; the role of actors' career interests; and the influence of the wider social context. Third, this study has implications for styles of evaluation of guidance. In particular, it cautions against 'classical' approaches, based on pre-specified criteria, and recommends in-depth case studies which can illuminate processes of re-interpretation of guidance, particularly at the 'classroom' level. Ideally, these would be co-ordinated collections of studies allowing scope for comparison.

The detailed practical implications can only be fruitfully explored by practitioners themselves, with reference to their particular concerns and the areas in which they work. However, two areas can be suggested as possible starting points for consideration: working *within* the process of determining guidance definitions, and working *on* the process. As regards the former, most simply it is important for practitioners to be aware of the extent of 'macro' and 'micro' political activity involved in the production of careers education and guidance at all levels and to be sceptical of current orthodoxies. While the latter may be persuasively supported by philosophical, psychological, sociological and economic arguments, the explanation of their success may owe as much, if not more, to their capacity to survive in particular political arenas as to their merits from the point-of-view of facilitating individual development. As regards the latter, this study raises the question of the acceptability and legitimacy of the types of political processes observed. This in turn opens the broader issue of what kinds of political processes for determining definitions of guidance are justifiable in terms of the ideals of the profession. In order to realise these ideals more fully, it would seem that those concerned need to explore and work upon not only models of guidance but also upon the processes through which such models are defined.

REFERENCES

Atkins, M.J. (1984) 'Pre-Vocational Courses: Tensions and Strategies'. *Journal of Curriculum Studies*, Volume 16, pp. 403–15.

Bates, I. (1984) 'From Vocational Guidance to Life Skills: Historical Perspectives on Careers Education', In Bates, I., Clarke, J., Cohen, P., Finn, D., Moore, R. and Willis, P., *Schooling for the Dole?: the New Vocationalism*. London: Macmillan.

Bates, I. (1985a) 'Curriculum Development in Careers Education: a Case Study'. PhD thesis, University of Leeds.

Bates, I. (1985b) 'Towards Theory of Social Influences on the Development of Curricula'. Paper given at 'Theory of School Subjects' Conference, University of Leeds, July.

Cooper, B. (1984) 'On Explaining Change in School Subjects'. In Goodson, I.F. and Ball, S.J. (eds), *Defining the Curriculum*. Lewes: Falmer.

Cooper, B. (1986) *Renegotiating Secondary School Mathematics: a Study of Curriculum Change and Stability*. Lewes: Falmer.

Goodson, I.F. (1983) *School Subjects and Curriculum Change*. London: Croom Helm.

Morton-Williams, R. and Finch, S. (1968) *Young School Leavers*. Schools Council Enquiry 1. London: HMSO.

Organisation for Economic Co-operation and Development (1983) *Education and Work: the Views of the Young*. Paris: OECD.

Pollock, G.J. and Nicholson, V.M. (1981) *Just the Job: a Study of the Employment and Training of Young School Leavers*. Sevenoaks: Hodder & Stoughton.

Roberts, K. (1977) 'The Social Conditions, Consequences and Limitations of Careers Guidance'. *British Journal of Guidance and Counselling*, Volume 5, No. 1.

Schools Council (1972) *Careers Education in the 1970s*. Working Paper 40. London: Evans/Methuen.

Speakman, M. (1976) 'A Sociological Perspective on the Developmental Theories of Occupational Choice'. *Careers Advisor*, Volume 3, No. 3.

Watts, A.G. and Herr, E.L. (1976) 'Careers Education in Britain and the USA: Contrasts and Common Problems'. *British Journal of Guidance and Counselling*, Volume 4, No. 2.

Whitty, G. (1987) 'Curriculum Research and Curricular Politics'. *British Journal of Sociology of Education*, Volume 8, pp. 109–17.

Willis, P. (1977) *Learning to Labour*. Farnborough: Saxon House.

Young, M.F.D. (ed.) (1971) *Knowledge and Control*. London: Collier Macmillan.

Chapter 14

Careers guidance in the knowledge society[†]

G. A. Wijers and F. Meijers

INTRODUCTION

According to Drucker (1993), the western world is being transformed from capitalism to a knowledge society:

> In the knowledge society the educated person is society's emblem, society's symbol, society's standard-bearer. . . . If the feudal knight was the clearest embodiment of society in the early Middle Ages, and the 'bourgeois' under capitalism, the educated person will represent society in the post-capitalist society in which knowledge has become the central resource. . . . *The educated person now matters.*
>
> (Drucker, 1993: 211)

In line with this vision, Watts (1993) stated recently that, due to the changing nature of learning and work, careers education and guidance are higher on the public agenda than ever before. In his opinion, a structure emerges in which education and employment are to a large degree mutually dependent: 'One works to learn; one learns to work. They are symbiotic: they depend upon one another. Both are continuing processes. In the post-industrial world, a society that wishes to work must be a learning society.' As a consequence, the concept of 'career' is redefined. Increasingly, a career cannot be defined as a structure: it has become 'boundaryless' (Arthur, 1994). Nowadays, a career has to be defined as a process, to describe an individual's lifetime of learning and work. In this process careers education and guidance can play an important role by offering opportunities for individuals to explore the relationship between what they are learning and their career development. However, Watts is not very explicit about how this role can be realised.

[†] This chapter is an edited version of an article in the *British Journal of Guidance and Counselling*, 1996, 24(2): 185–98.

In this chapter we try to be more concrete about the consequences which the changes in the nature of education and employment have (a) for the content of careers education and guidance and (b) for the role of the career counsellor. Our central thesis is that individuals are becoming responsible for their own work allocation. In order to bear this responsibility, they must acquire so-called 'actor competences', which can be considered as a specification of Drucker's concept of an 'educated person'. These actor competences resemble the 'process skills' mentioned by Kidd and Killeen (1992). They are qualities that enable individuals to appear on the social stage as an actor. An actor is someone who is no longer mainly passive, in the grip of psycho-social forces exerting influence on him or her. A lack of actor competences not only confronts individuals with a serious problem, but places the stable development of society as a whole at risk. It is for this reason that the role of the career counsellor is becoming more prominent. Traditionally the counsellor had only one client: the individual who had problems in choosing an occupation. In a post-industrial or – as we prefer to call it – a knowledge society, the main task of a career counsellor is to facilitate the ongoing process of work and learning. Therefore, institutions such as employers and schools are important clients too.

DEVELOPMENTS IN WORK ALLOCATION

In today's society, individuals are often confronted with complex career problems. Not only do most individuals face the problem of getting and holding a job, but they experience it repeatedly. Many are forced to review their career several times in the course of their working lives. Two or three decades ago this type of career problem scarcely existed. In the course of the socialisation process the average person gradually acquired a crystallised occupational identity. Parallel to the development of this identity, the person aimed at an ever-smaller range of occupations in the world of work that matched with their self-concept in the process of development (Gottfredson, 1981). At the end of education, individuals opted for one of the occupations available in their range of choice. Subsequently, without too much conscious effort, they usually landed in a working situation where the chosen occupation could be exercised for the rest of their life.

In other words, in the recent past people reached a working position by means of institutional forces. In various social institutions they were socialised for a specific occupational area, with each institution – in which the individual was present for varying lengths of time – making a (clearly defined) contribution to the overall process. These institutions provided the individual with an identity and a direction, and usually ensured that the individual reached and remained at a work destination that fitted his or her identity and direction. If you ask older people how they entered the work they are now doing, they often answer: 'I just rolled into it'. This answer illustrates perfectly how unaware individuals were in former times of the process by which they arrived at their work destination and how they were largely led by social forces.

In today's society the institutional forces give individuals a far less unambiguous picture of direction and identity, if only because their mutual interlinking has been weakened. Parents, school careers staff, occupational advisers, employment agencies and personnel officers now have far more to do. Children, pupils, clients, workseekers and staff members have no clear awareness of their direction and identity. In other words, they have no clear notion of what would be a fitting job and do not possess the negotiating skills required in order to gain and hold on to a job (Meijers, 1991). However, in many cases neither parents, nor school careers staff or other professionals, are capable of offering much sense of direction or identity. They too have difficulty in viewing the whole picture and understanding the direction of social change.

The changes in the allocation process can be summarised as follows. In earlier times individuals were largely objects in the process, but at present they are under growing pressure to become the subjects of their own work allocation. In the past the responsibility for work allocation lay with those acting on behalf of the worlds of education, job provision and business life, who did not shrink from assuming that responsibility. Now that responsibility is weighing more and more heavily on the shoulders of individuals themselves.

VIA LEARNING TASKS TO ACTOR COMPETENCES

In order to be a subject in their own work allocation, individuals must learn to perform three tasks: (a) to form an identity, (b) to determine a direction and (c) to plan a career and steer themselves on it. Once individuals have learnt this, they have become actors: people who have a hold on their own career.

Learning to form an identity

In the first post-war decades, formation of identity was a relatively unconscious process. Since the social context was still coherent, individuals were able to see themselves as single undivided personalities. But because the cultural context of present society is pluriform, the socialising forces are no longer unambiguous. The opportunities of living out one's selfhood are now so diverse that individuals no longer easily learn to know themselves as coherent, crystallised personalities, but perceive themselves much more as a collection of sub-identities (Luken, 1990).

Individuals are, in consequence, constantly facing the challenge not only of continually examining their self-knowledge with a critical eye but also – and at the same time – of organising the various parts of their own personality to constitute a functioning whole. This partly requires a rational approach: the various parts of the self-concept must be continually tested against experience and for logical consistency (Taborsky, 1992). However, there is also a partial need for a more literary approach. The various parts of the personality must be organised in a sensitively satisfying and sensible manner into a whole which fits into the individual's own life-story. Again, this is not just a one-off exercise but a constant requirement. New experiences and old, memories that flood back – these all require attention and processing into a self-concept, a life-story and a role which individuals wish to play.

Learning to determine one's own direction

To be able to form one's own identity is a condition for working on the second learning task: to determine one's own direction. In earlier times a sense of direction emerged in the course of the socialisation process. This gave individuals a sense of orientation in the part of the world of work corresponding to their own identities by the time the choice of an occupation had to be made (Gottfredson, 1981; Wijers, 1987). When the occupational structures become more vague and the relationship between occupations and opportunities for work in work organisations weakens, it becomes extremely difficult to gain, via images of occupations, a picture of work opportunities appropriate to the individual's personality. In addition, the lengthening youth phase gives learning a significance in itself: learning is less and less directly related to the world of work, a world which has become largely opaque (Meijers, 1992). What is more, determining a direction for oneself becomes more difficult because individuals are required to choose more and more from a pluralistic perspective: much more than in the past, they have to attend to the problem of balance between work, family and free time (Super, 1990). Finally, determining one's direction is hampered by the lack of unity in the concept of self. The various partial identities often indicate a variety of occupational opportunities.

How, then, can individuals arrive at a realistic sense of direction? In earlier times the functions in work organisations constituted the dynamic aspects of the world of work which, because of their changing nature, were not suitable as long-term signposts. It was different with the occupations hiding 'behind' specific functions in concrete work organisations: these occupations formed a relatively stable structure. But now that changes in the world of work are succeeding one another at an ever-increasing rate and are affecting the deeper structures of work, occupations are no longer immune. This means that occupations can no longer function as direction-finders in the world of work, goals towards which the individuals can make their way. Not even the labour market itself can provide an indicator of direction. The qualifications required by the labour market, in fact, change as rapidly as the functions from which they are derived (Arthur, 1994).

As far as we can see, there is but one aspect of the world of work that has remained reasonably stable (and can thus offer some orientation): the collection of domains at which the processes of production and distribution are aimed. By 'domain' we mean a collective area of needs vital to society, such as food, clothing, housing and health. The concrete production and distribution processes targeted on, for instance, the food requirement change continually over time. Even the nature of the food changes. But there is no essential change in the *need* for food. In this way, fourteen domains can be distinguished on which labour capacity is always targeted, generation after generation: food, housing, environment, tools, clothing, transportation, communication/information, education, security (justice/police), art/culture, recreation, health, economics and energy. Because of their stable nature, such domains can replace occupations as the key landmarks in the world of work.

Learning to plan and adjust one's own career

The responsibility placed on individuals for their own work allocation consists of more than the continual organisation of their personality and determining the direction they wish to take in the world of work. Individuals are also responsible for the development of skills necessary in order to gain and retain a place in work. These skills are to be found in three areas: that of work, that of education, and that of the labour market.

As far as the *work* area is concerned, this implies that individuals gain insight into the changes within the domain of their preference. How and in which direction are markets, products, organisations, functions and qualification requirements changing? In order to reply to this question, individuals need some sociological and economic insight. The sociological perception is required in order to be able to follow how the dominant actors in their domain are redefining the problems involved in satisfying needs within the domain. The economic perception is required in order to understand how, in the course of time, a change of market demands and production will occur as a response to the changes in the definition of the problem. Individuals can in this way come to obtain a picture of the future labour market demands in their domain: the technical-instrumental qualifications needed in order to be able to participate in the changed production process. Finally, individuals will require the skills needed to translate the acquired perceptions into concrete (strategic) action.

As far as *education* is concerned, individuals have to learn to tune the development of their qualifications to their talents, interests and

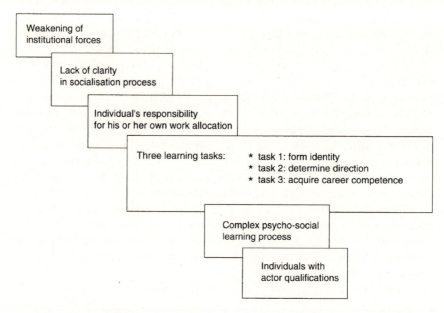

Figure 14.1 Model of how the individual carries the responsibility for his/her own work allocation

motivation (identity) on the one hand and to future market demands in the domain of their preference on the other. Since the changes in identity and in the domain will continue, the tuning of the qualification development will also have to be brought up-to-date from time to time. Qualification development must not only be tuned, but tuned in a planned way: individuals have to learn to opt for the correct educational trajectory on the basis of a qualification plan. Appropriate implementation of this plan requires not only learning skills and the skill to learn with others, but also learning to reinforce one's own weak sides (usually including the acquisition of the ability to cope with stress and fear).

If the qualification process progresses satisfactorily, individuals can in principle make a valuable offer to the *labour market*. In order to translate such an offer into a good labour agreement, however, more is required than simply technical-instrumental qualifications. Individuals need to learn to communicate their offer, to build up a network, to negotiate, to draw up contracts, and to establish a balance between work and free time. Such qualities can be grouped under the title of 'social-normative competences'.

The active competence required is clearly targeted on obtaining and keeping a job, we can call it *career competence*. Career competence should be seen as the fruit of the third learning task ('learn to plan a career and to guide oneself') which individuals have to perform in order to carry the responsibility of their own work allocation.

Actor competences

Developments in the domain of work allocation are shown in diagrammatic form in Figure 14.1. The learning result achieved by individuals who carry the responsibility for their own work allocation can be termed 'actor competences'. Earlier, we defined actor competences as qualities enabling individuals to appear on the social stage as actors, as persons who are no longer mainly passive. Actors do not only learn like animals, by means of conditioning and imitation: they also reflect on what they have experienced and learned. They have knowledge, skills and attitudes, but they also reflect on these on a metacognitive level. The result is that they know what they know and can do, and at the same time are aware of the shortcomings in their knowledge, skills and attitudes. It should be noticed that all these competences are based on a communicative capacity (an actor does not appear alone but always with others) and especially on the capacity to learn.

When people talk of actor competences, the criticism is often heard that the competences in question are the exclusive property of an élite and lie far above the capacities of the 'ordinary person'. But actor competences can, in principle, be acquired by everyone.

PROBLEMS IN THE DOMAIN OF WORK ALLOCATION

When we examine the development of the person/work relationship in five institutional contexts – namely, the primary community forms (family etc.), education, the labour market, the labour system and the care sector (i.e. the 'extended' social security system, including all institutionalised care) – the suspicion becomes stronger that many people cannot cope with their new responsibility of being a subject.

In *families*, it would seem that young people are finding it difficult to develop for themselves a more or less stable plan of action regarding work and working, while their parents feel powerless to help them in this. But it is not only young people and their parents who experience problems: many older men and women sit at home with nothing to do because they have no chance in the labour market.

In *education*, not only drop-outs constitute a growing problem but also the many pupils who opt for an educational trajectory without any hope of an appropriate destination in the work process. These pupils, too, represent a vulnerable group which is far from able to make a clear and well-

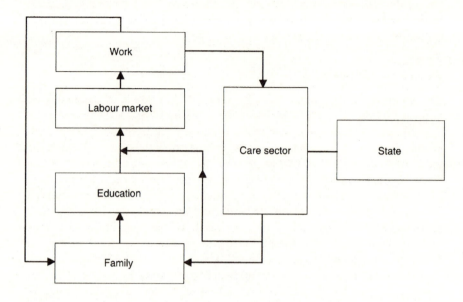

Figure 14.2 The social trajectory of the industrial society

motivated 'offer' on the labour market. Concern in the educational world regarding these problems is expressed in the increase in careers guidance offered to students in higher education.

On the *labour market*, it is becoming more than clear how difficult it is at the moment for many to get a job. In the industrial society, the labour market presented itself for individuals as an (often local or regional) opportunity structure. In post-industrial society, however, for more and more individuals the labour market has become a parking place 'guarded' by the officials of the labour exchange system. The familiar target groups for this system – racial minorities, women returning to the world of work, the handicapped and the long-term unemployed – remain a problem despite all of the extra effort expended. But older people, too, and people in general with out-of-date technical-instrumental qualifications and few social-normative competences, have little chance on the labour market. The rise in the number of re-training sessions, job application courses and other types of training where marketing techniques are applied show the recognition that there are shortcomings in those individuals trying to gain employment.

In the *work process*, it is quite evident that there are problems involved in holding on to work once it has been obtained. Reorganisation carried out in companies often reveals that part of the staff no longer have an 'offer'

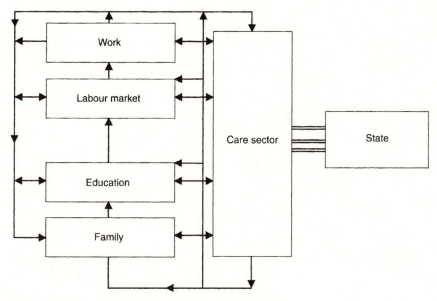

Figure 14.3 The social trajectory of the knowledge society

to make that fits with the demands of the internal labour market. In many cases this means that their 'offer' on the external labour market will be no stronger.

Finally, in the *care sector*, the problem of work allocation grows greater as the demands made on care increase while budgets remain static or are cut. Many people, often living on social security, who have spent some time in therapy or in some other way have made use of the services offered by the care sector, are placed under pressure to make efforts towards participation in the world of work. This group, because it has no hopes for the future, runs a grave risk of falling back into the care sector.

The magnitude of the influence exerted by the shortage of actor competences on the mutual relationships between the institutional contexts we have distinguished can be clearly seen from an historical comparison. Figure 14.2 shows – in a greatly simplified form – the social trajectory normally followed by individuals in the industrial society. It indicates that in the first decades after the Second World War the social trajectory was, for many, an unbroken line running from parental family, via education, the labour market and work, back to the individuals' own family. In this trajectory we recognise the standard biography which was offered and accepted in the course of the socialisation and enculturation process (DuBois-Reymond and Meijers, 1988). The relatively small box for the care sector and the lines

Contexts	Actors		
	Individual	Organisation	Government
Family	Family member	Family	Social services
Education	Pupil/student	School/university principal, careers advisor, teacher	Education authorities
Labour market	Job seeker	Employment office	Employment authorities
Work	Employee	Employer, personnel supervisor	Economic affairs authorities
Care sector	Patient/client	Hospital, psychiatric services, prison	Health and welfare authorities

Figure 14.4 Fifteen actors who risk becoming overburdened by allocation/career problems

joining that institution with other institutions indicate that the care sector at the time fulfilled a relatively modest social role.

In Figure 14.3 we see – again, in extremely simplified form – a picture of the social trajectory which frequently occurs today. This diagram indicates that social development of individuals is far less direct than earlier. People fall out of an institutional framework far more frequently and then return – often via the care sector – to an institutional context that they had quit. What is noticeable is that the care sector is far larger and more frequently used. Family, education, labour market and work are no longer capable of keeping the individual on 'the straight and narrow'. Thus the passage from one context to another is no longer so obvious and there is a growing need for mutual communication and tuning. In the five institutional contexts we mentioned, there are three different kinds of actors who can be distinguished and who, each on a different level, are faced with allocation/career problems of individuals as a consequence of their lack of actor competences: individuals; the organisations of which individuals are part or on which they are dependent; and the government bodies responsible for the institutional context as a whole.

In the *family*, the husband who is on long-term sick leave and the daughter who does not know what she wants both clearly have a problem. Research has shown that a situation of this sort does not leave the other members of the family unaffected (Te Grotenhuis, 1993; Te Grotenhuis and Meijers, 1994). The individual and family problems posed by the situation exerts pressure on governmental agencies and on social partners via such bodies as the social services.

In *education*, the pupil with too few actor competences has problems of motivation. The school suffers because a pupil of this sort disturbs the teaching and causes low educational returns. The education authorities bear the burden in the form of criticism of the entire educational system, low educational returns and frustrated teachers.

On the *labour market*, the job-seeker without actor competences has great difficulty in finding work. At the meso-level, the employment office and other mediating bodies also experience difficulties; and of course the employer would prefer a potential staff member who knows what is going on in the sector and is motivated and qualified to contribute to it. On the macro-level, people with a weak market position constitute a structural problem for state agencies which are concerned with employment.

In the *work process*, an employee with few actor competences is vulnerable. If the organisation gets into difficulties, he or she goes into dysfunction. For the individual involved, this is a painful experience, reinforced by the threat of job loss. But a dysfunctioning employee is also a burden to the company. Management, the personnel department and other colleagues often do not know how to deal with the situation. For this reason, external careers guidance counsellors are brought in. On the macro-level, governments are increasingly confronted with an economy in which a principal factor is human resources development (HRD). People without actor competences fit badly into HRD programmes and will eventually – in their own good time – almost certainly call on the already overburdened social security system.

Finally, in the *care sector*, a patient or client without actor competences is someone with little hope of social rehabilitation and reintegration since this can often only be achieved through work. Yet work is very difficult to obtain after a stay in the care sector. Since the patient or client can provide sufficient legitimation for not working, and for attention and income, it is not surprising that people do not easily give up this role when there is no prospect of an attractive alternative, i.e. suitable work. The stagnating flow into the labour market caused by a lack of actor competences faces the institutions in the care sector with a problem of capacity and with growing frustration amongst their own staff. The unsatisfactory link between care sector and work (via education and/or labour market) confronts the government once again with the limits of the welfare system.

In summary, it can be said that there are at least fifteen actors who are confronted with the allocation/career problem as a result of the individual's shortage of actor competences. They have been placed in a framework in Figure 14.4. Anticipating the description of the possible role for the careers guidance counsellor in solving the allocation/career problem, we propose that these fifteen actors should constitute the future target group of the careers guidance counsellor.

Why are cultural and social forces, which in earlier times eased individuals into a job, becoming weaker and more unclear? The world in which individuals lived in the 1950s was relatively small and stable. Since then, increasing international connections, based on greatly increased opportunities for communication and transport, have led to the paradox of what is known as the 'global village': the whole world as one single village. In this large and pluriform world, the old cultural and social framework is insufficient: it offers too little opportunity for interpretation and action for individuals to face up to its burgeoning complexity.

Within typical industrial organisations in the past, people worked within a role pattern that provided room for no more than a small part of the employee's personality. Now staff members are expected to be flexible, creative, stress-proof, involved in the culture and policy of the organisation, and possessing both learning capacity and social skills.

This type of role pattern clearly matches up with the fact that people have to process a great deal of information in order to remain up-to-date in the new, turbulent and complex world in which work organisations are forced to operate. Here organisations are characterised as learning, production processes as knowledge-intensive, and knowledge constitutes the greatest source of power (Toffler, 1990). The widely-used terms 'knowledge' or 'information society' as characterising the society which has come into existence in response to the demands of the 'global village' are, in our view, well chosen.

In the knowledge society, individuals have to find their own way in education and occupational life, without the unquestioned support of the traditional cultural and social forces. In work organisations the realisation has dawned that employees at every functional level must dispose of special competences such as flexibility and creativity in order to respond to the situation. The relationship between these competences and what we have called 'actor competences' is evident (London, 1993).

THE NEW ROLE OF THE CAREERS GUIDANCE COUNSELLOR

If actor competences are a requirement for individuals who have to plan their educational and professional career in the knowledge society, it is obvious that the careers guidance counsellor should play a role in the development of these competences. The clarification of career problems will, in fact, lead more frequently to the diagnosis of 'lack of actor competences'. To contribute to the development of actor competences in the working-age population, designed to prevent and to resolve allocation/career problems: this is how the role of the careers guidance counsellor in the knowledge society can be formally defined.

The careers guidance counsellor will place the main emphasis on the determination of learning goals and the stimulation and planning of learning processes. The work – consisting of support offered to individuals in the implementation of three learning tasks (i.e. formation of identity, determination of direction, and career planning/self-guidance – will take on a more educational character. Because of the complexity of the psychosocial learning process leading to actor competences, the work will also be more labour-intensive.

Earlier we distinguished five institutional contexts in which individuals can be troubled by allocation/career problems. Support in the solution of these problems means that the expert (or, as will more frequently be the case, a team of experts) will have to take account of the factors in the context which can brake or stimulate the learning process. The context-bound nature of the individual also implies that the expert will have to give his or her attention to the actors at organisational and government level. At the organisational level, the expert will be able to contribute to the creation of facilities in the organisation which are likely to encourage the learning process. Included in this category will be such things as advice to and training of management in work organisations targeted at providing support in the implementation of employee's careers plans. At government level, the expert will be able to give information regarding the nature of the career/allocation problems, and advice on institutional policy likely to create conditions under which the problems can be resolved at individual and organisational level.

The role described here still has, naturally, characteristics of the old role, but there are also differences. Metaphorically, we can compare the old role(s) with that of a ferryman and the new role(s) with that of a pathfinder. We hope that the adventure offered by pathfinding will compensate for the loss of security and clarity enjoyed by the ferryman.

REFERENCES

Arthur, M. (1994) The boundaryless career: a new perspective for organizational inquiry, *Journal of Organizational Behavior*, 15, pp. 295–306.

Drucker, P.F. (1993) *Post-Capitalist Society*, New York: Harper Business.

DuBois-Reymond, M. and Meijers, F. (1988) Das 'Mass Youth Project': auf der Suche nach einer 'modernen' pädagogischen Norm, in: W. Ferchhof and Th. Olk (eds) *Jugend im Internationalen Vergleich: Sozialhistorische und Sozialkulturelle Perspektive*, München: Juventa, pp. 133–50.

Gottfredson, L.S. (1981) Circumscription and compromise: a developmental theory of occupational aspirations, *Journal of Counseling Psychology {Monograph}*, 28 (4), pp. 545–79.

Kidd, J. and Killeen, J. (1992) Are the effects of career guidance worth having?: changes in practice and outcomes, *Journal of Occupational and Organizational Psychology*, 65, pp. 219–34.

London, M. (1993) Relationships between career motivation, empowerment and support for career development, *Journal of Occupational and Organizational Psychology*, 66, pp. 55–69.

Luken, T. (1990) Zelfconceptverheldering [Clarification of the self-concept], in: R. Spijkerman, A. Vincken, and M. Weekenborg (eds) *Handboek Studie- en Beroepskeuzebegeleiding {Handbook of Educational and Occupational Guidance}*, Alphen a/d Rijn: Samsom H.D. Tjeenk Willink, ch. 1050, pp. 1–23.

Meijers, F. (1991) Van kiezen en gekozen worden: grenzen en mogelijkheden van beroepskeuze-begeleiding [Choose or being chosen: limits and possibilities of careers guidance], in: R. Spijkerman, A. Vincken and M. Weekenborg (eds) *Handboek Studie- en Beroepskeuzebegeleiding {Handbook of Educational and Occupational Guidance}*, Alphen a/d Rijn: Samsom H.D. Tjeenk Willink, ch. 1400, pp. 1–34.

Meijers, F. (1992) 'Being young' in the life perceptions of Dutch, Moroccan, Turkish and Surinam youngsters, in: W. Meeus, M. de Goede, W. Kox and K. Hurrelmann (eds) *Adolescence, Careers and Cultures*, Berlin/New York: De Gruyter, pp. 353–73.

Super, D.E. (1990) A life-span, life-space approach to career development, in: D. Brown, L. Brooks and Associates, *Career Choice and Development*, San Francisco: Jossey-Bass, pp. 197–262.

Taborsky, O. (1992) *Loopbaan in Balans {Career in Balance}*, Tilburg: AMA.

Te Grotenhuis, H. (1993) *Bijstandskinderen: Opgroeien aan de Rand van de Verzorgingsstaat {Children on Welfare: Growing Up at the Edge of the Welfare State}*, Amsterdam: Amsterdam University Press.

Te Grotenhuis, H. and Meijers, F. (1994) Societal consequences of youth unemployment, in: A.C. Petersen and J.T. Mortimer (eds) *Youth Unemployment and Society*, Cambridge: Cambridge University Press, pp. 227–48.

Toffler, A. (1990) *De Nieuwe Machtselite {The New Power Elite}*, Utrecht: Veen.

Watts A.G. (1993) Promoting careers: guidance for learning and work, *National Commission on Education Briefing*, 15.

Wijers, G.A. (1987) *Een ontwikkelingspsychologgisch concept van beroepskeuze en arbeidsmarktprognoses {A developmental psychological concept of occupational choice and labour market prognosis}*, 's-Gravenhage: OSA.

Chapter 15

Confessing all? A 'postmodern guide' to the guidance and counselling of adult learners[†]

Robin Usher and Richard Edwards

While the funding and provision of guidance for adult learners has waxed and waned in the last years, its importance, and some would argue centrality, to the learning process has been asserted on a regular basis and from a number of quarters. From the mid-1980s to the early 1990s, UDACE (1986), the FEU (now FEDA) (1988) and NIACE (1990), among others, have consistently argued for impartial guidance prior to, during and on exit from learning opportunities. In its early phases, this approach can be seen as consistent with welfare models of society, where guidance was needed to enable access and widen opportunity. Towards the later 1980s this shifted slightly to engage with the increasingly important role given to guidance in the functioning of the labour market. The emphasis here came from government and particularly focused on the provision of guidance to unemployed adults as part of the process of action planning. This was also marked by a shift towards market models in the conception of guidance with criteria of efficiency, effectiveness and quality rising to the fore. Here guidance plays a central role in making the market in learning opportunities work, for as the latter have proliferated, so the range of opportunities available to adults has increased making choice an increasingly complex task.

Our intention here is not to disentangle the debates that have developed in this field. Our concern is more with the wider work which the discourses of guidance and counselling perform in relation to current social, economic and cultural processes. For while different strands in the discourses of guidance and counselling can be identified, there is a certain commonality in the assumption that these practices as well as being more efficient provide a more 'human', 'democratic' and 'empowering' form of educational experience than more traditional 'take it or leave it' educational provision. The argument is that the more individuals are given the opportunity to engage

---

[†] This chapter is an edited version of an article in *Studies in the Education of Adults*, 1995, 27(1): 9–23.

in understanding the choices available to them and to make their own 'authentic' choices – the more power is given to the adult learner – then the greater the degree of personal 'development' and 'empowerment' from the educational experience.

The basis for this commonality is the humanistic psychology most commonly associated with Carl Rogers (for example, 1980 and 1983). Here therapeutic notions of the importance of feelings to the authentic all-round expression of self are translated into educational discourses and practices with self-development and self-realisation constructed as a central normative goal. Individual experience and feelings are inserted into the educational processes and become the means by which rationality, skills and attitudes are developed. Thus, it is the whole 'person' rather than simply the 'head' and/or 'hands' which engages in and is affected by the educational process. This notion has had a very powerful effect, not only influencing liberal education, but also the fields of training, vocational education and human resource development. It has been one of the means by which the discursive and practical barriers between what were traditionally seen as different sectors have been elided.

The humanistic discourses of guidance and counselling can therefore be seen as playing a very important role in the contemporary structuring of learning opportunities. However, it is not our purpose to explain this discourse, evaluate its success or failure, or suggest ways in which it might be improved. Rather, we take Foucault's position that discourses are not to be explained in terms of their causes, the intentions of their 'authors' or the interests they appear to serve. Discourses are the means by which power is disseminated, the means by which power is given effect. They are imbued with power and have powerful effects. Thus they need to be 'named' and explored (Foucault, 1986a). It is precisely such a 'naming' we offer here. What we propose to do is to subject some of the central assumptions in the discourses of guidance and counselling to displacement – to see them in another way – because we would argue that their self-understandings and the understandings which they constitute are in danger of becoming an orthodoxy undermining the potential for a critical engagement with educational practice.

To effect this displacement we will situate person-centred guidance and counselling within two different yet related alternative discourses. The first of these is centred on the notion of 'confession' to be found in the later work of Foucault. We will draw on this to suggest that person-centred guidance and counselling and its empowering effects can be seen as an example of the 'pastoral power' at work in contemporary social formations where subjects are enabled to engage and identify with their own regulation or governing of themselves. The second is related to the more general question regarding modern and postmodern identities, and here we explore the paradox that guidance and counselling is becoming more central in a period when the achievement of its goals appears to be more unlikely. In respect of the notion of a postmodern identity, we suggest that guidance and counselling are a positional good in the construction of a lifestyle and are therefore more to do with desire than empowerment. In essence, we are suggesting, in line with work which has been done elsewhere (see, for example, Howley and Hartnett, 1992; and Metcalfe, 1992), that the field of guidance and counselling needs to go beyond the boundaries of its 'normal' discourses of 'skills', 'experience', 'contracts' and 'client-centredness' to construct more critical self-understandings.

CONFESSION AND PASTORAL POWER

The work of Foucault has started to receive more attention in the field of education in recent years and this is slowly extending into the field of adult learning. Here we wish to focus on Foucault's analysis of the ways in which power in modern society is extended and becomes ever more pervasive even as its discourses and practices become ever more 'humane'.

Foucault's work on sexuality is important here (Foucault, 1981 and 1986b). Rejecting the dominant view of the Victorian era as a period of sexual repression, Foucault (1981) charts the massive increase in discourses on sexuality in that period and argues that in bringing forth the body as an object of knowledge, 'sexuality' became ever more closely subject to regulation. Foucault describes the dominant notion of repressed sexuality as an example of the 'repressive hypothesis', the view that power is always a constraint wielded by the powerful over the powerless. Foucault argues that power should instead be seen as an active, productive force which 'creates' subjects (or subject positions), a process which while empowering also serves as a means for the more effective regulation of subjects. The notion of repression therefore misconstrues this growth of regulation, which in the process hides the 'work' that discourses of sexuality do in constructing the notion of autonomous self-expressing subjects freed from constraints. One effect of the repressive hypothesis is that a particular view of sexuality is 'naturalised', made an inherent characteristic of the embodied subject, thus concealing the effects of discursive practices in constructing sexuality.

In this view, people are positioned through discourses in a variety of subject positions, such as 'woman', 'man', 'child', 'parent', 'teacher', 'lover', 'clever', 'pushy'. It is through this positioning by a network of multiple determinations that discourses secure the affective and effective governing of people. The notion of a 'person' is therefore itself a discursive construct; to be a person is to occupy a subject position within a discourse. Persons are not 'natural' givens in the world, nor is knowledge of them a process of discovering or uncovering their 'reality', an assumption which lies at the heart of the notion that guidance and counselling allows individuals to express their own true feelings, interests and circumstances. Persons are rather constructed through 'knowledgeable' or expert discourses such as humanistic and psycho-dynamic psychology and their accompanying practices. This knowledge and expertise is thus conditional upon and a condition of the exercise of power, even as it is presented as a neutral process.

Bringing forth one's self as an object of knowledge through guidance and counselling is therefore a form of educational practice whose purpose is to make open for intervention those aspects of a person which have hitherto remained unspoken. To constitute the self as an object of knowledge is to discover the 'truth' about oneself where the guide/counsellor plays an active and powerful role; a process Foucault refers to as 'confession'.

> The confession has spread its effects far and wide. It plays a part in justice, medicine, education, family relationships, and love relations, in the most ordinary affairs of everyday life, and in the most solemn rites. . . . One confesses in public and in private, to one's parents, one's educators, one's doctors, to those one loves . . .
>
> (Foucault, 1981: 59)

With the spread of confession, its purpose shifts from one of salvation to self-regulation, self-improvement and self-development. In other words, confession actively constitutes a productive and autonomous subject *already* governed and thereby not requiring externally imposed discipline and regulation.

Confession works on the basis that there is something to be confessed, a deep truth or meaning hidden within subjects which once discovered opens the door to personal development, autonomy and emancipation. It is in this sense that confession is said to lead to 'empowerment'. Practices of guidance and counselling can be seen as forms of confession but where the meanings ascribed to self and experience are *already* effects of power. In order to participate 'successfully' in the process of confession subjects need to have already accepted, or be brought to accept, the legitimacy and 'truth' of confessional practices and the particular meanings that these invoke. Thus, in guiding and counselling adult learners, people need to be brought to accept themselves as 'learners' and as in 'need of learning' for their further development. Here, as Metcalfe (1992) suggests in relation to careers guidance, the aim is to help align student subjectivity with the various educational and psychological discourses available to help them reach a 'realistic' decision. 'Realism' already assumes certain forms of power which, as Wrench (1990) has suggested, systematically disadvantage minority ethnic groups through their humanistic focus on individual development.

Confession also works on the basis that there is someone to confess to.

Foucault (1981: 61) argues that confession is a 'ritual that unfolds within a power relationship, for one does not confess without the presence (or virtual presence) of a partner who is not simply the interlocutor but the authority who requires the confession'. It is in the very process of confessing that people are constituted as speaking and desiring subjects, and at the same time are enfolded in power as they become subject to the authority and authoritative discourse of the partner (the confessor) within the transaction. The confessional transaction generates 'material' spoken by the confessing subject, a body of knowledge through which subjects are inscribed in particular ways – for example, as a 'case' (Foucault, 1979a) – and thus become a site of intervention by the expert (the confessor). Through the expertise of the guide/counsellor, subjects become enfolded within a discursive matrix of practices which constitute their 'learning needs' and paths of self-development.

Even as confession has become central to modern forms of governance, its position as a 'regime of truth', a particular power-knowledge formation has been masked. In this sense the most effective forms of power are those which are not recognised as powerful because they are cloaked in the esoteric but 'objective' knowledge of expertise and the humanistic discourse of helping and empowerment. This power-knowledge formation of expertise and empowerment displaces the need for active containment and overt oppression; it is a form of power that spreads throughout the 'capillaries' of the social formation. Thus, an active, autonomous and productive subjectivity is brought forth in confessional practices even as it remains subject to the power-knowledge formations which 'bring forth' this form of subjectivity and invest it with significance. Confession therefore functions as regulation through self-regulation, discipline through self-discipline, a process which is pleasurable and even 'empowering', but only within a matrix of emancipation/oppression from which power is never absent.

The power of modern social formations can be analytically separated into disciplinary and pastoral aspects. Disciplinary power describes those processes through which knowledge about the population is gained by the nation state as a condition for the effective management and governance of the people. These processes are embedded in the knowledgeable (expert) discourses of the human sciences, sciences which provide knowledge about madness, deviancy, crime, and of course education. These discourses and their accompanying practices are power-knowledge formations which constitute the objects of their disciplinary gaze – for example, the deviant, the prisoner, the learner – and provide the basis for intervention, for programmatic action. Pastoral power, working through confession, enables individuals to actively participate in disciplinary regimes by investing their own identity, subjectivity and desires with those ascribed to them through certain knowledgeable discourses.

Pastoral power is a component, and a very important one, of contemporary governmentality which Foucault (1979b: 20) defines as 'an ensemble formed by the institutions, procedures, analyses and reflections, the calculations and tactics, that allow the exercise of this very specific albeit complex form of power'. For Foucault the notion of governmentality is a way of thinking power differently. Governmentality is discursive, 'a technology of thought' which constitutes a domain for programmatic action. However, it is not confined simply to the workings or deliberate policies of governments, but exists wherever 'the political programmes and objectives of government have been aligned to the personal and collective conduct of subjects' (Gane and Johnson, 1993: 9). In its most contemporary form governmentality is characterised by 'the entry of the soul of the citizen into the sphere of government' (Rose, 1990: 113). Through certain practices and techniques people's 'inner' lives are brought into the domain of power. This then is a governmentality where power seeks not only to govern bodies but also subjectivity and intersubjectivity and to do so not through force and repression but through 'educating' people to govern themselves.

Our argument is therefore that pastoral power is the contemporary form taken by governmentality. As Miller and Rose (1993: 102) point out, people's self-regulating capacities become allied with economic objectives. To realise oneself, to find the 'truth' about oneself becomes both personally and economically desirable – individuals, themselves ... can be mobilised in alliance with political objectives, in order to deliver economic growth, successful enterprise and optimum personal happiness'. Thus, it is not entirely surprising that pastoral power has developed at a time of economic crisis, when oppositional and resistant discourses and practices could potentially be highly disruptive to dominant patterns of economic and social change. Central to this form of 'governing' is the spread of guidance and counselling practices.

We would argue therefore that in the contemporary period the shift from disciplinary to pastoral power is particularly noticeable in the field of education. This shift is embodied in a wide range of practices to which guidance and counselling are central, for example action-planning, the accreditation of prior learning, portfolio-based assessment, learning contracts, records of achievement, continuous assessment, self-evaluation. Nor is this form of governmentality restricted to students. It also operates in relation to staff where increased importance is given to staff appraisal and human resource development. Thus, people are being encouraged to drive themselves ever harder, to accept even greater individual responsibility for themselves and their contributions to organisations and the social formation. 'Choice' and 'development' govern the guidance and counselling process, yet the senses of autonomy, responsibility and 'empowerment' this constitutes engenders an even greater requirement for guidance and counselling as the stress and anxiety of the apparent self-government engendered by confession creates its own problems. In other words, pastoral power becomes self-replicating, creating the conditions for its own proliferation, as the form of 'empowerment' engendered is a basis for the 'problems' it seeks to resolve. Guidance and counselling may therefore be considered a symptom of the contemporary form of governmentality rather than a cure for its ailments.

It is for such reasons that we have witnessed the spread of guidance and counselling throughout the social formation and within the discourses of adult learning. This development is also deeply paradoxical, as due to their basis in the process of confession and circulation of pastoral power, the very guidance and counselling processes through which people's difficulties are meant to be resolved actually result in further dislocation, as the sense of individual responsibility for one's condition, for the development of an autonomous and individualistic subjectivity and its accompanying stress displaces more 'social' sensibilities. Thus, confession can be seen to play a central aspect in the individualisation characteristic of modern society.

At one level individualisation provides the grounds for greater responsibility for self and enterprise as ties of kinship, community and tradition break down. This is a common enough argument. However, Foucault suggests that we ought to see this more as the shaping of a new form of identity and a reconfiguration of the way in which power is exercised rather than its transcendence. In this sense, the very breakdown of alternative ties is the result of the shaping and displacement introduced by pastoral power. The humanistic discourses of guidance and counselling which individualise adult learners are already part of an edifice of pastoral power, of a new form of governmentality which itself needs to be addressed.

IDENTITY, MODERNITY AND POSTMODERNITY

The displacement of the subject in contemporary social formations and the question of identity has been much debated in recent years (see, for example, Lash and Friedman, 1993; Keith and Pile, 1993). The work of Foucault and others, such as Lacan and Derrida, have provided a critical thrust in that displacement, one which has spread into the wider question of whether the changes we are experiencing in the contemporary world signify a shift from a modern to a postmodern condition.

Giddens (1990 and 1991) has argued that modernity – which as a historical period is held to have developed between the fifteenth and eighteenth centuries – is a process of constantly breaking with tradition, through a reflexive monitoring in an onward drive to progress and develop 'the new'. In this process of self-constitution, modern society and the modern nation state produces more information about itself as a condition for its ongoing development. This is not only true for nation states but also for individuals, a characteristic of the governmentality of modern social formations we discussed earlier. Modernity therefore signifies the loss of tradition at a personal as well as societal level where 'in the context of a post-traditional order, the self becomes a reflexive project' (Giddens, 1991: 32). In the contemporary context of what Giddens refers to as late modernity this process of reflexivity has been radicalised by the amount of information available, the media through which it is not only disseminated but also constituted, for example, printed text and electronic signal, and the range of options over which certain choices can and indeed have to be made. As Giddens (1991) and Bauman (1993) argue self-identity therefore becomes conditional upon a choice of lifestyles making life planning an integral component of modern existence.

Giddens (1991: 21) argues that this situation is 'existentially troubling' as the very uncertainty and reflexivity upon which modernity is grounded means that the choices confronting people are ambiguous and insecure. The assumption of a privileged position where the rational person presented with all the choices available is able to decide which is 'in their best interests' or which 'best meets their needs' becomes problematic as the process of reflexive self-questioning and existential anxiety becomes unstoppable. As people can never have complete information about all the conditions and possibilities of existence, they become dependent upon the expert systems which constitute the context and provide pre-packaged information for their life-planning and for direct guidance of their choices.

Although Giddens sees the place and functions of expert systems as part of modernity, they can perhaps be more readily seen as part of the attempt to keep modernity on the road, that is, to put some closure around what is existentially troubling. In this sense, life planning might be said to provide the grounds of identity – a sense of security – within the discourses through which people are constituted; the pastoral power we discussed above. Thus, life planning books and programmes are as much subject to a limiting of options within certain parameters as they are expanders of opportunity – the rainbows and parachutes people are invited to build for themselves only have so many colours, and people's personal constructs already assume a certain embeddedness in discourses of the self. It is the problematic nature of such groundings in the contemporary period which the notion of postmodernity addresses.

To a certain degree, Giddens' view of identity in late modernity is shared by writers on postmodernity, but there are differences of emphasis and explanation. For postmodernists, culture is no longer simply a form of representation, but has itself become commodified and central to the 'success' of flexible accumulation, the period of capital accumulation emerging from the crisis of inflation and low productivity in the 1970s (Harvey, 1991). In postmodernity, the notions of 'lifestyle' and 'image', and the proliferation and circulation of the latter through the media, are central. Image here is important in two senses, as a form of communication through the media

and as an expression of identity. Images help people to constitute an identity, a self-image. 'Life' itself is held to have become subject to
aestheticisation – a 'playfulness' where identity is formed (and re-formed)
by constantly unfolding desires expressed in lifestyle choices. Existential
anxiety is a function of desires which can never be satisfied, even with ever-
increasing knowledge about the self.

Postmodernity is therefore not simply restricted to a cultural domain,
but is part of a wider condition, where the increased volatility of image
results in an increased volatility of identity – 'as the pace, extension, and
complexity of modern societies accelerate, identity becomes more and more
unstable, more and more fragile' (Kellner, 1993: 143). This is the basis of
the argument that the contemporary subject has become decentred. Some,
for example Baudrillard (1988), take this even further and argue that the
very notion of 'identity' has itself become problematic.

In relation to life-planning, the paradox we referred to in relation to
confession is repeated, as the very volatility of the contemporary world
means that long-term planning is impossible. The particular emphasis on
consumption, lifestyle and image associated with the electronic media and
post-Fordist forms of production, distribution and consumption engender
new forms and possibilities for identity which are specifically postmodern.
'Life' is constituted through the global proliferation of images where taste
is produced and satisfied in new forms of production and marketing. The
new media enable image to be given greater cultural significance even as
images are commodified and consumed – 'the effect is to make it seem as
if we are living in a world of ephemeral created images' (Harvey, 1991:
289). Thus, while postmodern identity shares the reflexivity of modern identity, the former 'tends more to be constructed from the images of leisure
and consumption and tends to be more unstable and subject to change'
(Kellner, 1993: 153). Here, the uncertainties of identity which are troubling and require guidance and counselling as a form of alleviation can give
way to an excitement and pleasure in the constant forming and re-forming
of identities, a pleasure of which the confessional practices of guidance and
counselling may only be a part. In other words, in relation to postmodern
identity, guidance and counselling may not be a 'need', but a satisfaction
of desire, a pleasure to be consumed like any other (Bauman, 1993). The
search for the truth about oneself, the search for autonomous subjectivity
and 'self-realisation' is perhaps never-ending because it is a response to
desires which can never be fully and finally satisfied in this form.

For postmodernists, the discontinuity and fragmentation of identity has
in its extreme form been termed a kind of schizophrenia. The centred
rational subject at the heart of the reflexive project of self-identity in
modernity is decentred and subject to the production of images in which
'the serial and recursive replication of identities (individual, corporate,
institutional, and political) becomes a very real possibility and problem'

(Harvey, 1991: 289). In other words, reflexivity is not a transcendental activity undertaken by individuals, but is embedded in a particular image context or sign system. Identity is not an expression of self, but constituted (and re-constituted) through image(s). In working with adult learners therefore, rather than taking self-expressions as the reflection of an authentic, 'core' self, it is images and their significations which need to be challenged and deconstructed.

Harvey identifies two possible responses to the 'problem' of postmodern identity. The first is to become highly adaptable, basing choices upon short-term planning in order to maximise immediate possibilities. This is a position inscribed in much of the discussion of the need for a multi-skilled and flexible workforce and guidance and counselling practices associated with action-planning, individual training plans and records of achievement. However, the problems facing even this strategy have been made manifest in education by the length of time it can take to achieve certain courses of action, as the 1993 high levels of unemployed architectural and law students demonstrated. The second response is to become part of the production of volatility. This 'entails manipulation of taste and opinion, either through being a fashion leader or by so saturating the market with images as to shape the volatility to particular ends' (Harvey, 1991: 287), the position associated with what has been termed the 'new middle class' of which educational practitioners are themselves a part.

The relative merits of modern and postmodern conceptions of identity cannot be explored here. There is a sense in which both modern and post-modern, and maybe even traditional forms of identity can be said to co-exist in the contemporary world providing a complex pattern of overlaying and interaction. Any simple notion of the displacement of a modern by a post-modern condition therefore needs questioning. Both conceptions of identity articulate the paradox that life-planning is both a necessary and impossible response to the contemporary condition. This is consistent with the tension at the heart of pastoral power that produces consequences requiring the further development and extension of confessional practices. This is reinforced in postmodernity as confessional practices themselves become objects to be consumed by some in the construction of a lifestyle.

However, there is a fundamental difference between the modern view of the transcendental self for whom the finding of a stable identity is a normative goal and the postmodern perspective of the self as subject to image in which there is a 'playful' construction of multiple identities. Postmodernity is a world where people have to make their way without fixed reference points and traditional anchoring points. Consequently, as Kellner points out (1993: 158):

> identity today thus becomes a freely chosen game, a theatrical presentation of the self, in which one is able to present oneself in a variety

of roles, images, and activities, relatively unconcerned about shifts, transformations, and dramatic changes.

The differing conceptions of modern and postmodern identity therefore present great problems, as they affect how we view the purpose, content and means of engagement in the process of life planning. To conceive of the guidance process as at least partially about the mediation of image is a far cry from the dominant person-centred notions of choice, self-development and autonomous subjectivity. To articulate identity with desire, consumption and lifestyle may take many too close to an apparent market view of guidance and counselling. Yet if identity is not simply a matter of reason and autonomy, the postmodern reconstitution of identity can only be ignored or spurned on the very elitist grounds that many practitioners understand themselves to be struggling against.

END NOTE

We would want to stress that we value much of the practices of guidance and counselling that have developed in the field of adult learning and would wish to see more comprehensive and extensive provision than is currently possible. However, what we have suggested above is that the dominant humanistic and modernistic self-understandings which shape these practices need to be problematised. The discourses associated with these self-understandings marginalise and exclude important questions surrounding power and identity, questions which need to be constantly foregrounded amidst the uncertainties of the contemporary world.

REFERENCES

Baudrillard, J. (1988) 'Simulacra and Simulations', in M. Poster (ed.) *Jean Baudrillard: Selected Writings*, Cambridge: Polity Press.

Bauman, Z. (1993) *Modernity and Ambivalence*, Cambridge: Polity Press.

Foucault, M. (1979a) *Discipline and Punish: the Birth of the Prison*, Harmondsworth: Penguin Books.

Foucault, M. (1979b) 'On governmentality', *Ideology and Consciousness* 6, pp. 5–22.

Foucault, M. (1981) *The History of Sexuality Volume One: An Introduction*, Harmondsworth: Penguin Books.

Foucault, M. (1986a) 'On the genealogy of ethics', in P. Rabinow (ed.), *The Foucault Reader*, Harmondsworth: Penguin Books.

Foucault, M. (1986b) *The History of Sexuality Volume Three: The Care of the Self*, Harmondsworth: Penguin Books.

Further Education Unit (FEU) (1988) *Guidance and FEU REPLAN*, London: FEU.

Gane, M. and Johnson, T. (1993) 'Introduction', in M. Gane and T. Johnson (eds), *Foucault's New Domains*, London: Routledge.

Giddens, A. (1990) *The Consequences of Modernity*, Cambridge: Polity Press.

Giddens, A. (1991) *Modernity and Self-Identity: Self and Society in the Late Modern Age*, Cambridge: Polity Press.

Harvey, D. (1991) *The Condition of Postmodernity*, Oxford: Basil Blackwell.

Howley, A. and Hartnett, R. (1992) 'Pastoral power and the contemporary university: A Foucauldian analysis', *Educational Theory* 42, 3, pp. 271–84.

Keith, M. and Pile, S. (eds) (1993) *Place and the Politics of Identity*, London: Routledge.

Kellner, D. (1993) 'Popular culture and the construction of postmodern identities', in S. Lash and J. Friedman (eds) *Modernity and Identity*, Oxford: Blackwell.

Lash, S. and Friedman, J. (eds) (1993) *Modernity and Identity*, Oxford: Blackwell.

Metcalfe, A. (1992) 'The curriculum vitae: confessions of a wage-labourer', *Work, Employment and Society* 6, pp. 619–41.

Miller, P. and Rose, N. (1993) 'Governing economic life', in M. Gane and T. Johnson (eds) *Foucault's New Domains*, London: Routledge.

NIACE (1990) *Learning throughout Adult Life*, Leicester: NIACE.

Rogers, C. (1980) *A Way of Being*, Boston: Houghton Mifflin.

Rogers, C. (1983) *Freedom to Learn for the 80s*, Ohio: Charles E. Merrill.

Rose, N. (1990) 'Psychology as a "social" science', in I. Parker and J. Shotter (eds) *Deconstructing Social Psychology*, London: Routledge.

UDACE (1986) *The Challenge of Change: Developing Educational Guidance for Adults*, Leicester: NIACE.

Wrench, J. (1990) 'New vocationalism, old racism and the careers service', *New Community* 16, pp. 425–40.

Chapter 16

Accounts and the development of shared understanding in employment training interviews†

Neil Mercer and Jo Longman

INTRODUCTION

This chapter uses data from recorded interviews to offer an analysis of discourse which is focused on content rather than structure, and which is qualitative rather than quantitative. By bringing together concepts from two distinct areas of research, one concerned with 'accounts' and the other concerned with the development of shared understanding, we hope to shed new light on ways that talk functions as a medium for the presentation, sharing and reconstruction of knowledge.

Through talk, people are able to share experience, to create shared knowledge from individual resources. The body of 'common knowledge' which accumulates then provides a contextual foundation, a referential framework, which can support future talk (for example Edwards and Mercer, 1987; Mercer and Edwards, 1987). It is particularly relevant here because we approach our data as applied researchers, concerned with the extent to which the interviews in question – which have been carried out as part of an occupational skills training programme for unemployed adults – are successful as events in which a counsellor and a client share knowledge, negotiate a course of intended action and produce a written summary of the outcomes of their discussion.

Our analysis will consider the nature and communicative functions of the accounts which participants offer, and the ways that these accounts contribute to the body of common knowledge which provides the substantive and contextual basis for the talk in the interview. However, our analysis will also deal with other matters such as how interviewer and interviewee exercise power in the process whereby knowledge is shared and publicly presented. In particular, we will point to ways in which accounts offered by interviewees may subsequently be *appropriated* and *reformulated* by interviewers.

---

† This chapter is an edited version of an article in *Text*, 1992, 12(1): 103–25.

On a different level, we believe that our analysis offers useful insights into the relationship between official, institutional representations of interview procedures and how those procedures are realized in practice.

THE RESEARCH SETTING

Our data comes from a series of recorded interviews within a British national vocational training scheme called Employment Training operated from 1988. It is not necessary to describe this scheme here in any detail. Basically, it is one designed to facilitate the return of long-term unemployed people to the workforce by placing them in a suitable course of training. For people entering this scheme (known as 'clients'), the first substantial contact is with a counsellor whose job it is to (a) elicit clients' preferences for specific kinds of work, (b) identify clients' relevant vocational strengths and weaknesses, special needs and so on, and (c) propose suitable training (which may include such things as help with literacy and numeracy, as well as explicitly job-related skill training). It is a requirement of the scheme that each new client completes a 'Personal Training Plan' – a form which contains the information (a)–(c) above, and also an 'Action Plan' which summarizes an agreed course of action and is endorsed by the signature of both client and counsellor. The forum for completing the Personal Training Plan is an interview, usually lasting between 30 minutes and an hour, which each counsellor holds with each of their new clients. In the official manual of practice on the conduct of these interviews (Training Commission, 1988: 9), its aims are introduced to counsellors as follows:

> There are many ways to start people talking about themselves and their achievements, and the Initial Assessment interviews are about just doing that. You will be working with clients to identify their strengths and weaknesses in a number of different areas, to help them decide the options and opportunities best suited to their needs and abilities. . . . Your job is to be the client's advocate: to encourage each individual to present him or herself in the best possible light.

The philosophy underlying these procedures is thus represented as a 'client-centred' one, and one that is intended to encourage in clients an ability to take individual responsibility for their actions. Elsewhere (p. 4) the same manual says: 'The role of the TA [Training Agent, represented here by the counsellor] is to help clients make their own decisions so that they feel responsible for implementing the Action Plan.'

There is also an implication in this guidance that the counsellor should act as a kind of 'public relations' advisor to the client, helping them create in the Personal Training Plan a positive image of themselves as a potential worker. However, the counsellor is also charged with responsibility for obtaining information of a certain quality from the client. The manual says (p. 16): 'It is important to remember that, throughout the interview, you will be looking for EVIDENCE – real proof of what a person has achieved. It is only by identifying this evidence, based on what you are told, that you can actually determine what has been achieved.'

It is audio and video recordings of Initial Assessment interviews which constitute our main data. We also use interviews carried out by one of us with counsellors and clients to gain additional background information about the aims and expectations of the individuals involved; but this information will not be drawn on directly in this chapter.

PROCEDURE

How the interviews were recorded

Formal approaches through the Training Agent Network gained us access to interviews in seven locations, spread around the Midlands and north of England. One of the main interests of our project as a whole was in the appraisal of clients' literacy and numeracy through initial interviews. This means that while our intention to analyse recorded discourse was made clear to all participants, its purpose would almost certainly be perceived in terms of examining how literacy and numeracy skills were discussed by clients and counsellors. In total, seven weeks were spent on observation, with twenty nine interviews being recorded. A researcher was present at six of these interviews. On the other occasions the tape recorder was simply handed to the counsellor or placed in the room at the start of the interview, in view of participants. On two occasions, proceedings were recorded by a video-recorder set up in the interview room: the researcher was not present in the room on these occasions. Fourteen supplementary interviews of the same researcher talking with clients and counsellors both before and after interviews were also recorded.

Transcription conventions

In our transcripts the dialogue has been presented in a column format because we felt this revealed most clearly those features of the talk in which we were interested. For example, continuous talk by one speaker is more conspicuous as it is not broken up by supportive words like 'yeah' or 'I see' as it would be in script format. When the flow of talk is uninterrupted it is easier to focus upon issues of content and meaning as opposed to structure and turn-taking (although these are adequately represented for the purposes of our analysis).

The interviewee's talk is located in the left-hand column and is labelled as 'client', the interviewer's talk is found in the right-hand column, labelled 'counsellor'. Because we read from left to right, we may be predisposed to place more importance on the talk on the left of the page (see Ochs, 1979). We therefore took a conscious decision to locate the client's talk in the left-hand column to try to elevate its status in the eyes of the reader. When the two participants speak simultaneously the dialogue is on the same line. A square bracket marks the point at which the first speaker was joined by the second speaker. The dialogue has been punctuated to aid under-standing. A speaker pausing noticeably (i.e. at a point or for a duration which it did not seem appropriate to represent by standard punctuation) is represented by (.), or if the pause was longer than 1 second, by (n secs). Where the examples start off or finish in the middle of a speaker's turn, this is represented by (. . .). Words emphasized by the speaker are underlined. Any relevant non-verbal features are in parentheses (for example (laughs)) and comments about the dialogue that we have made are in italics.

THE CONCEPT OF 'ACCOUNT' IN PREVIOUS RESEARCH

The notion of an 'account' is potentially very broad: any report, story or explanation could reasonably be termed an account. However, as Potter and Wetherell (1987: 74) explain:

> there is a more restricted technical sense of this term marking out the discourse produced when people are explaining actions which are unusual, bizarre or in some way reprehensible (Scott and Lyman, 1968). If you are caught doing something which appears odd – perhaps someone walks into your room while you are wearing your underwear on your head – you will want to account for your behaviour: you might, for example, explain that you are exploring possibilities for Saturday night's fancy dress ball. If this account is successful, your behaviour will seem rather less odd.

The analysis of these kinds of accounts in conversation can be traced back directly to the work of the philosopher Austin (1961). Within the research tradition this generated, accounts have been defined as statements made to explain behaviour which is viewed as untoward, inappropriate or unex-pected. Sociologists, psychologists and linguists followed philosophers in studying accounts.

Conversation analysis, as referred to by Potter and Wetherell (1987), takes everyday 'trivial' conversation as the archetype for the analysis of all interactional talk. It is essentially naturalistic microsociological research, emerging from ethnomethodology (see Heritage, 1984), and within it there is an overriding emphasis on the importance of language in the creation and maintenance of the social world. Discourse is treated as a 'potent, action-orientated medium, not a transparent information channel' (Potter and Wetherell, 1987: 160). Conversation analysts attempt to describe how the talk of individual speakers contributes to the construction of conversational discourse. With regard to accounts, their interest has focused on the points at which accounts (especially those which act as 'explanations for one's conduct', McLaughlin, 1990) are normally introduced. Some interesting work in this field is that of Atkinson and Drew (1979), whose analyses of the discourse of law courts show how accounts are elicited and offered and the 'conversational work' that is thereby accomplished. In strict conversation-analytical terms an account is identified as one element of a particular type of interactional talk sequence. For example, question and answer normally go together to constitute what would be termed an *adjacency pair*. On some occasions, a speaker responds to a question or statement with a remark which is not the expected one. This is what is called a *dispreferred response*. This unexpected response is then often followed by an explanatory account. An example from our own data would be as follows:

Client	*Counsellor*
	You also experienced operating machinery. Was it on like a production line? The kind of work you were doing?
Well, I just put that down (*dispreferred response*). But now you said that, I used to work on a production line (*offers an account*).	

For us, the relevance of the conversation analysis approach lies in its depiction of accounts as conversational events which, although produced by individual speakers, are most properly understood as elements of a social, interactional process. Our prime interest is in the content of conversations and how knowledge is shared; accounts offered by one speaker are an obvious source of information to the other. But what information is included, and how that information becomes part of the knowledge shared by both speakers, cannot be explained simply in terms of the kinds of accounts that are offered. We need also to know how accounts are elicited, and what use, if any, is made of the information contained in an account in the subsequent conversation.

The variability of accounts

Also relevant to our interests is the research of Potter and Mulkay (1985). They examine how scientists account for the nature and outcomes of their research endeavours in different talk settings – comparing, for example, the accounts offered in the official arena of a conference with those given in informal, one-to-one conversations. One of the most striking aspects of their findings is the variability of the accounts offered by the same speakers in different settings. Potter and Mulkay use their findings to argue that there are no valid criteria for taking one conversational event, any one account, as the 'definitive version'. They suggest that, instead of trying to overcome this variability of account, researchers should focus their attention on it, as an indication of what the speaker is trying to achieve through talk in a particular setting.

For us, this research emphasises that accounts are normally highly context specific. They are sensitive to the social settings in which they are produced, and depend for their meaning on a contextual framework created by the earlier conversation and other shared activity of the speakers involved. Potter and Mulkay thus account for the 'inconsistency' of speakers across settings. But equally interesting, perhaps, is the issue of how listeners – the recipients of accounts – are able to comprehend and judge the adequacy of accounts in such variable circumstances. As McLaughlin (1990: 66) points out in her discussion of explanations, an 'obvious feature of explanations is that they are often explicitly solicited. What is less apparent is that the form of these solicitations influences the shape the explanation takes'. Listeners will collaborate with the speaker in the creation of a suitable framework of shared understanding within which any particular account will appear normal to both participants. This highlights an essential feature of accounts: they will only be effective if they are constructed to take account of the limitations of that shared contextual framework. An account which is at odds with the contextual flow of a conversation may be, at first hearing, incomprehensible, as the following example from our data shows:

Client	*Counsellor*
	So you left school when you were sixteen?
Yes.	
	That's going back to 1977. You don't look that old.
I've had a haircut and a shave.	
	You've had what?
I've had a haircut and a shave.	
	(Laughs) You left in '77, that's what 12 or 13 years ago now isn't it . . .

ANALYSIS

What do we mean by an account?

Despite those relevant features discussed above, we found that the body of previous research on accounts did not offer any single analytic approach which was well-suited to our research interests. We were indeed interested in how participants accounted for themselves, but had no particular interest in developing or using a comprehensive typology of accounts. We were not so much interested in accounts as identifiable structural features of conversations, but in the process of accounting and how this related to the development of shared understanding. This interest relates to a point made by Cody and McLaughlin (1990: 232) about the benefits of doing a 'fine-grained analysis of what actors actually say', thereby examining accounts in conversational contexts. Moreover, although we were interested in how the participants did the 'conversational work' of the interview, revealing how discourse was being structured through, for example, the creation of 'adjacency pairs' seemed to carry us only part of the way towards the explanations we sought. From an applied perspective, our interest was in how the interview functioned as a forum for (a) allowing the counsellor to gather information from the client, (b) allowing the client to express their own perceived training aims and needs, and (c) constructing a Personal Training Plan for the client which was considered appropriate by and acceptable to both parties (with the counsellor's criteria for acceptability reflecting their professional, institutionally grounded responsibilities). Our interest in accounts had developed when the preliminary examination of our data showed that interviews rarely functioned as a straightforward information sharing and gathering event, culminating in the completion of a suitable plan of action. We saw that clients had to 'account for' their employment histories, their training needs and vocational aims. To a lesser extent, counsellors 'accounted for' the procedures they were following and the proposals they made. Much of the joint activity in the interview conversations pivoted on and developed from utterances which explained or justified something said or done by the speaker. These utterances were, then, our 'accounts'.

Accounts as 'common knowledge'

It also seemed to us that earlier research on accounts had paid little attention to the function of talk as a medium for creating joint accounts of events. Through talk, people may strive for mutuality and consensus, using discussion and argument to achieve a shared world-view, a 'common knowledge'. In such ways are opinions and explanations tested and validated, different perspectives compared and perhaps reconciled, and (in some

settings) 'official' versions of events constructed from shared individual rec-
ollections. Earlier research had shown clearly how 'conversational work' may
be directed towards such ends (for example Edwards and Mercer, 1987;
Mercer and Edwards, 1987). In the study of interviews which were explicitly aimed at achieving a mutually agreed 'Personal Training Plan', this aspect
of talk seemed of potentially crucial significance. Moreover, as mentioned
earlier, the institutional definition of these interviews depicted a collaborative venture, with the counsellor as a facilitating agent for the expression of
the client's abilities, aspirations and training needs.

Power in the interview: the reformulation of accounts

Most of the research by us and our associates referred to above was conducted in educational settings, and was concerned with the analysis of
teacher–pupil discourse. A common finding in such research, and by others
before us (for example, Edwards and Furlong, 1978), is that teachers exercise considerable control, through talk, over which ideas and information
offered by pupils are to be considered as legitimate contributions to the
lesson. This is much more than a matter of acknowledging pupils' answers
to questions as correct or incorrect. Edwards and Mercer (1987: chapter 7)
offer a list of features of classroom discourse which reflect teachers' control
over the expression of knowledge. For example, contributions made by pupils
may be acknowledged as worthy, and yet in some ways not adequate to
the teacher's requirements of the discourse as a teaching-and-learning
activity. In such circumstances, teachers may re-cast or *reformulate* pupils'
statements, offering them back to the class in a form which better suits
their (normally implicit) teaching purposes and goals. At other points in
the discourse, teachers may exercise similar control by *reconstructively recapping* earlier talk and activity in class, presenting a revised, edited version
of past experience shared by teacher and children which is in accord with
educational requirements.

In the interview setting, we were similarly interested to see if counsellors' professional aims and agendas were reflected in the re-casting of clients'
contributions to the discourse, and in the reconstructive recapping of earlier
discussion. We were also interested to test the extent to which the formulation of what purports to be the client's own Personal Training Plan and
Action Plan is in fact under the strong control of the counsellor. Thus we
wished to know if the participants collaborated to construct joint accounts,
and if in that constructive process counsellors could be seen to control the
ways clients' accounts were 'officially' represented in the process and
outcomes of the interview.

A case in point

We will use the content of one interview to explore the above matters further. This is an interview between a white, female counsellor (in her late twenties) and a male client (early thirties, also white). The accents of both participants reveal that they are indigenous members of the local community (a north Midlands industrial town).

As she begins the interview, the counsellor already has before her some brief preliminary information, provided by the client, about his employment training aspirations. As they sit down, the counsellor begins the interview by referring to this information:

Client	*Counsellor*
	Let's have a look.
I were gonna change sommat on there actually. Thinking about it, I filled in HGV or PSV, crossing out PSV and shoving in (.) cos I'm quite interested in Household Electronics.	

It thus becomes clear that one of the goals the client has in mind is becoming qualified to drive commercial road vehicles, either heavy goods vehicles (HGV) or buses (PSV), with another being training as an electrician. The counsellor moves on to ask the client about his employment history. She asks questions like:

'So have you ever worked before?'
'Where was the last firm you worked for?'
'And what did you do there?'
'So that'd take you back to, not '83, late '84?'

It seems clear that the kind of information she requires in order to fill in the form is brief and factual: job titles, job descriptions, names of firms and dates of periods of employment. However, the client's response to such enquiries do not always match these requirements. He sometimes seems loth to, or unable to, provide exact dates and other information as these responses show:

'I was only there for a few months'
'Haven't a clue'
'But I was only there for uhhh six weeks'

On the other hand, he sometimes offers quite elaborate responses to enquiries. For example, in the following passage, he is responding to an enquiry about his experience as a general labourer in the construction industry:

Client	Counsellor
Well, it started off as being employed as a general labourer,	Yeah
[by the end of it I was dumper driver, forklift driver, tractor driver, scaffolder.	
	So it's really sort of like construction then.] construction worker.
Yeah I got collared for everything.	
	Kept you busy.
Well it's uhh (.) I <u>knew</u> what I was <u>doing</u>.	

This short passage has a number of interesting features. First, the client's account of his labouring experience is in terms of skilled roles he performs, three of which involve driving. The client thus offers an account of his experience in a labouring job which presents it as, in essence, a driving job, relevant experience for someone who wishes to train as a lorry driver. However, the counsellor re-formulates this as 'construction worker'. Two compatible explanations for this seem likely. One is that she simply feels that this is the best way to summarize that experience on the form. A second is that it is well known amongst counsellors that HGV training is heavily oversubscribed: it is unlikely she will be able to find her client a place, and so wishes to steer him away from that option and towards the more 'realistic' goal of training related to construction work.

The counsellor goes on to make an interesting interpretation of the client's next, elaborating remark. The idea of being 'kept busy' has very different connotations from the idea that a person is so skilled and adaptable that they get asked to do everything. The client responds with a kind of account. Within the framework of conversation analysis (Atkinson and Drew, 1979), his account has certain characteristic delivery features which mark it as a particular kind of disagreement, a 'dispreferred response' in an adjacent pair. First, the remark begins with 'Well . . .'; and there is a delay component (the pause marked (.)) before the disagreement is broached. The client thus voices his dissatisfaction with the counsellor's gloss on his earlier remark. The potential disjunction is not addressed, as the counsellor turns her attention back to the form, and to dates.

The conversation in the extract above embodies a struggle between conflicting accounts and representations, and it is a struggle which continues throughout this transcript. Later on in the interview, the counsellor again takes up the option of construction work, and presents it in a positive light.

Client	Counsellor
	. . . Would you not think of considering the construction trade and actually getting trained up in some aspects of that, see]ing as how you've done a long time in that.
Ummm	
I spent quite a lot of time on it and it's [	Would you like to get the actual proper skills, you know the qualified skills.
Well, I'm [I'm not very good in (.) mm brickwork and whatever, or anything like that I like joinery.	cos
	Yeah, you see what I'm thinking of is (.) um driving, it always is one of the hardest places to get a placement in, you know, that type of work. Ummm to go on to to to HGV driving . . .

Following our own definition, there is a lot of accounting going on in this extract. The counsellor explains to the client why she believes construction work training is a sensible option: she points out that he has considerable relevant experience, and makes explicit her knowledge about the relative unavailability of HGV training placements. The client, on his part, voices his lack of enthusiasm for that option both through the style of his responses and the disclaimer of some relevant skills. There is quite a lot of negotiation going on at this point. We can see here information being offered, knowledge being made joint. It also seems as if both parties recognize that this is a particularly sensitive part of the discussion: they 'tread carefully', expressing ideas tentatively, and the talk is marked by pauses and stammers.

At other points, both parties offer accounts in ways which, while still offering personal knowledge for joint consideration, are less mutually supportive, more antagonistic:

Client	Counsellor
	I'm just thinking that like in the construction trade, if if you were applying for a job you've got sort of

Yeah but I mean in, it's the majority of time in the construction business I've been driving.

Yeah.

Yeah. I've been driving them for years now 'n never needed one.

Yeah

like, 20 months experience there, um,] you've got the experience there as well.

Mm (.) yeah, what about getting uh like a forklift certificate or something like that.

Cos you could you could go through for something, um of that nature. I could ring through.

Mm, well apparently there's new rules that have just come out to say that you need, you know you've got to have a certificate to be able to do that type of work.

Eventually, the interview moves into a discussion of the client's 'hobbies and interests' (its content following the sequence of items on the Personal Training Plan form).

Client

Yeah, and well I like D.I.Y.

So, I'm forever doing jobs for friends.

Ummm
Woodworking, glazing, ummm, bit of electrics bit of plumbing.

(4 secs) It's cos I've [
It's mainly cos I've got quite a few tools as well.

So I can do these jobs.

Yeah.

Counsellor
. . . Right, hobbies and interests. So, you like hiking and walking do you.

Yeah

Yeah, so what sort of D.I.Y. things do you] do is it like woodworking that sort of side or].

Mm, right so um
I'll put do it yourself home] maintenance.

Yeah.

Right so I'll put do it yourself home maintenance that sort of
like covers all, all] aspects of the type of things.

Here the client rejects the first formulation by the counsellor of his hobbies and interests. Instead, he goes on to offer examples which fit more into a 'work experience' rather than a 'leisure' frame ('bit of electrics, bit of plumbing'). However, the counsellor, while accepting the new content, is not drawn into a 'work' frame. This is probably because she is at that point filling in the 'hobbies and interests' section of the form; but her reluctance may also reflect an unwillingness to consider another possible field of training for the client. Nevertheless, as the interview continues, the client continues to invoke this experience, and the discussion eventually moves into a direct consideration of training in carpentry and joinery. In this respect, the client can be seen to exercise control over the content and direction of the discussion, an influence comparable to that of the counsellor when shifting the focus of the interview away from HGV driving.

Where the counsellor's influence remains strong throughout the interview is in deciding how information offered by the client should be re-presented on the form. For example, following the introduction of joinery as a topic, this interchange occurs:

Client	Counsellor
I've still got quite a few of me tools	
	Yeah. Now (.) that's involved in
Yeah	construction industry and in] sort of like your D.I.Y. So put that in.
(3 secs) I've still got me scaffolding (.) spanners.	
	Right. Ummm (.) right so you've got quite a lot of things down there. Looking at the um, jobs that you've done when you were refitting at the
Er jackhammering mainly	hotel what sort of work were you
Ripping out	doing there was it any]
	So it was sort of like ta]king it ripping it out and sort of like so it's um (.) I'm just trying to think.
Gutting	
	Yeah (.) um so its (2 secs) preparation of premises, make it sound nice.
Full refurbishment	
	Full refurbishment.

Having rejected her own ('ripping it out') and the client's even more graphic description of his work ('gutting'), she reformulates this experience in terms which, in her informed judgement, better fits the requirement of the form (which, as mentioned earlier, is officially defined as a rhetorical document, part of a 'marketing exercise' on the client). To the client, she briefly accounts for this reformulation by saying that she is 'making it sound nice'. The client collaborates in this reformulation, offering 'full refurbishment'.

As in most of the interviews we observed, there are many instances of this counsellor referring to the requirements of representing what is discussed on 'the form'. Indeed, the sequence of content headings on the Personal Training Plan form is probably the strongest single determinant of the path taken by the discussion in all the interviews in our sample. Often, references to the form being filled in by the counsellor are coupled with references to the client's supposed ownership of it and/or collaborative role in its completion:

'put yourself down then as "quick" . . . Put that down OK.'
'so we'll put that down on there and we'll put it on this other form that we were completing.'

It is eventually agreed that the client should sign up for a course in carpentry and joinery. The counsellor completes the form accordingly, and as she does reconstructively recaps the client's contribution to the discussion as an account of why this is a suitable option. Note that the client has made no mention in the interview of seeking formal qualifications:

Client	Counsellor
	So obviously you want to get a qualification so that you can prove to people that you can do the job, and you hope it'll sort of lead you into a job. So I'll just read this through to you, I put that you've had past experience and that you feel that you've got the skills and tools to be able to complete the training, gain qualifications and eventually to get a full-time job. Does that sound]
Yep (*said very quietly*)	all right to you?
	Right, do you want any help brushing up on your metric conversions?
No, I'm all right, thanks.	

Towards the end of the interview, after the decision about training has been made and consolidated, the counsellor says:

'But I don't want to dissuade you from your original choice.' (i.e., *training to drive heavy goods vehicles*).

Her choice of the word 'original' here is interesting. It suggests that HGV driving was not the client's first choice in terms of priority, but simply his first choice in terms of time. This therefore implies that the client has changed his mind rather than compromised his preferences. In the closing stages of the interview, the counsellor offers the form to the client and says:

'I need you to . . . pop a signature just there on that one. That's to say that we've gone through all the paperwork and that you're happy with what we've decided. All right?'

DISCUSSION

The quality of accounts

The purpose and procedure of the interview clearly requires the client to account for his employment history, to explain what he did in particular jobs. The counsellor elicits such accounts from the client asking for information which can be written down, whose status thus is that of documentation: it becomes public, albeit *restrictively*, and so might be held up by some authority for verification. The counsellor elicits information in ways which directly reflect the content headings of the form she is completing on his behalf. She is thus visible as – and indeed, sometimes accounts for herself as – the agent of a greater authority (that which produces the forms, and which no doubt holds their completed versions in its files). This authority might well be assumed by clients to have access to, or be seeking, other information about their histories and present circumstances (for example, whether they were really unemployed, or in fact following some clandestine occupation). It is to this authority that both participants in the interview are, ultimately, accountable for the outcome of the interview.

The interview procedure elicits accounts by the clients of two kinds (a) those explanations and elaborations of past experiences which are offered in direct response to the enquiries of the counsellor, and (b) accounts of a more 'structural' kind, the 'dispreferred responses' of conversational analysts, in which the client disagrees with a formulation offered by the counsellor and justifies his disagreement. The counsellor offers relatively fewer of both kinds of account. She sometimes justifies her views by sharing professional knowledge with the client (for example regarding HGV training being over subscribed), and sometimes explains what she is doing by reference to the requirements of 'the form'.

Reformulation and control

Despite frequent references by the counsellor to the client's supposed active participation in completing the form there is little evidence in the discourse of the client treating this task as one which is within his control. And, as accounts are elicited, offered and discussed, the process which we observe is better described as one of negotiation, rather than collaboration. The counsellor enquires, the client responds. The counsellor offers reformulated versions of the accounts of personal experience provided by the client, and the client corroborates or disagrees with these accounts. The counsellor proposes courses of action, the client accepts or declines these proposals. When the client offers new, unsolicited information, its relevance to and inclusion in the discussion, (i.e. its status as relevant 'common knowledge') must be negotiated with – made accountable to – the counsellor.

All our data confirm that counsellors exert enormous control over what is included in the written outcome of the interview, and they do so both in terms of content (what is included and what is left out) and in terms of style (how things are represented). The final section of the official form asks for succinct 'reasons for employment aim', and the counsellor in the above interview is typical of those we have observed in drawing the interview to a close with a reconstructive recap of the client's deliberations in making a final decision about training. Despite the official rhetoric of the Personal Training Plan being in the ownership of the client, its production most certainly remains in the control of the counsellor.

The institutional context

In terms of functional effectiveness in its institutional context, the interview we have analysed above can be considered to have achieved a reasonably positive outcome. While the client's initial and preferred choice for a course of training was not realized, the content of the agreed course (carpentry and joinery) does reflect the client's own declarations of interest and experience. For the counsellor, the agreed course represents a realistic, practical option, as it takes account of their professional knowledge about where training and employment opportunities lie. Accounts have been effectively elicited, knowledge has been shared, representations negotiated and agreement reached about outcomes. We would not evaluate all of the interviews in our sample so positively. In many, counsellors are less successful in eliciting accounts, and clients are less articulate and forthright in expressing their aspirations and preferences. In some, the course of action eventually agreed seems more an outcome imposed by the counsellor, rather than one emerging genuinely from the negotiation of shared ideas and expectations.

But however positive its outcome, our analysis of the above interview reveals some interesting and problematic aspects of the procedures being followed. These aspects are common to most, if not all, of the interviews we have observed. It seems likely that these aspects will be features of many other institutional settings for talk besides those of occupational training, because of the nature of these social encounters and the institutional procedures and ideological framework which generate them.

One of the most significant kinds of work performed by counsellors in the interviews is one which receives no explicit mention in the official manual of interview practice. This is the task of reformulation, taking information obtained from clients and recasting it to create a version of the clients' experience and their 'strengths and weaknesses' which is suitable for inclusion on the form. There is more to this than the completion of discrete sections of the form. Counsellors are in fact faced with a rhetorical task, using information provided by the client to construct within the constraints of the form a potted history and character sketch of someone who is well-matched to the course of training they are going to follow.

Professional responsibilities and ideological dilemmas

Other aspects of the particular encounters we observed also have an interesting relationship to the institutional representation of these encounters, as set out in the official manual of practice (Training Commission, 1988). The manual makes clear that the counsellor is responsible for – professionally accountable for – the quality of the information, the 'evidence', in the client's form. The completion of the form is clearly given the utmost priority by counsellors, and notwithstanding the official rhetoric of its ownership by the client, they maintain strict control over how it is completed and what it contains. Yet the manual also emphasises that the philosophy of the interview should be client-led. Although counsellors maintain strong control over the content of the form, this philosophy is strongly reflected in stylistic features of counsellors' talk. Reformulated accounts are typically offered back to clients as either joint constructions ('We can put . . .') or as the client's own words.

On the one hand, counsellors are expected to exercise their own greater knowledge of the system and guard their professional accountability through exercising strong control over proceedings. They work under pressure of time: the form is long, they are required to achieve a completed form for each client, but they are paid according to numbers of clients successfully dealt with. On the other hand, they are expected to allow clients to determine their own course of action, and even to run the interview itself as training which will encourage clients to make their own decisions so that they feel responsible for implementing the Action Plan to which they eventually put their signature.

In facing such a dilemma, these counsellors share a problem with other professionals who are responsible for both the elicitation through dialogue of information from their 'clients' and professionally accountable for the quality of that information. School teachers provide an obvious example.

Oral and literate dimensions of the interview

However, Initial Assessment Interviews make some requirements of counsellors which are not experienced by teachers in the day-to-day business of the classroom. The most obvious of these is the obligation to produce for each conversation a documented outcome. An important part of counsellors' professional work is the vicarious conversion of information gained through talk into a written product, the client's Personal Training Plan form. We have seen that the structure of the form shapes and dominates the discourse, and that counsellors give very high priority to its completion. The information required is initially in the hands of the interviewee, and that person will be required to sign to acknowledge ownership of the accounts thus represented. And again the professional is accountable for the kind and quality of information required, and may in the process of interview make selective judgements about what should be written down, and render accounts given into a quite different style of language while still retaining the format of a first-person singular account.

CONCLUSIONS

Early research on accounts was mainly concerned with types of account and their informative function. More recent research has focused on how accounts operate as structural elements in the creation and maintenance of conversation. Such research has recognized the essentially interactive, responsive nature of accounts, but has not given particular attention to the content of accounts or to the ways in which content is intimately related to the historical, contextual framework of conversation. Other recent research has examined the content of accounts which are offered in specific cultural contexts, and contrasted and compared accounts offered in different contexts. None of this research, however, has directly addressed the ways that conversational patterns elicit or respond to accounts, and in particular the ways that the information provided by speakers in accounts may be selectively *appropriated* and *reformulated* by partners in subsequent conversation. That is, no prior research has given direct consideration to accounts as dynamic elements of the content of conversations. We hope that in this chapter we have shown that accounts represent an important raw material for 'conversational work', and that the elicitation, presentation, and reformulation of accounts is a process which is shaped by the roles and relationships of conversational partners. In particular, an analysis of this process can reveal ways in which one or other partner controls the development of the content of a conversation. In practical terms, we see this approach as providing a basis for the development of techniques for the evaluation of counselling interviews and similar institutional forms of discourse, and for the in-service training of counselling staff.

REFERENCES

Atkinson, J.M. and Drew, P. (1979) *Order in Court: The Organization of Verbal Interaction in Judicial Settings*, London: Macmillan.

Austin, J. (1961) *Philosophical Papers*, Oxford: Clarendon Press.

Cody, M.J. and McLaughlin, M.L. (1990) Interpersonal accounting. In *Handbook of Social Psychology*, H. Giles and W.P. Robinson (eds), 227–55. Chichester: John Wiley & Sons.

Edwards, A.D. and Furlong, V.J. (1978) *The Language of Teaching*, London: Heinemann.

Edwards, D. and Mercer, N. (1987) *Common Knowledge: The Development of Understanding in the Classroom*, London: Methuen/Routledge.

Heritage, J. (1984) *Garfunkel and Ethnomethodology*, Cambridge: Polity Press.

McLaughlin, M. (1990) Explanatory discourse and causal attribution, *Text* 10 (1/2): 63–8.

Mercer, N. and Edwards, D. (1987) The development of understanding in a group of adults working together, *Open Learning* 2 (2): 18–24.

Ochs, E. (1979) Transcription as theory. In *Developmental Pragmatics*, E. Ochs and B.B. Schieffelin (eds), London: Academic Press, 43–72.

Potter, J. and Mulkay, M. (1985) Scientists' interview talk: Interviews as a technique for revealing participants' interpretative practices. In *The Research Interview: Uses and Approaches*, M. Brenner, J. Brown and D. Canter (eds), New York: Academic Press, 247–71.

Potter, J. and Wetherell, M. (1987) *Discourse and Social Psychology: Beyond Attitudes and Behaviour*, London: Sage.

Scott, M.B. and Lyman, S. (1968) Accounts, *American Sociological Review* 33: 46–62.

Training Commission (1988) *The Employment Training Interview: Identifying Personal Strengths and Past Achievements* (Achieving Quality No. 2), Sheffield: Her Majesty's Stationery Office.

Author index

Subject index